Beyond Postmodernism

Beyond Postmodernism identifies ways in which psychoanalysis has moved beyond the postmodern debate and discusses how this can be applied to contemporary practice.

Roger Frie and Donna Orange bring together many of the leading authorities on psychoanalytic theory and practice to provide a broad scope of psychoanalytic viewpoints and perspectives on the growing interdisciplinary discourse between psychoanalysis, continental philosophy, social theory and philosophy of mind. Divided into two parts, Psychoanalytic Encounters with Postmodernism and Psychoanalysis Beyond Postmodernism, this book

- elaborates and clarifies aspects of the postmodern turn in psychoanalysis
- furthers an interdisciplinary perspective on clinical theory and practice
- contributes to new understandings of theory and practice beyond postmodernism.

Beyond Postmodernism: New Dimensions in Clinical Theory and Practice provides a fresh perspective on the relationship between psychoanalysis and postmodernism and raises new issues for the future. It will be of interest to practicing psychoanalysts and psychologists as well as students interested in psychoanalysis, postmodernism and philosophy.

Roger Frie is Associate Professor of Human Development and Educational Psychology, Simon Fraser University, Vancouver; and faculty member at the William Alanson White Institute, New York.

Donna Orange is supervisor and faculty member at the Institute for the Psychoanalytic Study of Subjectivity, New York, and the Institute for Specialization in Self Psychology and Relational Psychoanalysis in Rome/Milan.

Beyond Postmodernism

New dimensions in clinical theory and practice

Edited by Roger Frie and
Donna Orange

Routledge
Taylor & Francis Group

LONDON AND NEW YORK

First published 2009
by Routledge
27 Church Road, Hove, East Sussex BN3 2FA

Simultaneously published in the USA and Canada
by Routledge
270 Madison Avenue, New York, NY 10016

Routledge is an imprint of the Taylor & Francis Group, an Informa business

Typeset in Times by Garfield Morgan, Swansea, West Glamorgan
Printed and bound in Great Britain by T J International Ltd, Padstow,
Cornwall
Paperback cover design by Lisa Dynan
Paperback cover image by Mark Houtzager (www.markhout.com)

This publication has been produced with paper manufactured to strict
environmental standards and with pulp derived from sustainable forests.

British Library Cataloguing in Publication Data
A catalogue record for this book is available from the British Library

Library of Congress Cataloging in Publication Data
Beyond postmodernism : new dimensions in theory and practice / edited by
Roger Frie and Donna Orange.
    p. ; cm.
  Includes bibliographical references and index.
  ISBN 978-0-415-46687-5 (hbk.) – ISBN 978-0-415-46688-2 (pbk.) 1.
Psychoanalysis. 2. Postmodernism. I. Frie, Roger, 1965– II. Orange, Donna M.
  [DNLM: 1. Postmodernism. 2. Psychoanalysis—trends. WM 460 B5736
2009]
  BF175.4.P45B49 2009
  150.19′5—dc22
                                             2008032520

ISBN: 978-0-415-46687-5 (hbk)
ISBN: 978-0-415-46688-2 (pbk)

Contents

Notes on contributors

William J. Coburn, Ph.D., Psy.D. is supervising and training analyst and faculty member at the Institute of Contemporary Psychoanalysis, Los Angeles and at the Northwestern Center for Psychoanalysis, Portland, Oregon. He is Editor-in-Chief, *International Journal of Psychoanalytic Self Psychology* and is an editorial board member of *Psychoanalytic Inquiry*.

Morris N. Eagle, Ph.D. is Professor Emeritus, Derner Institute of Advanced Psychological Studies, Adelphi University, New York. He was previously Professor of Psychology at York University, Toronto. He is the author of *Recent Developments in Psychoanalysis: A Critical Evaluation* (McGraw-Hill, 1984) and has written more than 100 articles in psychoanalysis and psychology.

Anthony Elliott, Ph.D. is Chair of Sociology at Flinders University, Australia, and Visiting Research Professor at the Open University, UK. He is the author and editor of twenty books, including most recently: *Concepts of the Self* (Polity, 2007, 2nd edition), *The New Individualism* (Routledge, 2005, with Charles Lemert), *Subject to Ourselves: Social Theory, Psychoanalysis and Postmodernity* (Paradigm, 2004, 2nd edition), and *Social Theory since Freud* (Routledge, 2004).

Jon Frederickson, M.S.W. is a faculty member of the Washington School of Psychiatry, Washington, DC, where he has been chair of the Advanced Psychotherapy Training Program and Co-chair of the Supervision Training Program. He is author of *Psychodynamic Psychotherapy: Learning to Listen from Multiple Perspectives* (Taylor and Francis, 1999) and several articles and book chapters on the relationship between postmodern theories and the concept of the person in psychoanalysis.

Roger Frie, Ph.D., Psy.D. is Associate Professor of Educational Psychology and Human Development at Simon Fraser University, Vancouver, and supervisor and faculty member at the William Alanson White Institute, New York. His recent books include *Psychotherapy as a Human Science*

(Duquesne University Press, 2006, with Daniel Burston) and *Psychological Agency: Theory, Practice, and Culture* (The MIT Press, 2008).

Arnold H. Modell, M.D. is Clinical Professor of Psychiatry, Harvard Medical School, and training and supervising analyst at the Boston Psychoanalytic Institute. His most recent books include *Imagination and the Meaningful Brain* (MIT Press, 2003), *The Private Self* (Harvard University Press, 1993), and *Other Times, Other Realities* (Harvard University Press, 1990).

Donna Orange, Ph.D., Psy.D. is supervisor and faculty member at the Institute for the Psychoanalytic Study of Subjectivity and the Institute for Specialization in Self Psychology and Relational Psychoanalysis in Rome. She is co-author with Robert Stolorow and George Atwood of *Worlds of Experience* (Basic Books, 2002) and *Working Intersubjectively* (Analytic Press, 1997), and author of *Emotional Understanding: Studies in Psychoanalytic Epistemology* (Guilford Press, 1995).

Robert D. Stolorow, Ph.D., Ph.D. is Clinical Professor of Psychiatry at the UCLA School of Medicine and training and supervising analyst at the Institute of Contemporary Psychoanalysis, Los Angeles. He is author of *Trauma and Human Existence* (Routledge, 2007) and co-author of *Worlds of Experience* (Basic Books, 2002, with Donna Orange and George Atwood).

Judith Guss Teicholz, Ed.D. is supervising analyst and faculty member at the Massachusetts Institute for Psychoanalysis. She is author of *Kohut, Loewald, and the Postmoderns* (Analytic Press, 1999) and co-editor of *Trauma, Repetition, and Affect Regulation* (Other Press, 1998, with Daniel Kriegman). She is on the editorial board of the *International Journal of Psychoanalytic Self Psychology*.

Heward Wilkinson, M.Sc. is Hon. Fellow, UK Council for Psychotherapy, and a UKCP Registered Integrative Psychotherapist. He was Editor of the *International Journal of Psychotherapy* 1994–2004. His book on the poetic paradigm for psychotherapy, *The Muse as Therapist: A New Poetic Paradigm for Psychotherapy*, is currently in press with Karnac Books.

Preface

Roger Frie and Donna Orange

Another book on postmodernism? Within the humanities, postmodernism is considered by many to be passé. Even such central figures as Foucault and Derrida, who early on heralded the death of the subject and the endless slippage of meaning, softened their positions towards the end of their careers. Yet within the world of psychology, and particularly within psychoanalytic theory and practice, postmodernism continues to be central – if not ascendant – in contemporary discussion and debate.

The considerable time lag between the emergence of postmodernism in late 1960s France and the embrace of postmodern ideas by psychologists and psychoanalysts decades later suggests the extent to which the mental health professions, especially in North America, remain insulated from the humanities. In our opinion, this is a profound limitation in the education of psychologists and psychoanalysts. Indeed, much of our writing to date has been motivated by a desire to demonstrate the importance of philosophy for clinical theory and practice. As scholars and practitioners, trained in philosophy, psychoanalysis and clinical psychology, we welcome the cross-disciplinary fertilization that the embrace of postmodernism signifies. But this cross-disciplinary approach also brings with it a host of challenges, not least because so many clinicians who embrace the label of postmodernism remain unfamiliar with philosophy and the humanities. Moreover, in our experience, clinicians still tend to believe that critical thinking is antithetical to psychoanalytic practice, with its emphases on the search for meaning, understanding, and healing.

Another way to understand the enthusiastic, if belated, reception of postmodernism into psychoanalysis is to consider the authoritarian and all-knowing heritage of traditional analytic approaches. An antidote to this authoritarianism was required and postmodern deconstructionism, with its skeptical unmasking of epistemological pretention, and of privilege and power, seemed to fill the need exactly. Within the North American context, the embrace of postmodernism is most evident in the school of relational psychoanalysis. Indeed, for many observers, postmodernism and relational psychoanalysis are today indelibly connected. Unfortunately, the postmodern tonic had its own authoritarian side-effects, as several contributors to our book point out.

In our view, the embrace of postmodernism by psychoanalysts has led to overuse, if not misuse of the term "postmodernism." The label of post-modernism is often used to describe and define the entire tradition of post-classical psychoanalysis, including ways of thinking and practicing that differ markedly from actual postmodern philosophy. While the postmodern turn has helped psychoanalysis move beyond the limits of modernism, it also brings to psychoanalysis a host of conceptual and theoretical problems, which either go unrecognized or remain unresolved. The unintended consequences include an aversion to "reality-talk" that can invalidate the patient's experience, including experiences of trauma and retraumatization in the treatment situation. Clearly the postmodern version of the principle of parsimony ("Occam's razor") needs to be wielded with considerable care and with awareness of its inherent limitations.

In the meantime, there are other developments in European philosophy and social theory that provide ways of conceptualizing psychoanalytic theory and practice that move beyond the strictures of the postmodern debate. As such, this book has a threefold purpose: first, to elaborate and clarify aspects of the postmodern turn in psychoanalysis; second, to further an interdisciplinary perspective on clinical theory and practice; and third, to contribute new ways of understanding theory and practice beyond postmodernism.

Books, whether edited or authored, often have a history all their own, and ours is no exception. The postmodern turn in psychoanalysis, like psychoanalytic history in general, tends to be a political affair. Unfortunately this means that the principles of difference and otherness that define postmodernism can be lost in the dogmatic nature of the debate. Proponents are often absolutely convinced of the rightness of their position, leading critics to become equally vocal in their opposition. As a result, the ability to listen to what the other says is frequently lacking. Publishing a book on the postmodern debate can be a similarly risky undertaking. This book was initially conceived as a dialogue between proponents and critics of the postmodern turn in relational psychoanalysis, but fell prey to the doctrinal politics of psychoanalytic publishing. Given the uncertainties over the current status of psychoanalysis as a profession, this kind of continued sectarian thinking seems to us unfortunate.

We firmly believe in the need for more discussion and debate with the aim of making contemporary clinical theory and practice an inclusive, rather than exclusive undertaking. It is in this spirit that we invited post-modern relational analysts to contribute, but they declined. Although we were saddened by this response, we do not believe that this detracts from the scope of the scholarship of our book, which includes among its contributors many of the leading authorities on psychoanalytic theory and practice today. Notably, the contributors hail from different psychoanalytic perspectives, and each develops a unique perspective on the issue of post-modernism and interdisciplinary scholarship. The chapters themselves represent a variety of viewpoints: some develop a compatiblist position through which the constructive interaction between postmodernism and psychoanalysis is illustrated, and others offer a constructive, respectful critique of aspects of postmodernism, especially as it appears in contem-porary relational psychoanalysis. We have also sought to extend discussion over the postmodern turn beyond relational psychoanalysis and to this end, we include some recent developments in Derridian and post-Lacanian theory and practice. The result is a book that includes a broad scope of psychoanalytic viewpoints and perspectives, and presents a rich and growing interdisciplinary discourse between psychoanalysis, continental philosophy, social theory, and the philosophy of mind.

Our own backgrounds in continental philosophy, with its non-reductive phenomenological spirit, as well as our work in clinical psychoanalysis, have shaped this book. We are interested above all in a philosophy and psychology of human experience and of an emergent and agentic post-Cartesian subjectivity. Above all, and in contrast to radical postmodernists, we take our patients' suffering as something to understand and to heal, not to deconstruct or co-construct.

As with any lengthy, scholarly undertaking, we are indebted to a number of different people. We thank Kate Hawes at Routledge for taking up and supporting this project, and Jane Harris for her excellent advice as we sought to shepherd it through its various stages to completion. Our stu-dents and our patients have been instrumental in helping us to develop the ideas and practical injunctions that we present in this book. Above all, we are indebted to our families, to whom we dedicate this book. For their support and enthusiasm, Roger wishes to thank Emily, Elena and Andreas, and Donna thanks Don and Henny.

Introduction

Coherence or fragmentation? Modernism, postmodernism, and the search for continuity

Roger Frie

The intersection of postmodernism and psychoanalysis is a dominant and, at times, divisive theme in contemporary clinical theory and practice.[1] This volume of original chapters brings together leading authorities in psychoanalysis who collectively seek to retain what is valuable in the so-called postmodern turn, while arguing for the need to move beyond postmodernism. The contributors enter into dialogue with psychoanalytic postmodernism in order to clarify its conceptual basis, its current status, and above all, introduce new ways of thinking and practicing analytically that move beyond the strictures of the postmodern debate. In the process, they seek to extend the reach of clinical theory and practice beyond the current fascination – and continued fixation – with postmodernism.

The emphasis on social constructivism, ambiguity, difference, and the dissolution of the subject has both destabilized and created unquestioned touchstones in much contemporary psychoanalytic writing. Indeed, a central motive for this book is to address the lack of sufficient, rigorous analysis of what postmodern ideas actually mean in clinical practice. This difficulty exists, in part, because postmodernism is itself a cluster of ideas, hints, and suggestions that often resist precise definition; this makes questions of relevance difficult to pin down and claims of relevance ubiquitous. American relational psychoanalysis in particular has relied on postmodern ideas, often uncritically referenced, to buttress its rejection of alternative psychoanalytic views, both classical and contemporary. This book sheds light on the assumptions that the reliance on postmodernism hides, and suggests that other philosophical options exist, choices perhaps more congenial to clinical work.

Of particular concern to the contributors is that much of what is currently being written about and debated in psychoanalysis can no longer be defined within the parameters of postmodernism. They propose a new vocabulary in order to capture the developments from the fields of continental philosophy, social theory and the philosophy of mind. Such a language includes a greater focus on experiences of agency and embodiment, the application of systems, chaos, and complexity theories, and a reexamination of the dialogic nature of the "talking cure." Continental philosophies of phenomenology and hermeneutics provide important sources, and voices from philosophy and social theory like those of Martin Heidegger, Hans-Georg Gadamer, Maurice Merleau-Ponty, Cornelius Castoriadis and Anthony Giddens make themselves heard.

Above all, this book seeks to broaden the scope of interdisciplinary thinking in psychoanalysis. While the embrace of postmodernism in psychoanalysis has spurred the growth of interdisciplinary scholarship, the lack of clear and rigorous theory has caused some to question the value of introducing ideas from philosophy, literature, and related disciplines into analytic theory and practice. By moving beyond the postmodern debate to embrace both new and neglected theories and thinkers, this book seeks to substantiate the relevance of interdisciplinary psychoanalytic theory.

The objective of this Introduction is to provide a context for understanding the interdisciplinary nature of the debate over postmodernism in psychoanalysis. Just as there is no single school of psychoanalysis that exhaustively defines theory and practice, neither is there a single overarching perspective on postmodernism. By extension, this book will present a range of viewpoints on postmodernism in psychoanalysis. The chapters in Part I of the book explore the integration of postmodernism and psychoanalysis and provide a contrast between critical and compatible positions. The chapters in Part II of the book explore clinical, philosophical and social theories, many of which are outside of common psychoanalytic parlance, with the aim of mapping out ways to move beyond postmodernism.

It will not have escaped notice that psychoanalysis today appears as an embattled profession. From a practice standpoint, psychoanalysts are confronted with myriad economic and political forces that pose serious challenges to the goals of clinical work. Yet from the perspective of theory and technique, psychoanalysts have long been divided and grouped into different theoretical and clinical schools. The obstacles that confront psychoanalysis nowadays are a result of changes in society at large, as well as fissures internal to the profession itself, and speak to the need to find a common ground upon which a more inclusive outlook on human experience and behavior can be established. We are by no means advocating a singular perspective, but neither do we think the current schisms, whether theoretical or practical in scope, are of benefit to the discipline.

The evolution of clinical theory and practice is important to establishing a shared purpose in psychoanalysis and securing its relevance in the clinical setting and beyond. Ironically, the recent bifurcation of much contemporary psychoanalytic theory and practice between modernism and postmodernism has only further exacerbated preexisting oppositions and done relatively little to bring about inclusive change. The emergence of a postmodern psychoanalysis has been described as akin to a "pendulum swing," which for some observers has swung too far (Eagle 2003), and for others, perhaps, not quite far enough (Fairfield et al. 2002).

The distinction between modernism and postmodernism in psychoanalysis takes many forms, affecting the way in which clinicians formulate theory and view technique. The reliance on the analytic neutrality and objectivity that defined classical psychoanalysis has given way in postmodern assumptions about the analytic relationship that is based on mutuality. Classical assumptions about authority and reason are infused with ambiguity and uncertainty. In place of foundational concepts such as objectivity and truth, postmodernists emphasize constructivism. And in contrast to the materialistic, isolated entity that characterizes the so-called modernist self, the postmodernist sees the self as generated and maintained by the relational, linguistic, and cultural contexts which are outside of awareness.

The bifurcation of modernism and postmodernism thus is a reflection of changing theory and practice in contemporary psychoanalysis. Yet attempts to differentiate so stringently between varying perspectives inevitably raise questions about whether our culturally and historically situated models of theory and practice are continuous or disconnected. Do modernists really adhere to the notion of an immutable core self and do postmodernists always see the self as illusory? Is there a place for modernist concepts such as agency and authenticity in postmodernism? Is experience characterized by coherence, fragmentation, or some combination of the two? And as the nature of these questions suggests, the notion of dualistic thinking continues to be pervasive in psychoanalytic theory and practice. I will suggest that there is inevitably a considerable blurring of boundaries between modernism and postmodernism, so that the very definitions we use are open to question. Yet in the formulation of clinical theory and technique these boundaries continue to assert considerable influence. At times, the differences between modernism and postmodernism appear to be so exaggerated that the value of such generalizing labels must be doubted. Given the lack of clarity within psychoanalysis about what modernism and postmodernism actually mean, the sections that follow shall seek to define these terms in their historical and philosophical contexts. Subsequent sections then examine the way in which the postmodern turn in psychoanalysis has been carried out, and the extent to which it is both similar to and different from postmodern philosophy.

Enlightenment beginnings

To the extent that postmodernism is viewed as a reaction to modernism, it is necessary to begin with an exploration of what modernism means. For most observers, modernism is identified with a set of ideas and traditions that stem from the Enlightenment era. Indeed, most of the central ideas associated with the Enlightenment are the object of postmodern criticism.

Broadly defined, the Enlightenment consists of a compilation of thinkers from Descartes through Kant, who celebrate such foundational ideas as reason, truth, and freedom.

The Enlightenment is frequently presented by proponents of post-modernism as the source of modern society's dilemmas. The notion of the unified subject; the triumph of reason over nature; the imperial expansion of Western ideas of self-interest and autonomy to the exclusion of non-Western notions of community and selflessness; the celebration of scientific rationalism at the expense of the perils of modern technology; and the homogeneity of such values as universality and equality, which fail to account for differences in gender, race, culture, power and social class. But as with all stereotypes, the actual facts are rather more complex: the Enlightenment is neither as simple nor as straightforward as its postmodern detractors suggest. Indeed, a variegated reading of the Enlightenment (Eagleton 1996, 2005) demonstrates that there are at least two Enlightenment views of the self and its place in society, both of which weigh heavily in the evolution of psychoanalysis.

The first view sees humans as fundamentally equal in a society in which tolerance and respect for difference is held in the highest esteem. Conflicts are resolved through the use of reason and rationality itself is seen as something individuals can wield through autonomous thought and action. Rather than bow to authority, individuals seek knowledge and truth on their own. When bound together with others in the form of an egalitarian community, this quest leads to the progressive development of both the self and society.

The second view is rather different, and presents a society in which individuals are solitary beings, living in their own private spheres. According to this view, all that can be known with any certainty is one's own immediate experience. Dialogue, friendship and the very notion of community are considered perilous. Here the other person is experienced as a threat to individual liberty; as a result, the social order is based on self-protection. Reason is used to ensure the continued existence of one's private sphere and the progression of self-interest. Rationality is essentially a form of domination over other persons and nature itself. Human beings are at the apex of creation, all-powerful and only too willing to wield their power to further their own individual ends.

Both of these views of the Englightenment are indelibly connected. Just as the Enlightenment is justifiably called the "Age of Reason," with Voltaire and Diderot as its greatest proponents, so too was it the era of senti-mentality and feeling, as evidenced in the works of Rousseau. Whereas some, like Descartes, were dualists who emphasized the absolute division of body and mind, others like Hume were unbridled materialists for whom the mind consisted entirely of material matter. Whereas political thinkers such as Hobbes imagined life with his fellow humans as "brutish, nasty, and short," in which we would ultimately succumb to unbridled aggression, others such as Locke envisaged a community based on the recognition of intrinsic natural rights to life, liberty, and happiness. Here, then, are myriad contrasts: of reason and irrationalism, of altruism and self-interest, and of community and absolute privacy.

This pattern of Enlightenment contrasts is perhaps best exemplified in the work of Freud. As a representative of the modernist thinking, Freud believed that the power of reason could be used to strengthen the conscious mind. At the same time, Freud sought to do justice to the underside of reason, namely the unconscious. By demonstrating the inevitability of distortion in our thinking, Freud presented a more variable picture of the human mind than certain of his Enlightenment predecessors. His conception of the mind put rationalism in a constant tension with irrationalism. The importance of Freud's theory of the unconscious cannot be overestimated. The radicality of Freud's project lay in his Nietzschean assertion that the capacity to reason is undermined by unconscious, instinctual forces. In the process, Freud subverted the Cartesian belief in rational self-mastery.

Psychoanalysis reveals the ways in which human motivations are multi-determined and often hidden. Classical psychoanalytic treatment seeks to heal splits and to restore and enlarge the unity of the ego to the greatest possible extent. As Freud states:

> In actual fact, indeed, the neurotic patient presents us with a torn mind, divided by resistances. As we analyze it and remove the resistances, it grows together; the greater unity which we call his ego fits into itself all the instinctual impulses which before had been split off and held apart from it.
>
> (Freud 1919: 161)

Thus, Freud's project is at once radical in its celebration of the human instincts and bourgeois in its emphasis on the need to control the passions.

From its inception, therefore, psychoanalysis both challenged and carried forward modernist assumptions about the nature of the human mind. Freud's science of the mind was a radical investigation that sought to shed light on the psychically excluded and explain the roots of human behavior. Freud hailed the methods of late nineteenth century science, which spawned scientific rationality, and held forth the belief that eventually science would uncover the secrets of the mind. Not surprisingly, Freud retained the concept of objectivity as the cornerstone of classical psychoanalytic treatment. In his view, the analyst is an objective scientist who is able to observe and identify the constituents of the mental processes working within the patient. A crucial aspect of this process rests on the analyst's ability to bracket out distorting prejudices and thereby maintain a neutral stance that allows for objective, scientific observation.

As sociologists of science have shown, however, every observation has an implicit agenda. Scientists need to have pre-existing theories and suppositions in order to ask the questions which will lead to data; it is the shape of a question that produces the data that will answer it. The scientist is always situated in a specific time and place and his or her scientific theory is itself is a product of that culture. When applied to the psychoanalytic treatment setting, this suggests that the analyst's subjectivity and clinical perspective will inevitably influence what the analyst knows about his or her patient. The notion of objectivity is thereby placed in question. From a postmodernist perspective, the search for a latent psychic reality beyond analytic interaction – and with it, the belief that the analyst can "know" the content of a patient's unconscious – appears misguided.

Over time, classical psychoanalysis was confronted by other intellectual and scientific developments, yet largely continued to rely on its own modernist foundations. It is perhaps not surprising therefore that the introduction of postmodern ideas in psychoanalysis has resulted in many new challenges and opportunities. As a broad style of thinking, postmodernism is deeply suspicious of such notions as objectivity, truth, and reason, because it sees the world as ungrounded, fragmented, diverse and contingent. Postmodernism rightly questions such liberal ideals as freedom and self-determination and rejects the modernist belief in essentialism and universals. Postmodernism in psychoanalysis is associated as much with the philosophical rejection of such notions as autonomy, objectivity, and an ultimate truth, as it is with the clinical implications of fluid and shifting centers of meaning and identity.

Postmodernity and postmodern theory

To understand the impact of postmodernity for psychoanalysis and beyond, it is important to recognize that postmodern skepticism is not simply an intellectual pursuit. The ideas that make up postmodernism are actually grounded in the social and economic shifts of contemporary Western culture and the process of globalization more broadly. Postmodernity refers to a specific decentralized world of culture, technology, industry, and politics. A persuasive feature of contemporary social life is its ever-increasing capacity to enmesh human subjects in destructive relations of power, in situations of conflict and in processes of domination. In the midst of these changes, the human subject has undergone a radical transformation, in which personal identity and subjectivity have been utterly refashioned to the point at which they are believed to be mere fictions. The contrast to the Enlightenment thinking that characterized the so-called modern period could hardly be more striking.

Postmodern theorists seek to decenter or deconstruct such foundational or objective concepts as truth and knowledge in an attempt to account for the heterogeneity, multiplicity, and difference of our time. Despite the spectrum of opinions they encompass, all varieties of postmodernism share a basic rejection of the isolated thinking subject and its solipsistic perspective on our relationship to the world. Postmodernists celebrate the dissolution and dispersion of the self-determining subject, and view the self not in isolation, but as a product of history, culture, and language. Indeed, some radical versions of postmodernism go so far as to herald the "death of the subject."

The central ideas that make up the concept of postmodernism – at least in its American iteration (Cusset 2008) – are developed in the work of such thinkers as Jacques Derrida, Michel Foucault, Jacques Lacan and Jean-François Lyotard. Known collectively as "poststructuralists," these philosophers argue that humans are born into a system of languages that they neither invent nor control. The notion of linguistic structure is replaced by the play of "difference." Meaning is seen as multiple, unstable and open to various interpretations. In place of the traditional separation between the speaker and spoken language, the subject is understood to exist within the symbolic order and is constituted by language. For poststructuralism there is essentially no world beyond text, a sentiment expressed famously by Roland Barthes who states:

> Linguistically, the author is never more than the instance of writing, just as I is nothing other than the instance of saying I: language knows "subject," not a "person," and this subject, empty outside of the very enunciation which defines it, suffices to make language "hold together," suffices, that is to say, to exhaust it.
>
> (Barthes 1984: 145)

Poststructuralists reject outright any concept of the self or subjectivity that is not understood as discursive or interpreted. The understanding of the self as embedded in the social field also enables poststructuralists to uncover the effects of power and domination. The poststructuralist critique of the asymmetrical and inegalitarian features of modern society owes much to Foucault's model of the social field, constituted by myriad shifting relations, and multiple centers of power confronting multiple centers of resistance. Foucault analyzes the way in which the person is constructed within dominant discourses and becomes an "effect" of "regimes" of ideology, power, and knowledge.

Postmodernism thus fundamentally challenges the Cartesian view of the self-determining and self-transparent subject. Yet, it is questionable whether there is a single overarching conception of the modern subject that succumbs to the sweeping generalizations made by postmodernists. Indeed, there are many substantive accounts of post-Cartesian thinking that predate the emergence of postmodernism, and are excluded from its critique of the subject. Beginning with early German Romanticism, F. W. J. Schelling, and Novalis (Friedrich von Hardenberg) focus on the prereflective nature of experience upon which reflective self-knowledge necessarily depends. Heinrich Jacobi's philosophy of dialogue and G. W. F. Hegel's theory of mutual recognition directly oppose the isolated nature of the Cartesian subject, claiming that there can be no I without an Other. Similarly, a whole tradition of dialogical philosophers from Karl Marx and Ludwig Feuerbach through Martin Buber, emphasize the relational and communal nature of human experience. More recently, existential-phenomenological philosophers challenge the notion of unity, when they argue for a lack of self-identity (Sartre), for embodiment (Merleau-Ponty), and for context (Heidegger).

Just as the meta-narrative of the postmodern critique of the subject is open to question, so too are some of its basic tenets. In philosophy, contemporary thinkers such as Manfred Frank (1989), Peter Dews (1987), Juergen Habermas (1985) and others have all developed salient critiques of postmodernism, both as a philosophical tradition and as a set of normative assumptions. In social theory, meanwhile, Anthony Giddens (1991) and Zygmunt Bauman (2000) have each questioned the relevance of the term "postmodernism." For Giddens, what is commonly known as postmodernism is perhaps better understood as late modernism, since many of the ideas are an extension of modernism. As Giddens states:

> to live in the "world" produced by high modernity has the feeling of riding a juggernaut. It is not just that more or less continuous and profound change occur; rather change does not consistently conform either to human expectation or to human control.
>
> (Giddens 1991: 28)

Giddens critiques the notion of postmodernism as a separate paradigm, and particularly takes issue with its undermining of the reflective capabilities of the subject. For Bauman, the notion of postmodernism has itself been wrung dry by misuse and overuse. He substitutes the term "liquid modernism," by which he seeks to capture the inherent ambivalence and uncertainty of contemporary social life. According to Bauman (2000), it is the unstructured and fluid state of life that calls for a rethinking of the cognitive framework used to narrate individual experience.

In view of the broad-scale critiques of postmodern theory and the fact that there is no single way of conceptualizing subjective experience, it is also important to emphasize that there is no single monolithic definition of postmodernism. This is evidenced not least by the fact that Foucault and Derrida reinstate a version of subjectivity late in their work, after earlier altogether rejecting any notion of the subject. Given the perplexing reversals of philosophy, it is noteworthy that the theories developed by

Derrida, Foucault, and Lacan are derived from earlier thinkers, whose views on the subject were no less ambiguous or dramatic. Thus Derrida draws on Heidegger's later philosophy, in which Heidegger examines the relation of language and being. Foucault takes his inspiration from Friedrich Nietzsche, who addresses such issues as power and reason. And Lacan is often referred to as the "French Freud" since he sought to reinterpret Freudian psychoanalysis from the perspective of structuralism and linguistics. In fact, as we have seen, Freud himself sought to do justice to the other of reason, namely the unconscious, and played no small part in the decentering of the individual mind.

To complicate the definition of postmodernism still further, many observers (cf. Epstein 1997) distinguish between "radical" and "moderate" versions of postmodernism. Radical postmodernism can take various forms, arguing for example, that there is no such thing as truth; that all experience is constructed through language and discursive interpretation; and that gender is wholly constructed. Each of these positions is open to question. While there is general agreement that there may be no ultimate or essential truth, and that the perception of reality is always mediated, to conclude that there is nothing against which truth can be measured, or that all claims to truth are equal is problematic. Similarly, while interpretation plays a crucial role in the construction of experience, there still needs to be something against which interpretations can be judged and comparisons made, otherwise the slide into relativism may become inevitable. In regard to the social construction of gender, the experience of sexual difference is undoubtedly filtered through the lens of societal power relations and cultural practices, yet it is questionable that more basic biological differences are merely cultural artifacts.

The reservations about the radical postmodern viewpoint form the basis of a moderate, more restrained version of postmodern thinking. According to this moderate viewpoint, which the contributors to this book share, social, cultural and discursive forces mold experience in ways that are often outside of awareness. Yet experience itself can never be reduced to a mere epiphenomenon of the social and cultural contexts in which it takes place. Reflecting on the perils of reductionism in radical versions of postmodernism, Barbara Epstein (1997) observes:

> It is no better to argue that everything can be understood in terms of culture or language than to argue that everything is driven by economic forces, or by the quest for political power. The project that frames postmodernism is the critique of the Enlightenment rationality; there are aspects of that tradition that deserve to be criticized, such as the tendency to take the white male as the model of rational subjectivity, and the equation of truth with the discoveries of Western science, excluding other contributions. But the postmodernist critique

of the Enlightenment is one-sided. It forgets that a universalist view of humanity was a major (and only partially accomplished) step away from narrow nationalisms, and that the concept of truth is a weapon in the hands of progressive social movements, that they rely on opposing the truth of oppression to hollow official claims that society is just.

(Epstein 1997: 23)

From this perspective, moderate postmodernism stops short of the whole-scale reductionism that seems to work against the nature of progressive politics. The problem is that when subjects have no voices other than the "echo" of prevailing discourses, the potential for action is undermined and the possibility of social change placed in doubt (cf. Eagleton 1996).

Clearly the appreciation of some elements of postmodernism, but rejection of others is a risky undertaking (Elliott 2004). When there is too much toleration for difference, the risk of fragmentation becomes very real. On the other hand, when difference is insufficiently acknowledged, the result can be a spurious, modernist homogeneity. Habermas, for example, agrees with postmodern critics of the Enlightenment when they argue that the notion of a self-determining subject is no longer feasible. Like them, Habermas (1985) views reason as inescapably situated in history, society, and language. In contrast to postmodern critics, however, Habermas argues that the totalizing critique of reason undermines the capacity of reason to be critical and bring about progressive change. He suggests that the problems of the Enlightenment can be overcome only by a further Enlightenment, a position he develops in his theory of "communicative action."

The difficulty for many critics of postmodernism who hail from the political left is that they are often seen by proponents as wrong-headed, or worse, as engaged in a willful misreading. When Derrida's politics were challenged in the 1980s, supporters of deconstructionism vilified the critics. Derrida's proclamations concerning the "death of the subject" seem to undermine the idea of political agency and place in question the prospect of meaningful change. If all meaning were, as Derrida claimed, indeterminate, if moral and epistemological questions were ultimately "undecidable," what was the point of political commitment? Each time the tenets of deconstruction were questioned, supporters of Derridian postmodernism lashed out at critics with religious zeal. At moments it seemed almost as though postmodernism had become a new religion. Anyone who was not a believer was branded a heathen.

Unfortunately, discussion and debate over the nature of postmodernism in psychoanalysis is not immune to this kind of interchange. Given the acrimonious political history of psychoanalysis, this is hardly surprising. Yet it surely flies in the face of the openness to difference that forms the basis of the postmodern outlook. The section that follows traces the emergence of a postmodern viewpoint in psychoanalysis, focusing especially on the American relational tradition. Given the complexity and diversity of approaches, discussion will be limited to an outline of the central postmodern positions; these are more fully elaborated in the individual chapters of the book.

From postmodern theory to clinical practice

Postmodernism in psychoanalysis, like philosophy, takes many forms. Indeed, there is no overarching "postmodern" theory of psychoanalysis, just as there is no single way of practicing analytic technique. In the broadest sense, the emergence of a postmodern position in psychoanalysis has played a constructive role in calling attention to many of Cartesian rationalism's oversights. Within the North American context, postmodernism is most frequently linked to the emergence of the relational school of psychoanalysis. In Europe and South America, by contrast, postmodernism is associated chiefly with Lacanian and post-Lacanian versions of psychoanalysis. While this book will focus primarily on the relational variant of postmodern psychoanalysis, a number of chapters address the postmodern analytic perspectives that derive from Lacan and Derrida.

Though relational psychoanalysis, like postmodernism, is a compilation of different perspectives, what unites these approaches is their thoroughgoing critique of classical psychoanalysis. Postmodernism has proven invaluable to this undertaking. Relationists draw on the postmodern critique of the self-determining subject, of reason, objectivity and truth, to question the Freudian conceptualization of the mind, of analytic technique, truth and authority, which are all central to the analytic endeavor.

There are a number of key themes that make up the postmodern perspective in relational psychoanalysis. In contrast to the structural model of the psyche, with its distinct mental functions, relationists (Bromberg 1998) have developed the theory of "multiple self-states." The notion of multiplicity is closely connected with dissociation (Stern 1997), as opposed to the classical notion of repression. The significance of this development is evident in the fact that while multiplicity and dissociation have long been important theories of psychopathology, they are now viewed as everyday states of mind. In other words, many relationists embrace a radically decentered view of the self.

Closely linked with the notion of multiplicity is the "co-construction" of the analytic situation. For Mitchell (1993), Hoffman (1998) and others, the social construction of experience not only subverts the notion of the self-determining subject, but also points to the mediated nature of all analytic knowledge. In other words, relationists question the privileged knowledge and authority assumed by the classical analyst. For postmodern psychoanalysts, knowledge and truth in the analytic setting are always mediated by subjective and mutually constructed experience.

As a result of this epistemological shift, it is not surprising that analytic technique has likewise been substantially revised. Such classical analytic notions as the "neutral," "blank slate," and "anonymous" analyst have given way to notions of mutuality and the opportunity for self-disclosure. In place of a one-person psychology, relationists understand psychoanalysis as a two-person endeavor, in which understanding and knowledge is co-constructed in the interactive matrix of the analytic setting.

Perhaps the area in which postmodern relationists most closely approximate the work of Lacanian postmodernist psychoanalysis is in the analysis of the construction of social identity and personal experience. The relationist reexamination of gender and race, for example, has developed out of poststructuralism, particularly the work of Foucault. The differences between relational and postmodern psychoanalytic feminism and Lacanian and post-Lacanian feminism are many. But certainly all embrace the potentially liberating aspects of the postmodern subversion of singular identities. Indeed, in our opinion this is one of postmodernism's most valuable contributions to clinical theory and practice. The uncovering of ideological forces, of power and repression in the determination of experience, fundamentally challenges the essentialism of fixed categories and identities and creates a space for new experiences that move beyond the strictures of existing rationalist and patriarchal norms and values. Interestingly, however, while Lacan and Derrida each focus on the dislocating impact of language and the indeterminacy of meaning in psychic experience, relationalists have not embraced the linguistic turn of poststructuralism, largely limiting their analysis to social forces and role of ideology in the construction of experience.

The influence of Lacan's rereading of Freud in terms of language and semiotics is widespread. Outside of the Anglo-American context, the work of Lacan shares the stage with the perspectives of Melanie Klein and Wilfred Bion as a dominant perspective in psychoanalysis. The Lacanian and post-Lacanian tradition provides a starkly different view of personal experience than relational psychoanalysis when it sees subjectivity as inscribed by the insatiable lack of human desire. In the Lacanian version of psychoanalysis, any notion of the subject with a fixed reference point is radically denied. The subject is rendered helpless, if not meaningless, by illusory imaginary identifications and the endless slippages of language.

To the extent that Lacan's ideas are a direct extension of Freud's, it can be argued that his work is not yet fully representative of the postmodern turn. The emphasis on distinguishing between fantasy and reality in the imaginary, in order to make objective interpretations of the unconscious is still characteristic of Enlightenment reasoning about reality and objectivity.

To the extent that Lacan is concerned with the displacement of subjectivity in the symbolic order of language and culture – as when he writes of "the incessant sliding of the signified under the signifier" (Lacan 1977: 154) – Lacan moves well beyond the Enlightenment concerns of Freud. Indeed, his work provides a foundation for poststructuralist accounts of the manifestation of unconscious fantasy in ideology. Thus for Slavoj Zizek (1988), the desires and fantasies that were once thought to be the private purview of the individual subject are actually experienced and subverted at the level of social and cultural ideology. Selfhood exists not in private spheres, but in ideological discourse.

In contrast to the relational perspective, the Lacanian and post-Lacanian account of personal experience is defined by lack, emptiness, and depletion. Indeed, as the chapters in this book suggest, there remains a considerable gap between the work of American postmodern relational analysts and the sizable body of work developed by Lacanian and post-Lacanian psychoanalysis. It is precisely this gap that also points to different interpretations of postmodern theory. Lacan and post-Lacanian psychoanalysis are often engaged in the generation of poststructuralist ideas. The Lacanian analyst is schooled in postmodern philosophy, since it would be quite impossible to appreciate Lacan's work, or that of his followers, without an understanding of the philosophical tenets that inform his theories.

Postmodern relational analysts, by contrast, are several steps removed, picking and choosing from postmodern philosophy as they go, depending on the needs of their theory, or to bolster their critique of classical psychoanalysis. On the whole, postmodern relationalists are not educated in philosophy, and indeed, it remains highly unusual for North American training institutes to provide formal courses in continental theory and philosophy. As some contributors to this book suggest, the lack of philosophical education is an enormous drawback for the development of contemporary psychoanalysis, and perhaps also one of the reasons that some postmodern relationists paint themselves into a corner when it comes to the development of a coherent relational theory. This gap also helps to explain the curious time lag between the emergence of postmodern philosophies during the late 1960s and early 1970s, and their adaptation by American psychoanalysts several decades later. Whereas postmodern philosophy has long been subjected to criticism, debate, and revision, postmodernism is arguably still ascendant in American psychoanalysis (Fairfield et al. 2002), leading in no small part to the nature of the current debate over its benefits and drawbacks.

While postmodern influence has been important for critically examining the essentialisms of classical psychoanalytic theory, it is a form of thinking in psychoanalysis with substantial limitations. It is this recognition that has led well-known relationists to laud the emancipatory social power of a postmodern approach, while at the same time cautioning against its over-reaching use. Stephen Mitchell and Lewis Aron, for example, argue that

> From our point of view, constructivism in political and gender theory, in its dialectical swing away from essentialism, often becomes too airy and ungrounded, missing the ways in which the past, the inner world, developmental continuities, all have claims on our present experience. In the emancipatory zeal to shed social impositions, more political forms of constructivism seem not to appreciate that *we are what we have been*, and that we construct ourselves out of the materials at hand, including our bodies and their attributes.
>
> (Mitchell and Aron 1999: xvi, original italics)

Mitchell and Aron thus articulate a measured embrace of postmodernism. Yet the potential confusions inherent in this position are exemplified by their use of the term "inner world," which points to the continued prevalence of the dualistic, Cartesian bifurcation between "inside" and "outside." Though "inner world" is clearly a popular metaphor for private experience, it illustrates the continued pervasiveness of the Cartesian doctrine in contemporary psychoanalytic thought and practice. Nor is there a coherence of positions within the relational school on postmodernism. Indeed, some relationists (Aron 1996) seek to avoid the radical aspects of postmodernism in an attempt to develop a more moderate, affirmative, postmodern perspective. Noting these differences Aron suggests that relational thought "may be better categorized as part of the tradition of critical modernism rather than of postmodernism" (Aron 1996: 26). Conversely, others such as Susan Fairfield (2002) argue that relational psychoanalysis needs to rid itself of the vestiges of modernist thinking.

Of course, for some observers, the perspective outlined by Mitchell and Aron (1999) begs the question of why relational analysts insist on continuing to use the label "postmodernism," given its sometimes problematic philosophical status and ambiguous clinical definition. For certain relational psychoanalysts, perhaps, the use of postmodernism to describe aspects of relational theory and technique amounts to an attempt to reclaim the revolutionary character of Freud's initial, subversive project. Psychoanalysts of virtually all stripes would agree with the necessity of radicalizing the psychoanalytic project and making it more applicable in a contemporary context. Given the difficulties of translating postmodern ideas into the clinical setting, however, it is doubtful whether continued reliance on postmodern theory will in fact help the achievement of this goal. As the contributors to this book suggest, there are alternative ways of conceptualizing experience, which are manifestly post-Cartesian in nature, yet do not succumb to the pitfalls of postmodern theorizing. To paraphrase Terry Eagleton (1966: ix) on this point, we are not proposing that we have some fully developed alternative to postmodernism at our fingertips, just that we should be able to do rather better.

The contributors to this book present a diversity of viewpoints in their dialogue with postmodernism. Yet all are in agreement that the postmodern turn has opened up a host of important new opportunities from the development of social and gender theories to innovative techniques. The contributors are united in their belief that psychoanalysis cannot move back to the modernist, Cartesian assumptions that have long informed the classical tradition. But neither are they convinced that postmodernism in psychoanalysis provides a satisfactory means to move forward.

Indeed, some contributors wonder whether the Cartesian absolutes of classical psychoanalysis have not simply been replaced by new, equally problematic contradictions characteristic of some postmodern thinking. Contrary to much of the existing discussion and debate over the merits of modernism and postmodernism, it is not a question of which is better suited to psychoanalysis. To celebrate one approach over the other only substantiates this problematic bifurcation. Indeed, the bifurcation between modernism and postmodernism is yet another in a long line of dualisms that hinder the conceptualization of human experience.

Perhaps the key issue in clarifying the debate over the postmodern turn in psychoanalysis is the ambiguous way in which postmodernism is defined by contemporary analytic theory and practice. For many postmodern psychoanalysts, especially those in the American relational school, postmodernism provides the means to distinguish themselves from classical Freudians and other analytic approaches. To be sure, the fragmentation, ambivalence, and uncertainty characteristic of the period of postmodernity also impacts upon the practice of contemporary psychoanalysis. Yet the uncritical adoption of postmodern thinking, and its implementation in psychoanalytic practice, necessarily gives rise to a series of questions: If we take on the postmodern mantra that personal experience exists only as fragmentation and disintegration, then how does this play out in a clinical theory that seeks to restore a measure of hope and basic continuity of experience in the individual who seeks therapy? How does the radical decentering of human subjectivity mesh with the reflective capacities of the person upon which therapeutic dialogue and understanding depends? Does the decentering and displacement of human experience and normative values conflict with the fundamental, ethical prescripts of therapeutic practice? Are the goals of restoring health and reducing symptoms merely a reflection of the dominant ideology in which we live and participate?

There are no easy or straightforward answers to these questions, but they point to the some of the tensions that exist between the different registers I have described: postmodernity, postmodern theory, and the actual practice of analytic therapy. This is not in any way to suggest that these registers are separate enterprises. As postmodern psychoanalysts have successfully demonstrated, the practice of analysis is always shot through with ideology, just as the analyst and patient are themselves experiencing the uncertainties and ambivalences of the postmodern age in which they find themselves.

But it is precisely the translation from postmodern theory to psycho-analytic practice that makes the navigation of this terrain such a tricky, difficult, and also exciting undertaking. The excitement I am describing sets in when postmodernism is understood and presented not as dogma (as it too often is), but as an openness to difference, contingency, and new possibilities. As Anthony Elliott suggests:

> What happens if we reject the linkage of fragmentation and subjectivity in postmodernity, and replace it with a conception of our psychic capacity for imaginative elaboration of self and world, a conception which suggests the possibility of some more facilitating agency in the reproduction of postmodern cultural forms?
>
> (Elliott 2004: 35)

It is precisely this generative, intersubjective potential for the creation of meaning and new forms of experience and understanding that lies at the heart of this book.

If there is a single or dominant theme in this book, it is a hermeneutic sensibility to theory and practice that views the self not as a concrete entity but as a fundamentally contextualized process. This Heideggerian reading (1996) is combined with a respect for a dialogical approach to technique that draws equally on the insights of Gadamer (1995). The self as being-in-the-world is at once embodied, intersubjective, and personal. In drawing on the work of the early Heidegger, the contributors distinguish their approach from the philosophy of the later Heidegger, which forms the conceptual backdrop of much poststructuralist theory.[2] In taking this approach, they also align themselves with a relatively unknown tradition of "existential analysis" which first sought to apply the insights of Heidegger and other existentially and phenomenologically inspired philosophers and psycho-analysts such as Buber, Binswanger, and Merleau-Ponty (see Frie 2003). However, in contrast to the existential-phenomenological tradition, the contributors to this book develop a more far-reaching contextualism and understanding that is grounded in respect for the intersubjective contexts in which all experience unfolds.

This contextualist, hermeneutic tradition of thinking and practice is fundamentally post-Cartesian in nature, yet also at odds with the reduc-tionism inherent in radical versions of postmodernism. As Gadamer (1994) states:

> Understanding is no method but rather a form of community . . . Thus a dimension is opened up that is not just one among other fields of

inquiry but rather constitutes the praxis of life itself . . . Hermeneutics encourages not objectification, but listening to one another.

(Gadamer 1994: x–xi)

The contextualist, hermeneutic approach described by Gadamer is reflected in a number of different contemporary psychoanalytic approaches, and is especially evident in the intersubjective perspective. Indeed, many of the contributors to this book have written about or practice within a broadly hermeneutic and intersubjective orientation. At the same time, there are also other approaches represented in this book, from objective relations through self psychology and interpersonal psychoanalysis. Together the contributors seek to combine what is of value in the postmodern turn with an openness to new ways of thinking about such enduring questions as truth, knowledge, embodiment, selfhood, agency, and complexity in psychoanalysis.

Chapter outline

In order to facilitate discussion, this book is divided into two parts. Part I is entitled "Psychoanalytic encounters with postmodernism" and contrasts different accounts of postmodern psychoanalysis. The first two chapters articulate what Eagle and Frederickson see as both the strengths and inherent limitations and confusions in relational versions of postmodern psychoanalysis. By contrast, the third and fourth chapters by Teiholz and Wilkinson develop a compatibilist position with the aim of illustrating the level of integration that is possible between contemporary psychoanalysis and postmodern thinking.

In Chapter 1, "Postmodern influences on contemporary psychoanalysis," Morris N. Eagle identifies the postmodern turn in psychoanalysis with the arguments developed by so-called new view theorists within the American relational school. Eagle argues that legitimate criticisms of some traditional psychoanalytic views have been transformed into untenable postmodern philosophical positions that do not constitute an adequate basis for psychoanalytic theory or practice. He suggests that legitimate skepticism toward the therapeutic value of insight and self-knowledge has been transformed into a reductionistic philosophical position that appears to rule out the possibilities of discovering truth about the mind. For Eagle, the difficulties of traditional theory identified by new view theorists do not obviate the need to recognize the existence of the patient's psychic reality independent of interpretive constructions and to attempt to understand that reality as fully and accurately as possible. Finally, drawing on the work of the historian A. B. Spitzer, Eagle discusses selected historical examples illustrating the pitfalls of overriding historical facts with considerations of political ideology, coherence of narratives, and desired goals. He concludes that similar challenges are inherent in some aspects of the mode of thinking of the "new view" psychoanalytic theorists.

In Chapter 2, "Multiplicity and relational psychoanalysis: a Heideggerian response," Jon Frederickson analyzes the postmodern perspective on multiplicity in relational psychoanalysis. Drawing on the early philosophy of Heidegger, Frederickson proposes that postmodern relational analysts who endorse multiplicity tend to conflate patients' representations of themselves with their ontology, their "Being" as persons. He suggests that the tendency to relate to representations of ourselves, rather than our Being as persons, constitutes an affliction. According to Frederickson, post-modern analysts who endorse multiplicity make this same category error, reinforcing their patients' illness. Frederickson explores the multiple impli-cations this category error poses for a postmodern relational psycho-analysis, focusing in particular on how the analyst listens, knows, and thinks relationally. Whereas some postmodern relational analysts hold that the goal of psychoanalysis is to help patients stand between their represen-tations of themselves, Frederickson proposes that the goal of analysis is to help patients listen to their Being: the wordless, bodily, pre-reflective awareness that derives from what Heidegger refers to as our "primordial attunement" to being-in-the-world.

In Chapter 3, "A strange convergence: postmodern theory, infant research, and psychoanalysis," Judith Guss Teicholz examines a certain convergence she perceives between postmodern psychoanalysis and recent empirical findings from infant–caregiver, attachment, and cognitive neuro-science research. She finds the convergence strange because, from a post-modern viewpoint, there is no scientific truth beyond what can be mutually agreed upon through intersubjective negotiation. And yet these two seemingly contradictory approaches to human experience – the scientific and post-scientific – seem to be moving toward each other as research findings provide "evidence" for some of the central tenets of postmodern thinking. Teicholz explores the relationships among these disparate yet overlapping approaches to human experience and considers where research findings might fall on a postmodern continuum. In the process, she explores the implications of these findings for contemporary relational psycho-analysis.

In Chapter 4, "Primary process of deconstruction: towards a Derridian psychotherapy," Heward Wilkinson seeks to show how a Derridian outlook would manifest itself clinically. The chapter presents Derrida's ideas in terms of their possible application to psychotherapy and draws comparisons to Daniel Stern's exploration of "the present moment." Wilkinson develops a poetic paradigm of psychotherapy, which also provides a means of under-standing and appreciating Derrida's philosophy. Central to Wilkinson's analysis is a non-reductive, meta-psychoanalytic, non-objectivized concept of *enactment*. He suggests that enactment parallels Derrida's concept of primary writing, and he grounds the conceptualization of enactment in a trans-cognitive mode of action. Wilkinson develops an analysis of William Blake's poem, *The Sick Rose*, and provides additional clinical examples in order to illustrate the enactive character of clinical experience. On this basis, suggestions are presented about the dialogical and integrative character of the Derridian approach to psychotherapy.

Part II of the book is entitled "Psychoanalysis beyond postmodernism" and its chapters are similarly divided into two groups. The first three chapters by Orange, Stolorow, and Frie develop a hermeneutic and existential-phenomenological sensibility that the authors feel is often absent in postmodern psychoanalysis. The second set of chapters by Coburn, Elliott, and Modell elaborate such notions as complexity, rolling identification, and embodiment, in ways that move well beyond the current preoccupations of postmodern psychoanalysis. The book ends with a postscript that considers the implications of a psychoanalytic trajectory beyond postmodernism.

In Chapter 5, "Toward the art of the living dialogue: constructivism and hermeneutics in psychoanalytic thinking," Donna Orange suggests that postmodern constructivism and hermeneutics are often merged in post-classical and relational psychoanalytic writing. Her chapter seeks to distinguish them by comparing their origins, claims, tones, and purposes. To do this, it traces a famous encounter between their most prominent philosophical representatives, Jacques Derrida and Hans-Georg Gadamer. Where the aim of postmodern approaches is mainly deconstructive, seeking confrontationally to unsettle familiar categories and presumptions, Orange argues that hermeneutics seeks historically conscious understanding through dialogue. Philosophical hermeneutics thus emerges as the more clinically useful approach for psychoanalytic understanding.

In Chapter 6, "Trauma and human existence: the mutual enrichment of Heidegger's existential analytic and a psychoanalytic understanding of trauma," Robert D. Stolorow explores Heidegger's investigative method and its relationship to psychoanalysis. This chapter focuses on Heidegger's early philosophy, which is seen to provide the ground for the contextualist interpretive perspective of intersubjective approaches in psychoanalysis. Using a clinical example of trauma, Stolorow demonstrates the relevance of Heidegger's conception of the existential anxiety for the understanding of emotional trauma and traumatized states. He suggests that psychological trauma produces an affective state whose features bear close similarity to the central elements in Heidegger's existential interpretation of anxiety. Reflecting on trauma's contextuality and its existentiality, Stolorow then seeks to enrich aspects of Heidegger's notion of "Being-with" (*Mitsein*), the existential structure underpinning relationality. Although Heidegger's philosophy may in some respects be regarded as a forerunner of postmodern thought, Stolorow argues that this enriched conception of *Mitsein* extends Heidegger's existential analytic far beyond the moral relativism characteristic of radical versions of postmodernism.

In Chapter 7, "Reconfiguring psychological agency: postmodernism, recursivity, and the politics of change," Roger Frie argues that traditional conceptions of agency in psychoanalysis need to be revised in order to account for the way in which human experience is characterized by shifts between centering and decentering, integration and fragmentation. Frie suggests that the complexity of the human experience complicates any simple or straightforward definition of psychological agency. In contrast to the static, materialistic self that informs traditional definitions of free will, this chapter develops a fluid, dynamic conception of agency which is fundamentally embedded in social and biological contexts. Contrasting views of agency from Freud through Lacan and Sullivan through contemporary relational psychoanalysis, Frie suggests that the emergence of postmodernism provides key insights into the reflective capabilities of the subject, but also presents challenges for the conceptualization of agency. Drawing on the work of the social theorist, Anthony Giddens, as well as on hermeneutic philosophy, this chapter proposes a post-Cartesian, situated theory of agency and examines the politics of change.

In Chapter 8, "Psychoanalytic complexity: alternatives to postmodernism in psychoanalysis," William J. Coburn explores the nature of complexity and its interface with and application to contemporary psychoanalysis. Coburn suggests that complexity provides a compelling alternative to more radical postmodern attitudes, such as relativism and the constructivist approach to understanding the emergence of emotional experience and meaning. Ideas about complexity posit a vision of the ongoing clinical narrative as an emergent property and product of the larger relational and historical system of which each of us is an integral constituent. In particular, Coburn highlights the philosophical and clinical attitudes that emanate from adopting such ideas. The chapter thus underscores the clinical implications of two interrelated attitudes: one of valuing the distinction among three levels of discourse – that of phenomenological description, interpretive understanding, and metaphysical/explanatory assumptions – and the other of valuing the conundrum of personal situatedness, emotional responsibility, and potential freedom. Coburn suggests that these attitudes provide a salutary alternative to postmodernist perspectives in psychoanalysis that underplay or dismiss the individuality of personal minds.

In Chapter 9, "Identity, identification, imagination: psychoanalysis and modern European thought after the postmodern turn," Anthony Elliott traces recent developments in European modern thought and psychoanalysis on the theory of the human subject. Critically examining the post-Lacanian psychoanalytic departures of Julia Kristeva and Jean Laplanche, Elliott reflects on the state of the subject in its unconscious relational world. The chapter suggests ways in which the analyses set out by Kristeva and

Laplanche can be further refined and developed, partly through a reconsideration of the intertwining of unconscious representation and repression as developed in the writings of Cornelius Castoriadis, Thomas Ogden, and others. For existing psychoanalytical accounts of primary repression as a condition for the constitution of subjectivity, Elliott suggests we should substitute the concept of "rolling identification", the psychical basis of the shift from self-referential representational activity to an elementary form of intersubjectivity. Rolling identifications are defined as a representational flux that permits human subjects to create a relation to the self-as-object and pre-object relations. Such primal identification, Elliott suggests, operates through a "representational wrapping of self and others." The chapter concludes with a consideration of the cultural significance of primary repression, and the politicization of identification.

In Chapter 10, "Naturalizing relational psychoanalytic theory," Arnold H. Modell suggests that the hard problem for relational psychoanalysis is to account for how meaning is constructed between two different subjectivities. The difficulty is that persons construct their worlds of private meaning in accordance with everything that they have experienced, everything that they know, and everything that they value. While postmodern views provide a means to approach the issue of how self-knowledge is constructed, they do not sufficiently account for the physiological basis of our embodiment. Drawing in equal measure on neuroscience, philosophy and psychoanalysis, Modell argues for the naturalization of relational theory. His wide-ranging perspective is indebted to the philosophies of Heidegger, Merleau-Ponty and Charles Sanders Peirce. Modell proposes that recent knowledge gained from infant observation and neurobiology provides a necessary basis for the conceptualization of relational theory. In particular, he includes the biological sources of empathy, the development of reflective self-consciousness and the unconscious communication of feelings.

Notes

1 While the intersection of psychoanalysis and postmodernism is still a fairly recent occurence, psychology has been engaged with postmodern ideas for some time, as illustrated above all in the work of Kenneth Gergen (1985, 1991) and the emergence of narrative and constructivist therapies.
2 Any discussion of Heidegger's philosophy within the context of psychotherapy must necessarily include an awareness of the debate over his political past. We have each addressed the issue at some length elsewhere: see Frie and Hoffmann (2002), Burston and Frie (2006), Atwood, Orange, and Stolorow (2008).

References

Aron, L. (1996) *A Meeting of Minds*, Hillsdale, NJ: Analytic Press.
Atwood, G., Orange, D., and Stolorow, R. (2008) Heidegger's Nazism and the

Hypostatization of Being. Workshop given at the 31st Annual International Conference on The Psychology of the Self, Baltimore, MD.

Barthes, R. (1984) *Image, Music, Text*, New York: Hill and Wang.

Bauman, Z. (2000) *Liquid Modernity*, Cambridge: Polity.

Bromberg, P. (1998) *Standing in the Spaces*, Hillsdale, NJ: Analytic Press.

Burston, D. and Frie, R. (2006) *Psychotherapy as a Human Science*, Pittsburgh, PA: Duquesne University Press.

Cusset, F. (2008) *French Theory: How Foucault, Derrida, Deleuze, and Co. Transformed the Intellectual Life of the United States*, Minneapolis, MN: University of Minnesota Press.

Dews, P. (1987) *Logics of Disintegration: Post-Structuralist Thought and the Claims of Critical Theory*, London: Verso.

Eagle, M. (2003) 'The postmodern turn in psychoanalysis: a critique', *Psychoanalytic Psychology*, 20: 411–424.

Eagleton, T. (1996) *The Illusions of Postmodernism*, Oxford: Blackwell.

—— (2005) 'The Enlightenment is dead! Long live the Enlightenment!' *Harper's Magazine*, March: 91–95.

Elliott, A. (2004) *Subject to Ourselves: Social Theory, Psychoanalysis and Postmodernity*, Boulder, CO: Paradigm.

Epstein, B. (1997) 'Postmodernism and the Left', *New Politics*, 6: 13–32.

Fairfield, S. (2002) 'Analyzing multiplicity: a postmodern perspective on some current psychoanalytic theories of subjectivity', in S. Fairfield, S. Layton and C. Stack (eds) *Bringing the Plague: Toward a Postmodern Psychoanalysis*, New York: Other Press.

Fairfield, S., Layton, S. and Stack, C. (eds) (2002) *Bringing the Plague: Toward a Postmodern Psychoanalysis*, New York: Other Press.

Frank, M. (1989) *What is Neostructuralism?* Minneapolis, MN: University of Minnesota Press.

Freud, S. (1919) 'Lines of advance in psycho-analytic therapy', in *The Standard Edition of the Complete Psychological Works of Sigmund Freud*, 17: 159–168, London: Hogarth Press.

Frie, R. (ed.) (2003) *Understanding Experience: Psychotherapy and Postmodernism*, London: Routledge.

Frie, R. and Hoffmann, K. (2002) 'Bridging psychiatry, philosophy and politics: Binswanger, Heidegger, and Antisemitism', *Journal of the British Society for Phenomenology*, 32: 231–240.

Gadamer, H.-G. (1994) 'Foreword' to J. Grodin, *Introduction to Philosophical Hermeneutics*, New Haven, CT: Yale University Press.

—— (1995) *Truth and Method*, trans. J. Weinsheimer and D. G. Marshall, 2nd edn, New York: Continuum (originally published in 1960).

Gergen, K. (1985) 'The social constructionist movement in modern psychology', *American Psychologist*, 40: 266–275.

—— (1991) *The Saturated Self*, New York: Basic Books.

Giddens, A. (1991) *Modernity and Self-Identity*, Cambridge: Polity.

Habermas, J. (1985) *The Philosophical Discourse of Modernity*, Cambridge, MA: MIT Press.

Heidegger, M. (1996) *Being and Time*, trans. J. Stambaugh, Albany, NY: State University of New York Press (originally published in 1927).

Hoffman, I. Z. (1998) *Ritual and Spontaneity in the Psychoanalytic Process*, Hillsdale, NJ: Analytic Press.

Lacan, J. (1977) *Ecrits*, New York: Norton.

Mitchell, S. A. (1993) *Hope and Dread in Psychoanalysis*, New York: Basic Books.

Mitchell, S. A. and Aron, L. (eds) (1999) *Relational Psychoanalysis: The Emergence of a Tradition*, Hillsdale, NJ: Analytic Press.

Stern, D. B. (1997) *Unformulated Experience*, Hillsdale, NJ: Analytic Press.

Zizek, S. (1988) *The Sublime Object of Ideology*, London: Verso.

Part I

Psychoanalytic encounters with postmodernism

Chapter 1

Postmodern influences on contemporary psychoanalysis

Morris N. Eagle

What is postmodernism?

The purpose of this chapter is to critically evaluate the influence of post-modern views on psychoanalytic theorizing. Postmodern is a fuzzy category and for some not a meaningful one. So, any discussion of postmodern influences should begin with an attempt at clarifying what one means by "postmodernism". A useful characterization of the term is given by Jon Snyder in his translation of Vattimo's (1985) *The End of Modernity*. He writes: "There is a widely shared sense that Western ways of seeing, knowing, and representing have irreversibly altered in recent times" (1985: vi). These alterations include the following: the view that supposed truths are no less subjective values than any other beliefs or opinions; the project "to unmask all systems of reason as systems of persuasion, and to show that logic – the very basis of rational thought – is in fact only a kind of rhetoric" (1985: xxii); the contention "that all distinctions between truth and falsehood must be dissolved" (1985: xii); the reduction of truth to value or a particular perspective, the "infinite interpretability of reality" (1985: xxi); and the assertion that both in science and in art the choice of a paradigm is "ultimately made on the basis of persuasive power" and rhetoric rather than through demonstration of the truth of the matter.

I would also include in the general category of postmodern the kind of neopragmatist views of Rorty (1991) who writes:

> The tradition in Western culture which centers around the notion of the search for truth, a tradition which runs from the Greek philosophers through the Enlightenment, is the clearest example of the attempt to find a sense of one's existence by turning away from solidarity to objectivity. The idea of truth as something to be pursued for its own sake, not because it will be good for oneself, or for one's real or imagined community, is the central theme of this tradition.
>
> (Rorty 1991: 21)

Rorty makes clear his belief that we should turn away from the Enlightenment tradition of valuing objectivity and return to the pursuit of solidarity. And it is the rejection of this Enlightenment tradition that is one of the central features of postmodernism.

As one can see from the material cited from both Snyder and Rorty, postmodernism is to be most sharply contrasted with what John Searle refers to as the "Enlightenment Vision" (Searle 1998: 10). Closely linked to this vision are a set of what Searle calls "default positions" that have come under attack, particularly postmodernist attack. In the present context, the most relevant of these are, first, the assumption that "there is a real world that exists independently of us, independently of our experiences, our thoughts, our language"; and second, that "our statements are typically true or false depending on whether they correspond to how things are, that is, to facts in the world". It is precisely these basic assumptions, along with some others, that, according to Snyder, have come to be "irreversibly altered in recent times". The challenges to and attacks on these default positions, as Searle notes, have been variously "called social constructionism, pragmatism, deconstructionism, relativism, and postmodernism".

Psychoanalysis and the "Enlightenment Vision"

How are postmodern influences expressed in the context of psychoanalytic theorizing? One can begin addressing this question by noting that the different expressions of postmodern influences on psychoanalysis have in common a rejection of certain central features of classical theory that are embedded in the "Enlightenment Vision". The clearest expression of this is found in the classical idea that lifting repression and making the unconscious conscious, that is, expanding conscious awareness and gaining self-knowledge, are liberating and curative. From the moment that Freud introduced the "cornerstone" concept of repression as the primary pathogen of hysteria and the lifting of repression as the primary goal of treatment, psychoanalysis joined the "Enlightenment Vision". Knowing oneself was now viewed not only as a Socratic virtue, but also as a clinical necessity if one was to be cured.

The conviction that the truth shall set ye free was embodied in the conceptualization of insight, self-knowledge, and self-awareness as the primary curative factors in psychoanalysis. Despite their criticisms of psychoanalysis, figures such as Perls (e.g. 1973), the father of Gestalt therapy, Beck et al. (e.g. 1979), the father of cognitive-behavior therapy (CBT) (both of whom began their professional life as psychoanalysts), and Rogers (e.g. 1951, 1961), the father of non-directive therapy nevertheless continued to emphasize the therapeutic value of expanded awareness and self-knowledge. For a long time, this conviction held and permeated the culture. For example, it was not that long ago that an eminent and influential philosopher like Habermas could hail psychoanalysis as a liberating discipline that could overcome and "dissolve" the repetition compulsion through lifting repression and the therapeutic "power of reflection" (Habermas 1971: 271). In short, these critics continued to subscribe to the Enlightenment project.

This conviction and the unanimity regarding the therapeutic value of awareness and self-knowledge began to crumble some time ago. As noted by Eagle et al. (2001), the contemporary disillusionment with the traditional Enlightenment ideas that making the unconscious conscious, acquiring insight, and learning truths about oneself are crucial to therapeutic change has been recruited to a general postmodernist stance. The dethroning of insight and self-knowledge and replacing them with the primacy of corrective emotional experiences, the therapeutic relationship, co-constructed coherent narratives, and so on as curative factors do not, in themselves, constitute a postmodernist stance. There is nothing postmodern about the straightforward empirical claim that insight, self-knowledge, and learning truths about oneself may not be as effective as was thought and may, indeed, be less effective than other factors. (Of course, as an empirical claim, this would need to be established, not merely asserted.)

However, what may have begun as an informal empirical claim, for those described as espousing the "new view" (Eagle et al. 2001), became transformed into a philosophical position which seemed to rule out the very possibility of discovering truths about the mind. For example, as Mitchell put it, "there are no clearly discernible processes corresponding to the phrase 'in the patient's mind' for either the patient or the analyst to be right or wrong about" (Mitchell 1998: 16). He also writes: "An individual mind is an oxymoron" (Mitchell 2000: 57); "the basic unity of study is not the individual as a separate entity . . . but an interactional field" (Mitchell 1998: 3). He also questions the "traditional claims to analytic knowledge and authority [which] presupposed that the central dynamics relevant to the analytic process are preorganized *in the patient's mind*" (Mitchell 1998: 18, original italics).

If the individual mind is an oxymoron; if the individual's central dynamics are not preorganized, but rather co-constructed in the analytic situation; if there no clearly discernible processes in the patient's mind to be right or wrong about, it would surely make little sense to posit uncovering or discovering truths about one's mind, acquiring self-knowledge and insight, and expanding awareness as therapeutic goals. Instead, the process goals of psychoanalytic treatment now became retellings of one's life (Schafer 1992), persuasive narratives labelled "narrative truth" (Spence 1980), new meanings to be constructed or co-constructed (Mitchell 1998), new perspectives to be taken (Renik 1998), and in one extreme but perhaps the most frank expression of postmodern influences, beautifully wrought "aesthetic fictions" to be formulated (Geha 1984; see also Eagle's 1984 critique of

Geha's position). Furthermore, we are told, the analyst cannot escape his or her "irreducible subjectivity" (Renik 1993).

I want to emphasize again that the issue is not whether new perspectives, meaning-making, retellings, persuasive narratives, and so on are more therapeutically effective than insight, awareness, and self-knowledge. They may or may not be and whether they are or not is an empirical question. The point rather that I want to note here is the parallel between the supposed impossibility of discovering truths about the patient's mind and the emphasis instead on such goals as constructing coherent and persuasive narratives and new meaning systems in the psychoanalytic context and the general postmodern position noted at the beginning of this chapter which argues against any essential distinction between supposed truths and persuasive power and rhetoric. The presumed impossibility of the analyst's escape from his or her subjectivity (Renik 1993, 1998) is paralleled by the postmodern insistence that supposed truths are no less subjective values than any other beliefs or opinions. Thus, the issue here is that the very possibility of learning truths about oneself – or the analyst learning truths about the patient – or acquiring self-knowledge seems to be ruled out by a conception of mind that bears the influences of a postmodern philosophical position.

Characteristic of the postmodern turn in psychoanalysis is the transformation of legitimate criticism into radical and, in my view, untenable philosophical positions. Thus, as we have seen, legitimate questions regarding the therapeutic efficacy of insight and self-knowledge are transformed into claims that there are no truths about the mind to be learned or discovered. One sees a similar pattern with regard to legitimate criticism in other areas. For example, as noted by Eagle et al. (2001), the "new view" theorists have justifiably argued against the naive and sometimes arrogant belief that, by virtue of his or her theoretical knowledge and training, the analyst has virtually infallible access to the Truth about the patient's mind. They have also, quite rightly, rejected what at times has seemed to be the implicit claim of classical theory that there is a singular canonical interpretation of the patient's material. However, it is one thing to reject the claims of infallible access to the truth and another thing to reject altogether the possibility that one can reliably infer certain truths about the patient's mind. It is one thing to reject the idea of a singular canonical interpretation; it is another thing to dissolve all distinctions among interpretations and to do away with Freud's concern that interpretations "tally with what is real (in the patient)" (Freud 1916–1917: 452). It is one thing to recognize the difficulty and uncertainty of inferences about the patients' unconscious mental contents and processes; it is another thing to argue that one "interpretively constructs" another's mind (Mitchell 1998: 16), that is, that one's interpretations, in effect, constitute the other's mind.

A recognition of the untenability of the blank screen model and of certain conceptions of analytic neutrality has become transformed into the claim that the patient–analyst interaction constitutes and organizes the patient's mind, as if there were no stable organization prior to and independent of these interactions. Or, to put it another way, the legitimate idea that the analyst constantly emits cues that may *influence* the patient's state of mind is radically extended and transformed into the proposition that the analytic interaction totally *organizes* the patient's mind. For example, Mitchell's (1998: 18) rejection of the "traditional claims . . . that the central dynamics relevant to the analytic process are preorganized *in the patient's mind*" has led Meissner to comment that

> It seems odd . . . that one would think of the patient, as he enters the consulting room for the first time, as without a history entirely of his own, without a developmental background, without a psychology and personality that he has acquired and developed in the course of a lifetime, all accomplished before he had any contact with the analyst.
> (Meissner 1998: 422)

Mitchell has tried to clarify his position by stating that he is arguing against "the assumption that there is a static organization to mind that manifests itself *whole cloth* across experiences" (Mitchell 2000: 155, original italics). He thinks of the mind, he goes on to say, "as preexisting but not preorganized" and refers to Ogden's (1997) description of

> the internal object relationship . . . [as a] fluid set of thoughts, feelings, and sensations that is continually in movement and is always susceptible to being shaped and restructured as it is *newly* experienced in the context of each new unconscious intersubjective relationship.
> (quoted in Mitchell 2000: 155, original italics)

To the extent that I understand the distinction between "preexisting" and "preorganized" – and I confess that this distinction makes little sense to me – and the passage from Ogden he refers to (and I am not at all sure that I really understand that either), I read Mitchell as arguing against the idea of a static organization of mind which he associates with traditional theory (e.g. with such concepts as core dynamic conflicts and the timelessness of certain unconscious infantile wishes). What he proposes instead, citing Ogden, is a conception of the mind that is fluid, "continually in movement," and shaped by each new intersubjective relationship, or perhaps one should say, by the unconscious meanings given to each new intersubjective relationship.

Postmodernism and relational psychoanalysis

We see here a marriage between postmodernism and the interactional–relational turn in psychoanalysis. The two are not *inherently* linked, but have become linked in some of the contemporary literature. One can take the eminently reasonable position, as, for example, Gill (1982, 1994) does, that the analyst cannot be – nor is there virtue in trying to be – a blank screen nor a fully objective observer and that patient and analyst are always emitting cues and are always influencing each other – in short, that the analytic situation is thoroughgoingly interactional and relational. But these observations themselves do not necessarily lead to a postmodernist perspective. The basis for the marriage between the relational–interactional turn and postmodernism does not lie in the claim that patient and analyst interact and influence each other – who would dispute that fact these days? Rather, it resides in the claims that the analyst constitutes the patient's mind through "interpretive construction", that there is nothing corresponding to the phrase "in the patient's mind" that the patient or analyst can be right or wrong about, that the patient's mind is organized by each new intersubjective relationship (why isn't the analyst's mind also organized by each new intersubjective relationship?), and that there are no essential organized and stable properties of mind that are independent of social interaction.

The argument that the patient's mind is constituted by "interpretive construction" and that it is organized by each new intersubjective relationship seems to me to be analogous to the general postmodern reluctance to acknowledge the "default position" (Searle 1998) of a physical reality independent of our experiences, our language, and our constructions. Instead of positing an enduring and stable independent reality, postmodernists favor the idea of constructions that vary with historical era and social convention. Analogously, the analyst who is inclined toward postmodernism also seems to favor a conception of the patient's mind, not as something that has a stable and enduring structure independently of patient–analyst (and other) interactions, but as something that is "interpretively constructed" and is characterized by momentary states of meaning that vary with each interpersonal interaction. Thus, just as the postmodernist does not accord physical reality a status independent of social constructions of it, similarly the "new view" analyst does not accord mental reality (i.e. the patient's mind) a status independent of interpretive construction and social interaction.

Some "new view" theorists attempt to support their social constructivist conception of mind by drawing on developmental evidence suggesting that social interactions shape the infant's mental states and even the very possibility of developing any mental states at all and apply such evidence to adult mental functioning. However, they draw on developmental data very selectively. Yes, the developmental literature strongly suggests that social interaction influences the infant's mental states. But an important distinction is made in that literature between caregiving that is characterized by a sensitive and attuned responsiveness to the infant's actual signals and caregiving characterized by the imposition and projection of the caregiver's mental states on to the infant (e.g. Lieberman 1999). In both cases, the caregiver is helping to shape the infant's mental states. But in one case, the caregiver is responding relatively accurately and sensitively to the infant's actual signals and, in the other case, the caregiver, unable to distinguish between her own and the infant's mental states, imposes her mental states on to the infant. Were the infant's mind totally shaped and constructed by the caregiver's behavior, there could be no meaningful distinction between sensitive responsiveness and imposition and projection.

So, even in infancy, there are limits to social influences which, when exceeded, violate the integrity and inner nature of the individual. The infant is not a tabula rasa who is infinitely malleable to social influence. Although "new view" theorists may be uncomfortable with anything that smacks of essentialism, each infant possesses essential characteristics to which the sensitive caregiver responds and the insensitive caregiver does not. Further, it should also be noted that by the time one gets to be an adult, one has developed relatively stable mental structures that are certinly not unlimitedly malleable and susceptible to being shaped by social interaction.

One is reminded here of Winnicott's (1975) concepts of true self and false self implicit in which is a distinction between sensitive and insensitive caregiving. It will be recalled that for Winnicott the false self is a self of social compliance. That is, it is the product of compliance with the caregiver's impositions – a kind of "I will be who you want and need me to be." By contrast, the true self flows from the spontaneous organic impulse of the infant. "New view" theorists have always been uncomfortable with Winnicott's concept of true self (e.g. Mitchell 1991). It is too essentialist and therefore anathema to them. It suggests that in optimal development, certain areas of the personality need to be relatively *unsusceptible* to social interactional influence. There is no room for this idea in a thoroughgoing social constructivist view of mind. From that point of view, there can be no meaningful distinction between true self and false self. Or, to put it more sharply, Winnicott's description of a false self is virtually equivalent to the social constructivist's normative conception of the development of self.

It seems to me that one can draw a useful analogy between the importance of a caregiver's accurate and attuned responsiveness to her infant's signals – which partly depends on *genuinely* knowing her baby – and the importance of the traditional idea that the analyst's interpretations need to "tally with what is real [in the patient]." In either case, if mind is entirely constituted by social interaction, then, respectively, there are no independent mental (or physical) states in the infant for the caregiver to be accurately responsive to, or, in the adult, nothing corresponding to the phrase "in the patient's mind" for the analyst (or the patient) to be right or wrong about.

The authority of the analyst in the "new view"

As noted earlier and also in our article (Eagle et al. 2001), one basis for the "new view" critique of traditional psychoanalysis is the latter's presumed unearned authority and arrogance implicit in its claim that analysts had privileged access to the truth about the patient's mind and therefore, provided singular canonical interpretations about what is going on in the patient's mind. One risk, among many, of such a stance was the imposition of the analyst's point of view on the patient. Following a tradition begun by Ferenczi (Ferenczi and Rank 1986) the positions taken by the "new view" theorists democratized and contributed to an increasing egalitarianism of the analytic relationship. The singular canonical truth about the patient's mind was no longer to be authoritatively, and perhaps, if I may coin an neologism, authoritarianly, pronounced by the supposedly knowledgeable and expert analyst. The only expertise the analyst had, we were told, by Mitchell, for example, was in "meaning making, self-reflection, and the organization–reorganization of experience" (Mitchell 1998: 2). Further, the creation of meaning systems and narratives was not to be imposed in authoritarian fashion, but to be co-constructed and negotiated.

Why would anyone object to this seemingly new humility and increasing democratization of the analytic relationship? There are a number of answers to this question. For one thing, I do not see any less arrogance in the claim that one is an expert in meaning-making and the organization and reorganization of experience than in the traditional claim that one is an expert in reading unconscious wishes, motives, and defenses. Indeed, I find the latter more modest. I am made more than a little uncomfortable by claims of expertness in meaning-making and organization and reorganization of experience – these latter areas are too close to the core of how each one of us defines oneself. I don't know that anyone can legitimately claim to be an expert in these areas.

The purported arrogance of some classical analysts in asserting special access to the truth about the patient's mind is not *inherently* linked to a theory that sets analysts the task of inferring unconscious contents and processes in the patient's mind, particularly if the ideal of the theory is that such inferences "tally with what is real [in the patient]" (Freud 1916–1917: 452). In principle, given this ideal, arrogance and other excesses are correctible. I worry more about the excesses of a theory and philosophical stance that takes the position that the patient's mind is constituted by the analyst's "interpretive construction" and that there is nothing corresponding to the phrase "in the patient's mind" about which patient or analyst can be right or wrong. I do not see much possibility for correctives in this kind of position. There is no adequate recognition of an independently existing mind against which to judge the adequacy or accuracy of one's interpretations insofar as these interpretations constitute and construct the very mind that is being interpreted. What an opportunity for a benevolent, well-meaning socially determined, intersubjective tyranny! How is such a tyranny to be resisted when the very mind that would do the resisting is supposedly constituted and organized by the interpretations to be resisted? If I were a patient in treatment, I would be inclined to say: Thanks, but I will do my own meaning-making and my own organization of my experiences.

The "new view" of transference

I want to address some nuances in the position of the "new view" theorists that I have not fully dealt with to this point. As noted earlier, these theorists are quite comfortable with the exploration of the patient's momentary and fluid mental states. Indeed, as noted earlier and as Friedman (1998) observes, they seem to take that as their main psychoanalytic task. Also, as noted, it is the positing of "preorganized" and relatively stable and static structures that they tend to reject. This focus on the momentary gives one an additional insight into the thinking of the "new view" theorists. For it is precisely momentary and fluid mental states that can be readily seen as the product of ongoing social interaction. It is far more difficult to attribute stable and enduring structures to ongoing and ever-changing social inter-action, insofar as, by definition, they cut across different interactional situations. The "new view" theorists seem to have faith in the idea that it is the exploration of the momentary states that are the product of ongoing and fluid social interactions that will lead to therapeutic change. It is not clear what this faith rests on nor is the nature of the carry over from these explorations to the ongoing life of the patient outside treatment clear.

One can understand the intuition that an exploration of the patient's ongoing here-and-now fluid experiences with the analyst are likely to be associated with a greater cognitive and emotional immediacy. This has been an important basis for arguing the greater mutative power of transference interpretation (Freud 1912; Strachey 1934). However, one cannot ignore the question of the carry over of these explorations to the ongoing life of the patient outside treatment. It should also be noted that exploration of the patient's momentary states that are linked to ongoing patient–analyst interaction cannot simply be equated with analysis of the transference. One major purpose of the latter is to identify, in the here and now immediacy of the analytic situation, the patient's enduring intrapsychic and interactional patterns that also characterize his or her life outside the treatment situation. Although, as Gill (1982, 1994) and others noted, these patterns may be influenced by the analyst's characteristics and cues, they are not simply idiosyncratic momentary states uniquely and entirely generated by the specific patient–analyst dyad. That is, they are not simply "newly experienced in the context of each new . . . intersubjective relationship." Rather, the particular transference that appears in the analytic situation is believed to be representative of the patient's relatively stable intrapsychic and inter-actional patterns with significant people in his or her past and present life. It is this representativeness that partly gives analysis of the transference a special therapeutic role in analytic treatment. It is not clear what the meaning of transference would be and why it would have any special role if the mind were organized by "each new intersubjective relationship".

The whole point about the concept of transference is that it points to a "stickiness" of mental structures and patterns. As Rapaport (1959) noted a long time ago, structures are defined by their slow rate of change, not by fluidity. On a more pragmatic and concrete level, the fact is that people, including and particularly people in treatment, do not change that easily and readily. As we note in our article (Eagle et al. 2001)

> People who come to treatment (and, to a certain extent, people in general) . . . show repetitive and "static" patterns of behaviors . . . Were people as readily susceptible to being shaped and restructured by each new intersubjective interaction therapeutic change would be much easier than it is.
>
> (Eagle et al. 2001: 476)

There is something disturbingly unrealistic and pollyanish in all this talk about psychic organization being "always susceptible to being shaped and restructured . . . in the context of each new unconscious intersubjective relationship" (Ogden 1997: 190).

There are other disturbing aspects of the current postmodern turn. As Sass (1992) asks, are "new view" analysts sharing their new conceptions of psychoanalytic treatment with their patients? Is the presumed impossibility of determining the veridicality of interpretations a secret being kept from the patients? And I would add, do patients really believe there is nothing corresponding to the phrase "in the patient's mind" about which neither they nor their analyst can be right or wrong? Do they accept the goal of becoming "relative historians" of their lives? Would they stay in treatment if they were told directly that the analyst does not believe that it is possible to discover any truths, but rather is offering beautifully wrought "aesthetic fictions" (Geha 1984)?

There is something disingenuous in the disjunction between, on the one hand, how "new view" theorists work and what they tell patients and, on the other hand, the stance they take in journal articles and books. Perhaps the disingenuousness is fortunate. For as we tried to demonstrate in an earlier article and as, for example, Smith (1999) has argued, the fact is that despite the rhetoric, their conceptualization of concrete clinical material and their description of what they do is not especially different from that of any analyst (for a further discussion of the issue, see Eagle et al. 2001).

The irreducible subjectivity of the analyst

Another example of the tendency of "new view" theorists to extend legitimate observation or criticism to a point of untenability is seen in Renik's (1993, 1998; see also Renik 1996) discussion of the analyst's "irreducible subjectivity". Certainly, the traditional claim that as a "blank screen," neutral observer, the analyst has privileged and fully objective knowledge of the patient's mind warrants serious criticisms. However, that one cannot warrantedly claim such privilege and such knowledge does not leave the sole alternative that one is mired in "irreducible subjectivity," nor does it mean that the analyst's attempts to "find the patient's views" rather than his or her "own idiosyncratic views" "are essentially versions of [an untenable] analytic neutrality" (Renik 1998: 509).

There is a good deal of ambiguity and confusion in Renik's discussion of the analyst's "irreducible subjectivity," some of it trading on the different possible meanings of subjectivity. First, in an important sense, all personal experience is "irreducibly subjective" – that is what first person experiences are. However, that my experience is irreducibly subjective – after all, only I can have my own experience – does not mean that what I am subjectively experiencing cannot also be objective. My experience of, say, a red ball in front of me, in one important sense, is irreducibly subjective – I am having the experience. But that subjective experience is also objective in the sense that there is a red ball in front of me which others can also see. So, thus far, there is no contradiction between an experience being both irreducibly subjective as well as objective (see Meissner 2000).

A similar point holds with regard to the issue of taking different perspectives. Much is made by postmodernists and "new view" theorists, including Renik, about the fact that each of us may have a particular personal perspective about a given event or phenomenon. Continuing with the simple red ball example, you may literally have a different perspective on the red ball because you are seeing it from a different position. Thus, your subjective experience will be somewhat different from mine. But, as Cavell (1998) has pointed out in her discussion of Renik's article,

> The idea of a perspective on the world that is partial and subjective makes sense only given the idea of a world that is objective, a world that is there, independently of my seeing, that can be seen from different points of view while remaining the same world.
>
> (Cavell 1998: 115)

There would be no sense in talking about different perspectives on the red ball unless there were an objective red ball about which one has different perspectives. As Searle (1998) asks, in order to know reality objectively, is it necessary that one know it from *no* point of view?[1]

Renik wants to emphasize that the analyst, under the guise of neutrality and objectivity, is hiding the fact that his or her activity consists "essentially of communicating his or her personal judgments" (1998: 509). For Renik, this means the analyst is somehow being misleading when he or she claims to be trying to "find the patient's views". Were the analyst fully open and honest, Renik implies, he or she would have to acknowledge that he or she is addressing his or her "own psychic reality" and his or her "own idiosyncratic views".

There is much confusion here that needs to be unraveled. First, of course, the analyst communicates his or her personal judgments about and to the patient. What else would he or she do, communicate someone else's judgment? But, one hopes that the judgment is a reasonably informed one, based on such considerations as material presented by the patient, knowledge of the literature, training, and past experience. Second, if I communicate my personal judgment of what is going on in your mind, it does not simply mean that I am addressing my own psychic reality rather than trying to find and understand yours. Although I may be mistaken in my judgments, I nevertheless am trying to find your views and your psychic reality. My personal judgment is subjective insofar as it is mine. But, as noted above, this does not mean that it cannot also be objective. It is directed toward understanding you, not me. And in the context of the analytic situation, even when I am trying to understand my psychic reality, it is in the service of better understanding you. I am making a personal judgment about what is going on in you. Furthermore, although it is a personal judgment, it may be one warranted by the evidence and one that, based on the evidence, others might reach. So, it might be objective in that sense too.

Implicit in Renik's view is the idea that because of one's "irreducible subjectivity", each analyst is hopelessly locked into a self-enclosed solipsistic world in which one may deceive oneself that one is trying to find and addressing the patient's psychic reality when, in fact, one is really addressing one's own psychic reality. One might as well, then, stop pretending and openly acknowledge that this is what one is doing. This seems to be Renik's basic message. As I have noted, this is a confused message and certainly not one on which analysts ought to base their approach to patients. Of course, all judgment is filtered through subjective experience and even subjective bias. But one can become mired in proclamations of "irreducible subjectivity" at every turn – as postmodernists and "new view" theorists tend to do – or one can try to recognize and deal with one's idiosyncratic biases, however incompletely and imperfectly, and get on with the business of trying to understand the patient as fully and accurately as possible. After all, isn't this what we do in our normal daily lives? Our subjective perceptions are generally directed toward objects in the world and are normally in the service of gaining as accurate an understanding of them as possible.

Parallels to historical context

In the remaining section of the chapter I want to examine certain parallels between the role of truth in the contemporary psychoanalytic viewpoints I have been discussing and in particular approaches to historical accounts. I want to try to demonstrate the kinds of difficulties and inconsistencies that a particular way of thinking about these matters leads to in both the psychoanalytic and historical contexts.

The issues discussed here – discovering truth versus "interpretive constructions"; reconceptualizations of truth; contradiction between theory and practice – are not limited to the psychoanalytic context, but also emerge in other contexts, including political and historical contexts. I have been struck by the parallels between, on the one hand, the claim that the analyst does not discover what is in the patient's mind but rather offers "interpretive constructions" and, on the other hand, the claim that historical accounts do not deal with "what really happened", but only with different perspectives and interpretive constructions. Just as in the psychoanalytic context, it is claimed that mind is constituted by "interpretive constructions", so similarly in the historical context is it claimed that historical events are constituted by the historians' constructions and perspectives.

In a fascinating book, Spitzer (1996) examines the very issues I have been discussing in the context of four politically charged debates (the Dewey Commission's evaluation of the charges against Leon Trotsky in the Moscow Purge Trials; the Dreyfus Affair; Paul De Man's complicity with the German occupation in wartime Belgium and Reagan's justification for his 1987 visit to Bitburg cemetery). He demonstrates convincingly that "the refutation of falsehood or error depends on some criteria of veracity and validity and that these criteria are exposed in the heat of debate regardless of the theoretical affirmation or repudiation of epistemological standards" (Spitzer 1996: 1). For example, although in his general philosophical writings, Dewey (1938: 287) adopted an instrumentalist version of inquiry (as does Renik) and writes that "truth-falsity is not a property of propositions", he nevertheless claims that the Dewey Commission was trying to get at the truth as to the specific charges upon which he (i.e. Trotsky) was convicted: "This work is one of evidence and objective fact, not of weighing theories against each other" (as quoted in Spitzer 1996: 27). As Spitzer observes, despite his general instrumentalist theory of truth and inquiry, in evaluating the specific question of Trotsky's guilt or innocence of the Moscow trial charges and "in his refutation of the Commission's critics, Dewey seems to grant a hard autonomy to the 'objective facts'." Spitzer goes on to question whether the latter position can be reconciled with Rorty's (1991) celebration of "Dewey's suspicion of attempts to contrast an objective given (i.e. 'the evidence,' 'the facts') with human takings" (Spitzer 1996: 27, quoting Rorty 1991: 65).

The contradiction between theory and practice in regard to historical accounts can be seen as analogous to the disjunction between conceptual stance and concrete clinical material that we have observed in the work of Mitchell and Renik. Thus, although rejecting traditional claims regarding patients' preorganized central dynamics, in discussing the specific case of Robert, Mitchell (1998) seems to have no hesitation in identifying such preorganized central dynamics. He writes:

> I also suggested that his struggles with his son were in some measure reflective of struggles with a part of himself that had long been buried . . . Yet his dreams of something important that has long been forgotten suggest to me that he is struggling with a sense that he has tragically mutilated his own inner resources and potential.
>
> (Mitchell 1998: 23)

And similarly, despite rhetoric about "alternative perspectives", when Renik (1996) interprets the patient's chronic anger at her sister as, in part, a defense against critical feelings towards her parents, one assumes that he believes that she actually harbors such feelings toward her parents; and one expects that evidence is, or will be, provided to justify the attribution of such feelings to the patient.

The nature of truth in psychoanalytic and historical accounts

The parallel between historical and psychoanalytic accounts and the issues raised by such accounts goes further. Characteristic of some contemporary psychoanalytic theorists is a reconceptualization of the nature of truths – for example, Spence's (1980) equation of truth with persuasiveness ("narrative truth") and Renik's (1998) definition of the truth of a proposition by its consequences (what is true is what works). Although one may be seduced by the latter when the consequences in question seem to be benevolent (e.g., increasing the patient's happiness), as Spitzer convincingly demonstrates, perversions of truth in historical accounts have also been justified by presumed benevolent consequences and the prevention of negative consequences. For example, at around the time of the Moscow trials, many on the American Left argued that it was imperative that Trotsky be declared guilty because the Soviet Union needed support against fascism and other reactionary forces. A February 13, 1937 issue of the *Worker's Age* analogized between the Moscow trials and the political trials of the French Revolution and concluded: "In effect, we practically ignore the charges, refutations and counter-charges and ask ourselves: Which tendency was carrying forward the interests of the revolution and which was obstructing it?" (quoted in Spitzer 1996: 30). This is a conception of truth by conse-quences with, both literally and figuratively, a vengeance.

A similar argument was launched by the Anti-Dreyfusards in the Dreyfus case. As Spitzer (1996: 10) describes it, the weaker position taken was that "no truth could be accepted that entailed deplorable consequences" (i.e. the weakening of the military and the French state); the stronger position was "that the consequences constituted the truth" (Spitzer 1996: 10). Given the consequences that presumably "followed from an affirmation of Dreyfus' innocence, he must have been guilty" (Spitzer 1996: 10). Note that in both the case of the Moscow trials and the Dreyfus affair, the question of the guilt or innocence of the individuals on trial – their intentions, their actions, was essentially irrelevant for those who adopted a thoroughgoing prag-matic conception of truth.

A favorite of the right, a leading anti-Dreyfusard, and someone whose novels were a precursor to fascist ideology, Maurice Barres maintained that "truth was to be located in a given community or, generally in a nation. There was a French truth and a Jewish truth, necessarily incommensurable and therefore beyond argument" (Spitzer 1996: 10). In essence, Barres was arguing that there is no objective truth that is independent of one's community interests, but only different truths determined by the interests and perspectives of one's particular community. As Spitzer (1996: 10) notes, "Barres' appeal to solidarity as the matrix of truth has a contemporary resonance, although present-day advocates of such a criterion would scarcely wish to be aligned with the Barres' version of it". (Here Spitzer is alluding to, among others, the work of Rorty, in particular, his attempt to replace the ideal of objectivity with solidarity.)

Despite the redefinitions of truth in terms of consequences and of com-munity interests, those who were engaged in the frame-up of both Trotsky and Dreyfus also appealed to "facts" and "objective evidence," even if certain evidence was concealed and other "evidence" manufactured. The point here, "is that despite the general rhetoric about the nature of truth, when the chips are down, even those involved in the frame-ups tried to make their case by appealing to generally accepted standards of relevant evidence and rational inference" (Spitzer 1996: back cover). This is so because rational discussion is not possible without such standards. For example, to assert openly and present as one's sole argument, that whatever the facts, Trotsky must be found guilty for the sake of the revolution or that Dreyfus must be found guilty for the good of the French state is already to acknowledge the frame-up and to lose one's case in what hopes is the judgment of a wide audience. One can hardly convincingly resort to the argument that the verdict of guilty "works" (i.e. it protects the revo-lution or the French state) and therefore, is true.

The conception of truth in terms of consequences and the claim that different subjective interests and different communities yield different truths are related to each other and both find contemporary resonance in the work of some contemporary psychoanalytic theorists. The former, truth as a function of consequences is clearly expressed in Renik's (1998: 492) assertion that what is true is what works, and the latter, that truth and objectivity vary with one's subjective interests, in Renik's (1996, 1998) argument that any claim to objectivity is necessarily from the perspective of one's subjective interests. However seductive these epistemological ideas may be to some, they break down and cannot be sustained when one deals with concrete historical or clinical case material. As Spitzer puts it and as cited earlier, in regard to the four "cases" he discusses, "the refutation of falsehood or error depends on some criteria of veracity and validity and . . . these criteria are exposed in the heat of debate regardless of the theoretical affirmation or repudiation of epistemological standards" (Spitzer 1996: 1).

Discrepancy between theoretical stance and clinical approach

I would maintain that this is also true when one deals with specific clinical material, that is, when one is trying to understand what is going on in the mind of the patient as fully and accurately as possible and have one's interventions guided by that understanding. As has been noted, their epistemological rhetoric notwithstanding, the specific clinical formulations of Mitchell and Renik are not appreciably different from the kinds of formulations any analyst would be likely to make. Or, to put it somewhat differently, if one were exposed only to their description of the clinical material, one would have little inkling of their epistemological position.

In commenting on Renik's redefinition of truth and objectivity, Smith writes:

> contrary to his theory, however, Renik's clinical example, like others he has published, suggests that he is still guided in part by a traditional model of objectivity and tries to establish what is more objectively "out there" or "in there"
>
> (Smith 1999: 468)

Just as, if one read only the Dewey Commission's report on Trotsky, one would have little idea of Dewey's general philosophical views regarding the nature of inquiry, truth, and objective fact. The point here is not that Dewey or Mitchell or Renik are being inconsistent. The point, rather, is that their general philosophical positions are *unsustainable* when one deals with concrete material and concrete questions such as: was Trotsky (or Dreyfus) guilty or innocent of the charges brought against him? Did Renik's patient, in fact, harbor unconscious hostile feelings toward her parents and defend against them by focusing exclusively on her resentment toward her sister or is Renik's interpretation simply an "alternative perspective" that will purportedly help pave the way for her greater happiness? Does Mitchell's (1998) patient Robert, *in fact*, struggle "with the sense that he has tragically mutilated his own inner resources and potentiality" or are he and his patient only co-constructing a "new mythology?" The bottom line is that answering these questions requires evidence and "criteria of veracity and validity", a fact that should not be obscured by talk about meaning systems, alternative perspectives, coherent narratives, narrative truth, and so on.

For many historical accounts, the question of "what really happened", its currently unfashionable status notwithstanding, is critical. We want to know whether Trotsky, *in fact*, intended and acted in accord with the accusations against him and whether Dreyfus, *in fact*, betrayed French military secrets to the German military attaché in Paris. The parallel critical question in psychoanalytic accounts is not what really happened in the patient's early history. That is often difficult, if not impossible to ascertain and in any case too much has been made of it. As far as clinical work is concerned, it may frequently not be that important. The critical question in the psychoanalytic context that parallels the historical question of "what really happened" is, so to speak, "what is happening". That is what is the nature of the patient's thoughts, feelings, desires, conflicts, defenses, etc. and how adequately do one's theories, one's inferences and interpretations help the patient identify and acknowledge them? Thus, contrary to Mitchell (1998), there is a great deal corresponding to the phrase in the patient's mind about which one can be right or wrong. And the great deal is nothing less than the independent existence of the patient, his or her wishes, desires, conflicts, defenses, representations and so on. This does not mean that there is one canonical correct account or that there cannot be different perspectives on historical and mental events or that any account is endowed with absolute certainty. But, and this is central – one must leave room for being right or wrong, even if probabilistically. We have seen what the alternative to that is in historical accounts: a definition of truth by its political consequences and by one's community and political interests, with the total irrelevance of the actions, intentions, and sufferings of the individual or individuals.

Tallying with what is real – a moral issue

In the psychoanalytic context, the consequences of rejecting or minimizing the question of whether one's accounts "tally with something real in the patient" (Freud 1916–1917: 452) are, of course, more subtle and less political. But, they nevertheless are present and as in the case of historical accounts, also have a moral dimension. Thus, unless Renik really believes that his patient, in fact, harbors unconscious hostile feelings toward her parents, which she defends against (and addresses evidence for this belief), his interpretation is an arbitrary one and, in an important sense, violates the integrity of the patient. It is not enough to say that it "works" and therefore, is true. It is very likely that, in fact, Renik made that interpretation because he had reason to believe that his patient actually harbored unconscious resentful feelings toward her parents. This interpretation does, indeed, provide a new perspective on the patient's chronic anger at her sister. But it is not only a new perspective – there are an indefinite number of new perspectives one can take; it is a new perspective based on the inference that certain defended against thoughts and feelings are "in the patient's mind". Were one to make this kind of interpretation without having good reason to believe that the patient, in fact, has such thoughts and feelings, one would be on questionable moral ground – however much the interpretation might contribute to the patient's happiness. Or, to put it more accurately, however much one believes that the interpretation contributes to the patient's happiness. That Renik himself would not be comfortable with an interpretation solely on the basis of whether it "works" (i.e., increases the patient's happiness) is indicated by his reluctance to relinquish considerations of truth (what is true is what works) and objectivity (objectivity is always from a subjective interest) even if they are redefined so as to become unrecognizable (for a further discussion of this issue, see Eagle et al. 2001).

A return to the historical context

In our contemporary age, the historical event that most disturbingly and profoundly challenges constructionist views of historical events is the Holocaust. As Friedlander writes, "the equivocation of postmodernism concerning 'reality' and 'truth' – that is, ultimately, its fundamental relativism confronts any discourse about Nazism and the Shoah with considerable difficulties" (Friedlander 1992: 20). Doubts about the historian's ability to represent "what really happened" is exemplified by the work of Hayden White (e.g. 1992) who writes, "It is possible to tell different stories about the past and there is no way, finally, to check them out against the facts of the matter, the criterion for evaluating them is moral or poetic" (as quoted in Spitzer 1996: 3). White attempts to deal with the implications of his position by confronting the question:

> Do you mean to say that the occurrence and nature of the Holocaust is only a matter of opinion and that one write its history in whatever way one pleases? Do you imply that any account of that event is as valid as any other account so long as it meets certain formal requirements of discursive practices and that one has no responsibility to the victims to tell the truth about the indignities and cruelties they suffered?
>
> (White, quoted in Spitzer 1996: 3–4)

His response to these questions is to acknowledge a "factual bedrock" and "a terrain of positive history [where] true opposes false quite simply independent of any kind of an interpretation" (as cited in Spitzer 1996: 4). However, as Spitzer observes, White "then qualifies this rather striking concession" with this caveat: "the distinction between a lie and an error or a mistake in interpretation may be more difficult to draw with respect to historical events less amply documented than the Holocaust" (as quoted in Spitzer 1996: 4).

White's equivocation reflects the tension and contradictions between general theoretical-philosophical stance, on the one hand, and the need to come to grips with the concrete, in this case, an extraordinary concrete historical event, on the other hand. White proclaims the possibility of "tell[ing] different stories about the past," the impossibility of checking out the stories "against the facts of the matter", and the final judgment that the "criterion for evaluating [these stories] is moral or poetic". However, when confronted with the reality of the concrete event, in this case, an extraordinary concrete event, White suddenly introduces the "factual bedrock" and the "terrain of positive history [where] true opposes false quite simply independent of any kind of an interpretation" (as quoted in Spitzer 1996: 4). Is this because, as White suggests, the Holocaust is more "amply documented" than other historical events? I do not think that this is the only or crucial difference between the Holocaust and other historical events. I suggest rather that the profound moral dimension of the Holocaust confronts one in a blinding way with the disturbing implications of a position that views history primarily in terms of "tell [ing] different stories about the past". Under the impact of confronting the concrete event of the Holocaust, with its ample documentation, White is forced to acknowledge a "factual bedrock" and "a terrain of [where] true opposes false quite simply independent of any kind of an interpretation" (Spitzer 1996: 4). Presumably, White is acknowledging that if they are to be counted as history, the different stories one can tell must not violate "factual bedrock".

In a remarkable parallel, Mitchell (1998), aware that he runs the risk of being seen as favoring an "anything goes" approach, that is, of simply telling different stories, remarks, first, that "interpretive constructions" must not contradict basic facts of the patient's life, and second, that interpretive constructions that do contradict known facts do not work well.[2] Mitchell then makes clear that what he means by known facts is limited to discrete physical events, such as Mother died when I was three, and does not include such psychological events as Mother was withdrawn and depressed. Although the latter is far more difficult to ascertain than the former – an epistemological issue – it is not clear why it is not granted any facticity – an ontological issue. Also, insofar as analysts deal with psychological phenomena rather than discrete physical events, there is little weight carried by the requirement that psychoanalytic interpretations do not contradict discrete physical events. In the psychoanalytic context, if one is to avoid an "anything goes" approach, it is far more important that interpretations be constrained, not so much by past discrete physical events, but by what is happening now, that is, by the patient's current inner world of thoughts, feelings, desires, conflicts, etc. Of course, if one's inner world is *constituted* by the analyst's interpretive constructions, then such constraints are difficult to come by (for further discussion, see Eagle et al. 2003).

In drawing an analogy between psychoanalytic interpretations and historical accounts, a fundamental question to be asked is whether mental contents and processes (i.e. thoughts, feelings, conflicts, intentions, representations) can be understood to have a claim to the status of factuality similar to historical events. That is, the evaluation of psychoanalytic interpretations in terms of whether they "tally with what is real in the patient" parallels the evaluation of historical accounts in terms of whether or not they correspond to "factual bedrock"? However, whereas in the case of historical events, the "factual bedrock" often consists, in large part, of documented events, in the case of psychoanalytic accounts, as I have noted, the "factual bedrock" is not primarily the delineated "factual events" of the patient's life, but rather the mental contents and processes that constitute the patient's mind, that is, the patient's psychic reality. Hence, to say that an interpretation "tallies with what is real in the patient" is not to say that it corresponds to certain autobiographical "factual events" in the patient's life, but rather to say that it corresponds to his or her thoughts, feelings, conflicts, defenses, representations, that is, to his or her actual mental contents and processes.

However, historical accounts are not limited to delineated (and documented) physical events, but also include an examination of the motives, intentions, goals, beliefs, etc. of the historical figures involved in the events (Collingwood 1956). For example, one wants to know, not only that Dreyfus did not give military secrets to the German military, but also that he never had any intention to betray France. Any adequate historical account would include the fact that the death of millions in the Holocaust was not primarily the byproduct of other circumstances (e.g., disease, malnutrition), but was rather the result of an *intentional plan* in the minds of Nazi leaders. An essential part, then, of the "factual bedrock" for historical accounts often includes what was in the minds of those figures who played key roles in the historical events being described and interpreted.

In the psychoanalytic context, the pertinent contrast is not that between "historical truth" and some account of the patient's life that is meant to be persuasive and is called "narrative truth", but rather between interpretations that more poorly correspond to what is going on in the patient's mind versus those that more adequately tally with what is real in the patient – when it is clear that "real in the patient" refers to mental contents and processes (i.e., thoughts, feelings, conflicts, defenses, representations) going on in the patient's mind.

In drawing parallels between historical and psychoanalytic accounts, obviously, I am not equating "new view" theorists with Holocaust deniers, just as Spitzer (1996) is not equating Rorty's and various historians' views with the views of Stalinists, anti-Dreyfusards, and Holocaust deniers. I am also aware that the contexts of historical accounts and individual treatment are different from each other. The therapist who focuses on serviceable and persuasive narratives ("narrative truth") or new perspectives is, after all, motivated by a desire to do good, that is, relieve the patient's distress. However, good intentions are not sufficient here. For one thing, from their perspective, anti-Dreyfusards who demanded a narrative that would strengthen the French army and the French state – without regard for whether the facts demonstrated Dreyfus' guilt or innocence, that is, without regard for whether the account tallied with what was real – also had good intentions, the welfare of the nation and the army. The problem is that in the long run the path of constructing narratives, without adequate regard for the truth of the matter, is a dangerous one to take. Ultimately, this is a question of values. To what degree does one want to base one's life on persuasive narratives, even if they are comforting, or on searching for the truth about onself, even if that can be discomforting? This question is pertinent at both the level of the individual and the collective level of society. With regard to the latter, one can ask to what extent is a society dedicated to persuasive narratives and comforting historical myths and narratives versus a dedication to free inquiry and a search for the truth of the matter.

What I am trying to show is the dilemma and blind alleys to which a particular way of thinking may lead, in the contexts of both historical and psychoanalytic accounts. As far as the latter is concerned, I do not believe that one can dispense with or tamper too much with pursuing the central goal of always trying to determine what "is real in the patient" and continue to remain psychoanalytic. But to try to understand "what is real in the patient" requires a conception of (the patient's) mind as something that exists and is organized and structured independently of interactions with the analyst,[3] just as, in the historical context, one cannot dispense with or tamper too much with the central goal of always trying to determine the truth of "what really happened" independently of one's "interpretive constructions" and still hope to generate valid history. In both cases, it may be difficult to determine the truth of the matter; there may be disagreements regarding it; and there may be different perspectives on the same set of phenomena and events. However, the considerable and complex epistemological issues aside, the rock bottom question is an ontological one: complex and however difficult to determine, is there a truth of the matter, independent of one's interest, theories and biases, to be ascertained?

In the case of historical events, the question is: can one present an account of what really happened relatively independently of one's interest and biases? For example, did Trotsky and Dreyfus do what they were accused of doing? In the case of psychoanalytic accounts, the question is: what is the nature of the patient's inner life (his or her desires, fears, conflicts, fantasies, representations, beliefs, expectations, etc.) relatively independently of my "interpretive constructions"? To even ask both questions requires a commitment to a belief in determinate events and phenomena that exist independently of one's constructions. In the case of historical events, this seems more concrete and evident. Either Trotsky or Dreyfus did or did not do X. Although the issue of determinate events is more complex and subtle in the context of the individual's inner psychological life, the ontological issue is the same. Are there determinate phenomena (desires, wishes, conflicts, etc.) to which my account must correspond if they are to "tally with what is real in the patient"?

It seems to me that, in principle, there is no reason to assign greater facticity to the statement, "A carried out action X" then to such statements as "A desired X" or "A believed Y" or "A was in conflict about Z". As Searle (1998) notes, to do so is to accept the metaphysical position that a physical action or physical event is somehow more part of nature and reality, more "objectively" true than a subjective desire or belief. As Searle (1998) points out, although the statement "I am thirsty" refers to a subjective experience, that I am thirsty is as objective a fact as physical event X occurred.

In coming to the end of this chapter, let me say that, in certain respects, the writings of the "new view" theorists have served a useful purpose in providing and encouraging correctives to certain traditional psychoanalytic assumptions. For example, they have helped dismantle the myth that the analyst is a purely objective, "blank screen" observer; they have sensitized us to the subtle and complex interactions and influences between patient and analyst; they have highlighted the role of the analyst's personal history and idiosyncratic subjectivity. However, in each case, in the course of offering useful and cogent critiques, they have taken philosophical positions that not only are philosophically untenable, but also do not provide a fruitful basis for the growth and development of psychoanalysis.

As long as one holds the ideal that one's inferences and interpretations need to be constrained and evaluated according to the degree to which they "tally with something real [in the patient]", we are answerable, in principle, to the independent reality and integrity of the patient. The "new view" theorists are sensitive to the abuses of traditional theory in which the analyst's conviction that he or she has privileged access to the Truth about the patient's mind leads to an imposition of his or her theoretical views on the patient. At least in that view, however, there are, in principle, as Kirshner (1999: 449) says, "limits to the extent of interpretive latitude." In the excessive swing of the pendulum that characterizes the position of the "new view" theorists, specifically, in maintaining that one constitutes the patient's mind through "interpretive construction", that there is no preorganized structure of the patient's mind, independent of the interaction with the analyst, that in trying to understand another, one is only address-ing one's own subjectivity, in all this, there is the danger that the very existence of the patient's mind structured independently of the analyst is called into question, and that one is in the business of creating, not under-standing the patient.

The point is not that "new view" theorists expressly want to theorize their patients out of existence. Rather, the point is that they take positions the implications of which carry these risks and abuses. It is not only traditional theory that can be abused. Indeed, as I have tried to show, many of the reactions of the "new view" theorists to problematic aspects of traditional theory entail even more serious problems. Psychoanalytic theorizing seems to be cursed with extreme swings of the pendulum, with each swing, while partly correctively reacting to difficulties of extant theories, often creates perhaps even more serious difficulties of its own. It seems to me that each of the problems identified by "new view" and other theorists – for example, the uncertainty of our knowledge of the other, the role of the analyst's idiosyncratic history, bias, and subjectivity, the indirect and inferential nature of our knowledge of another's mind, the mutual interactive influence between patient and analyst – all these do not obviate the need to recognize the existence of the patient's psychic reality inde-pendent of our "interpretive constructions" and the effort to understand that reality as fully and accurately as possible.

Acknowledgments

This is a revised and considerably extended version of an article, entitled 'The postmodern turn in psychoanalysis', published in 2003 in *Psycho-analytic Psychology*, 20: 411–424.

Notes

1 Nagel (1986) has devoted an entire book, *The View from Nowhere*, to, as he puts it, "a single problem: how to combine the perspective of a particular person inside the world with an objective view of the same world, the person and his viewpoint included" (Nagel 1986: 3). Nagel weaves complex and multifaceted arguments in addressing this problem. However, a number of important points that Nagel makes are relevant in the present context. For Nagel, "the wider range of subjective types to which a form of understanding is accessible – the less it depends on specific subjective capacities – the more objective it is." In other words, although there are limits to objectivity – we are finite and fallible and cannot get outside ourselves completely – one can increase one's objective

understanding by trying to transcend one's own particular viewpoint. Such a step involves an examination of the relation "between the world and ourselves which is responsible for our prior understanding." There is, of course, much more to be said on this deep issue, but this is obviously not the place for it.

2 With regard to the latter, a number of questions come to mind: One, how does Mitchell know that interpretations that contradict known facts do not work well? And two, what if such interpretations did work well, that is, were therapeutically helpful? Would they, as Renik maintains, thereby become true (Mitchell 1998)?

3 Although, of course, it is influenced by ongoing interactions with the analyst as well, of course, as with other figures.

References

Beck, A. T., Rush, A. and Shaw, J. (1979) *Cognitive Theory of Depression*, New York: Guilford.

Cavell, M. (1998) 'In response to Owen Renik's "The analyst's subjectivity and the analyst's objectivity"', *International Journal of Psychoanalysis*, 79: 1195–1202.

Collingwood, R. G. (1956) *The Idea of History*, Oxford: Oxford University Press.

Dewey, J. (1938) *The Logic of Inquiry*, New York: Holt.

Eagle, M.N. (1984) 'Geha's vision of psychoanalysis as fiction', *International Forum for Psychoanalysis*, 1(3–4), 141–162.

Eagle, M. N., Wolitzky, D. L. and Wakefield, J. C. (2001) 'The analyst's knowledge and authority: a critique of the "New View" in psychoanalysis', *Journal of the American Psychoanalytic Association*, 49(2): 457–488.

Eagle, M. N., Wakefield, J. C. and Wolitzky, D. L. (2003) 'Interpreting Mitchell's constructivism', *Journal of the American Psychoanalytic Association*, 51, supplement: 162–179.

Ferenczi, S. and Rank, O. (1986) *The Development of Psychoanalysis*, Classics in Psychoanalysis 4, Madison, CT: International Universities Press.

Freud, S. (1912) 'The dynamics of transference', *Standard Edition*, 12: 97–108, London: Hogarth Press.

—— (1916–1917) *Introductory Lectures on Psychoanalysis*, *Standard Edition*, 15 and 16, London: Hogarth Press.

Friedlander, S. (ed.) (1992) *Probing the Limits of Representation: Nazism and the "Final Solution"*, Cambridge, MA: Harvard University Press.

Friedman, L. (1998) 'Overview', in O. Renik (ed.) *Knowledge and Authority in the Psychoanalytic Relationship*, Northvale, NJ: Jason Aronson.

Geha, R. E. (1984) 'On psychoanalytic history and the "real" story of fictitious lives', *International Forum of Psychoanalysis*, 1: 221–229.

Gill, M. M. (1982) *The Analysis of Transference: Theory and Technique*, New York: International Universities Press.

—— (1994) *Psychoanalysis in Transition*, Hillsdale, NJ: Analytic Press.

Habermas, J. (1971) *Knowledge and Human Interests*, Boston, MA: Beacon.

Kirshner, L. A. (1999) 'Toward a postmodern realism for psychoanalysis', *Journal of the American Psychoanalytic Association*, 47: 445–463.

Lieberman, A. F. (1999) 'Negative maternal attributions: effects on toddlers' sense of self', *Psychoanalytic Inquiry*, 19(5): 737–756.

Meissner, W. W. (1998) Review of S. A. Mitchell's 'Influence and autonomy in psychoanalysis', *Psychoanalytic Books*, 94: 419–423.

—— (2000) 'Reflections on psychic reality', *International Journal of Psychoanalysis*, 81: 1117–1138.

Mitchell, S. A. (1991) 'Contemporary perspectives on self: toward an integration', *Psychoanalytic Dialogues*, 1(2): 121–147.

—— (1998) 'The analyst's knowledge and authority', *Psychoanalytic Quarterly*, 67: 1–31.

—— (2000) 'Reply to Silverman', *Psychoanalytic Psychology*, 17: 153–159.

Nagel, T. (1986) *The View from Nowhere*, New York: Oxford University Press.

Ogden, T. (1997) *Reverie and Interpretation: Sensing Something Human*, Northvale, NJ: Aronson.

Perls, F. (1973) *The Gestalt Approach and Eyewitness to Therapy*, Oxford: Science and Behavior Books.

Rapaport, D. (1959) 'The structure of psychoanalytic theory: a systematizing attempt', *Psychological Issues Monograph*, 6, New York: International Universities Press.

Renik, O. (1993) 'Analytic interaction: conceptualizing technique in light of the analyst's irreducible subjectivity', *Psychoanalytic Quarterly*, 62: 553–571.

—— (1996) 'The perils of neutrality', *Psychoanalytic Quarterly*, 65: 495–517.

—— (1998) 'The analyst's subjectivity and the analyst's objectivity', *International Journal of Psycho-Analysis*, 79: 487–498.

Rogers, C. R. (1951) *Client-Centered Therapy*, Boston, MA: Houghton-Mifflin.

—— (1961) *On Becoming a Person*, Boston, MA: Houghton-Mifflin.

Rorty, R. (1991) *Objectivity, Relativism, and Truth: Philosophical Papers*, Vol. 1, New York: Cambridge University Press.

Sass, L. A. (1992) 'The epic of disbelief: the postmodernist turn in contemporary psychoanalysis', in S. Kvale (ed.) *Psychology and Postmodernism*, London: Sage.

Schafer, R. (1992) *Retelling of a Life: Narration and Dialogue in Psychoanalysis*, New York: Basic Books.

Searle, J. (1998) *Mind, Language, and Society: Philosophy in the Real World*, New York: Basic Books.

Smith, H. (1999) 'Subjectivity and objectivity in analytic listening', *Journal of the American Psychoanalytic Association*, 47: 465–484.

Spence, D. P. (1980) *Narrative Truth and Historical Truth: Meaning and Interpretation in Psychoanalysis*, New York: Norton.

Spitzer, A. B. (1996) *Historical Truth and Lies about the Past*, Chapel Hill, NC: University of North Carolina Press.

Strachey, J. (1934) 'The nature of the therapeutic action of psychoanalysis', *International Journal of Psychoanalysis*, 15: 127–159.

Vattimo, J. (1985) *The End of Modernity*, trans. J. R. Snyder, Baltimore, MD: Johns Hopkins University Press.

White, H. (1992) 'Historical emplotment and the problem of truth', in S. Friedlander (ed.) *Probing the Limits of Representation: Nazism and the "Final Solution"*, Cambridge, MA: Harvard University Press.

Winnicott, D. W. (1975) *Through Pediatrics to Psycho-Analysis: Collected Papers*, Philadelphia, PA: Brunner/Mazel (1975, reprinted in 1992).

Chapter 2

Multiplicity and relational psychoanalysis

A Heideggerian response

Jon Frederickson

Postmodern and relational schools of psychoanalysis have been greatly influenced by Harry Stack Sullivan's constructivist concept of the self. Sullivan (1936–1937, 1950) exploded the myth of a person as a single self, proposing that we have as many personalities as interpersonal relations thereby anticipating the postmodernist movement in psychoanalysis with its emphasis on the decentered, multiple self. According to Sullivan, "[N]o such thing as the durable, unique, individual personality is ever clearly justified. For all I know every human being has as many personalities as he has interpersonal relations" (Sullivan 1950: 219–220). The "overweening conviction of authentic individual selfhood . . . amounts to a delusion of unique individuality" (Sullivan 1936–1937: 16).

Although this aspect of Sullivan's theory freed us to examine our multiplicity as persons, it also raised questions regarding our unity. Lionells (1999) has referred to this as the problem of the independent psychic existence in the midst of psychological flux. Given the centrality of the concept of "multiplicity" to the postmodern turn in relational psychoanalysis, this raises a number of important questions: If there is multiplicity, is unity in the person merely an illusion (Mitchell 1993; Bromberg 1998)? If I am merely an agglomeration of "personalities," is there no "I" (Bromberg 1998)? If there is no "I", is authenticity possible (Mitchell 1993)?

Numerous theorists have criticized Sullivan's omission of uniqueness as a valid quality of the human person (Wolstein 1971; Crowley 1973; Freidland 1978; Klenbort 1978; Greenberg and Mitchell 1983; Moore 1984). Mullahy (1947) held that our individuality was a prerequisite to authentic relatedness. In fact, he believed the inability to perceive the unique in another person was a sign of illness. According to Thompson (1957, quoted in Lionells 1999), if we are determined entirely by relationships, we cannot account for freedom, creativity, or the unfolding of latent potentials. Fromm (1941) likewise criticized deterministic theories, instead emphasizing our capacity for freedom and the organic unfolding of the unique nucleus of the integrated personality.

According to Fromm, Sullivan's view is based on the social character of our time, which he terms an alienated character in which adjustment and cooperation have taken the place of genuine relatedness, and the human personality is seen as entirely a product of interaction with external forces.

(Thompson 1964: 98)

The person could not be reduced to the interpersonal field as Sullivan's writings seemed to imply. However, neither is the person completely separate from the field.

Towards an ontology of the person

In this chapter I will explore some of the problems in the way multiplicity has been conceptualized in Sullivan's work and the work of Bromberg. Specifically, I will show that they conflate a representation of the ontic with the ontological dimensions of personhood. This conflation results in a model which is fundamentally non-relational because in this model the therapist and patient relate to representations of the patient, not to her Being. I will then show the implications of an ontological perspective for a relational psychoanalysis. To illustrate these points I will rely on the work of Martin Heidegger, a philosopher who was deeply concerned about these specific issues as they relate to the field of psychotherapy.

In his Zollikon seminars, which were given to a group of psychotherapists, Heidegger critiqued Sullivan's work.

When they assert that a human being is determined as a being [who stands] in a relationship to other humans, the American [psychologist] Harry Stack Sullivan and his similarly oriented colleagues make an essential assertion about the human being, the foundations of which are not even questioned. (Essential means a projection, an a priori determination made in advance.) They take human comportment toward other human beings as a statement of something *about* the human being and not as an essential assertion determining the human being as a human being in the first place.

Relationship to . . . the being-in-relation-to . . . characterizes the unfolding essence of the human being. "Characterize" is the correct word here and not "constitute" because this would imply that being-in-relation-to . . . is already a complete determination of the human being, while the relationship to the understanding of being refers to a yet "deeper" determination of the human being's unfolding essence.

(Heidegger 2001: 153, original italics)

Sullivan claimed that the self is determined by relationships, thereby making a claim about the being of a person. Heidegger disagreed. He asserted that my unfolding essence as a human being is not determined by my relationships. Rather, my being-in-relation to you merely characterizes the unfolding essence of my being. Some have viewed this problem as a failure to distinguish epistemology (the act of knowing) from ontology (that which is known). Heidegger suggests another distinction. We must always distinguish the ontological from the ontic. The ontic refers to our specific relationships with others. The ontological refers to our being-in-the-world within which these relationships take place. This existential relatedness precedes any particular ontic relations. Here we see one of Heidegger's central concerns: Sullivan equated the patient's ontic relationships with others with ontology, the being-within-the-world within which those relationships take place. If we define the human being only as a self, or a collection of selves, our understanding of only the ontic level prevents us from understanding the ontological level, the essential ground of our being. When we a priori define the human being utilizing this sociological method we exclude the special nature of a human being, our being.

For instance, let's imagine a Sullivanian patient who believes that she is comprised of multiple selves. To perceive herself first she must have a sense of herself, her presence, her thereness, her being. These ontological phenomena have priority. But viewing herself as an object, devoid of her being, she is no longer aware of her presence, her thereness, or her being. Instead, she is aware only of her representations of her ontic qualities, and then equates those representations with her Being, her ontology. Yet, as Heidegger points out, "The phenomenon of *being* is the condition for the possibility for the appearance of the ontic, for the appearance of beings as beings" (Heidegger 2001: 187, original itaics). Sullivan mistakes the ontic for the ontological. He views the patient's objectification of herself as an accurate representation of her being rather than as a way to foreclose the unfolding of her being.

Why does Sullivan mistake the patient's objectification of herself with her being? Fromm proposed that Sullivan's view was an illustration of the social character of the time. Heidegger went further. He proposed that Sullivan's mode of thinking, like much of psychological thinking, had become dominated by scientific method which has influenced our thinking *and relating*. In scientific method, I posit myself as an authoritative subject who investigates things which I relate to as objects. That is, they exist only insofar as they are measurable and calculable. What becomes real to me is not your being, but my representations of you. Then I call those representations "objective."

Of course, this is as true of my representations of you as of myself. For instance, if we go back to the patient with multiple selves, she understands her presencing of herself from within the confines of her representation of herself, her representedness. Her living presencing disappears. She is no longer someone who is "presencing." Rather, she is now "understood" as an object present-at-hand. Thereby, she is no longer open to her presencing as what is given by itself, but only as how she is an object for herself as the thinking subject. Or if we shift to you and me: our openness, our presencing, our being-with in a relational spatiality is transformed into a relationship in physical space where you are an object over and against me. "For modern experience, something is a being only insofar as I represent it. Modern science rests on *the transformation of the experience of the presence of beings into objectivity*" (Heidegger 2001: 99, original italics).

As an example of this problem, let's turn to a quote from Hans Loewald on the psychoanalytic process:

> Psychoanalytic interpretations establish or make explicit bridges between two minds, and within the patient bridges between different areas and layers of the mind that lack or have lost connections with each other, that are not encompassed within an overall contextual organization of the personality.
>
> (Loewald 1977: 382)

This quote was a favorite of Mitchell's (2000) used to illustrate the relational school's understanding of the internalization of the interpersonal process. But let's examine it carefully. First of all, I don't interpret to your mind. I talk to *you*. You don't merely hear my interpretation. You hear *me*. My interpretation does not "bridge two minds." A "bridge" of pre-reflective, non-conceptual bodily attunement always already exists between us before words can arise from our feeling attunement. The bridge is not created by my interpretation, but by my bodily emotional openness and receptivity to you. Yet you in your youeyness are here before me and I experience you insofar as you are presencing, emerging as you prior to all my representations of you. In objectivity, the presencing of your being is reduced to my relationship to my representation of you: mind. Likewise, for the patient who "has" multiple selves, truth no longer refers to the self-manifestation of *who is presencing*. Truth is characterized as *what is "certain* for a representing Ego" (Heidegger 2001: 106, original italics). But then for this poor patient the criterion for what truly exists is not her being as she manifests herself, but her representations of herself. Having stood apart from herself, "objectively," she treats herself as an object, and then presupposes the objectivity of these selves. For this patient, and for some therapists, what becomes decisive is *how* a person is represented, and not *who this person is*. This constitutes a failure to recognize that the Being of any person exceeds any attempt at articulation through language and resists this method of objectification.

Before we can perceive a person as this or that person, we must perceive that there is someone presencing. The ontological reality of the person is primary in the order of being. But for the representing ego, thought and sight are primary, and the ontological reality of the person is *secondary in the order of being*. We take our thinking *about* and seeing *of* someone, these approaches from the *outside*, as primary and only with difficulty recognize there is someone here presencing. For Heidegger, the abysmal, concealed ground of a person is always more than what can be conceptualized and represented.

By objectifying herself as multiple selves the patient may have a "useful" way of thinking about herself. But entranced by her representations, she loses sight of who she is as she is. For her thinking, she as this presencing person is no longer decisive, but rather this image she holds of herself. By relating to this image she is no longer open to herself, the world that addresses her, or to her own responses to the world. Instead, she possesses what Heidegger would call a "capsule-like representation of a psyche," but she has lost contact with her very being. This reductive image imposed on her prevents her from being open to what her experience is telling her on a pre-reflective, non-symbolic, non-verbal level.

Oddly enough, her relationship to herself has become scientized into one where she is simultaneously the subject and the object, the observer and the observed. She is no longer in relationship to herself but to a representation of herself which has become the substitute for a living experience of herself. Further, she understands herself as an isolated mind which can never be understood in isolation from the ontological reality that she lives within the context of being-with others.

The patient's and therapist's attempt to objectify herself and relate to her representations is a kind of "epistemological" attitude. But this proves to be very problematic for relational psychoanalysts: we run the risk of relating to representations our patients bring to us for our attention and forget to relate to their Being. As relational therapists we need to develop an ontological approach to our work. We need to maintain our awareness of the "ontological (i.e. of Being as a whole) *while being engaged with beings in our everyday life*" (Levin 1985: 22, original italics). For the central question for us should be whether our listening and concepts as psychoanalysts opens up our human being for Being as a whole. Regrettably, our use of representations, for instance of multiple selves, forecloses our potential-for-being in order to protect our framework.

Unfortunately, this kind of "understanding" is limited because it objectifies the patient into a measurable "form." But Heidegger reminds us that understanding is not merely intellectual comprehension of conceptual categories. Rather, understanding is "openness towards the possibilities of whatever we meet, and this includes our own possibilities" (Cohn 2002: 44). For Heidegger, the term Dasein should be understood as "openness-to-being" or a "being-which-opens." For instance, when you and I meet, I don't simply convey an experience inside me to inside you. I am an openness-to-being and you are an openness-to-being. Always already we are being-here-together and this being-here-together is essentially already manifest in our bodily attunement-with each other and ourselves. And out of this being-together and our mutual bodily attunement our understanding-with is also manifest. Our "being-with is 'explicitly' *shared* in discourse" but our being-with "already *is* – only unshared as something not grasped and appropriated" (Heidegger 2001: 152, original italics).

For instance, if I make a conscious effort to "make" the patient feel understood, I am operating as if she is a separate object outside me requiring an "input" of empathy. Yet, in fact, I am always already in bodily attunement with her in our being-together and my understanding on an implicit, non-verbal level is already being shared in our being-with. Sadly, the patient, who attempts to convey this idea of multiplicity as if from inside her to inside me, is treating herself as an isolated container as well. She is trying to grasp and appropriate her being by making it into an object for me to grasp, appropriate and control as well. We could both relate to a representation, but we would not be being-with one another. Neither of us would be attuning with and being open to her as a Dasein who is always presencing and concealing, always knowable and unknowable, always revealing a surplus beyond any attempts of objectification. Our task is to be open to each other as we are in this immediacy before we have explained and categorized ourselves away. It means giving the phenomena, ourselves, priority. Instead, she invites us to look away from her being and to stare at an image on the screen so that both of us will relate to this image, as if we are watching a video about multiple selves, but without her being present to herself or me and, if I don't see this, without my being present to her or myself.

She centers her understanding within her consciousness. Sullivan centered his understanding within the ontic relations. Heidegger suggests we center our understanding within the ontological wider context of which we are a part. Within this ontological context, the tacit language of your being addresses me. I remain receptive to the claim of your being manifesting itself, your presencing. In fact, my distinction and peril as a human being is precisely my openness in manifold ways to your being. For through my openness to your being, I am in an attunement, a bodily way of being (Heidegger 2001: 74–75). The fact of my being and your being, our being-with, our openness, our presencing is the ontological ground which alone makes possible the ontic features addressed in psychology. But when the ontic *ways* of being described by psychology are mistaken for the ontological *facticity* of being, what is secondary is mistaken for the primary. "The human being's being-open to being is so fundamental and decisive in being human that, due to its inconspicuousness and plainness, one can continuously overlook it in favor of contrived psychological theories" (Heidegger 2001: 74). So let us turn now to a contemporary theorist who, like Sullivan, misses the ontological ground of being.

Bromberg and the theory of multiple selves

Bromberg (1998) is renowned in the psychoanalytic community for his very astute and sensitive observations about patients suffering from the after effects of trauma, especially those who claim to have multiple selves. Bromberg views the self as "decentered, and the mind as a configuration of shifting, nonlinear states of consciousness in an ongoing dialectic with the necessary illusion of unitary selfhood" (Bromberg 1998: 7).

> Paradoxically, the goal of dissociation is to maintain personal continuity, coherence, and integrity of the sense of self and to avoid the traumatic dissolution of selfhood . . . Self experience originates in relatively unlinked self-states, each coherent in its own right, and the experience of being a unitary self . . . is an acquired, developmentally adaptive illusion. It is when this illusion of unity is traumatically threatened with unavoidable, precipitous disruption that it becomes in itself a liability because it is in jeopardy of being overwhelmed by input it cannot process symbolically and deal with as a state of conflict.
>
> (Bromberg 1998: 182)

For Bromberg "the 'self' is an interpersonal entity relationally structured as a multiplicity of self/other configurations that are developmentally 'integrated' by an illusion of unity" (Bromberg 1998: 192). Hence, integration

> is, in essence, no different from any other personality attribute – an interpersonal construction jointly shaped by the individual and the eye of the beholder. The "beholder" is frequently another person but is always, simultaneously, a dissociated voice of the self. "Integration" is thus relative to the context of external reality as well as to the shifting of the multiplicity of self–other representations that define the experience of selfhood at a given time . . . I thus equally believe, as Mitchell (1993) has commented that "the sense of authenticity is always a construction and as a construction, it is always relative to other possible self-constructions at any particular time."
>
> (Bromberg 1998: 195)

> Psychological "integration" . . . does not lead to a single "real you" or "true self." Rather, it is the ability to stand in the spaces between realities without losing any of them, the capacity to feel like one self while being many.
>
> (Bromberg 1998: 256)

A human being's ability to live a life with both authenticity and self awareness depends upon the presence of an ongoing dialectic between separateness and unity of one's self-states, allowing each self to function optimally without foreclosing communication and negotiation between them. When all goes well developmentally, a person is only dimly or momentarily aware of the existence of individual self-states and their respective realities because each functions as part of a healthy illusion of cohesive personal identity – an overarching cognitive and experiential state felt as "me."

(Bromberg 1998: 272–273)

Bromberg's formulations of a decentered self place him in the forefront of a group of relational psychoanalysts who have been deeply influenced by postmodernism. They privilege the multiple representations of a patient's epistemology and deny any ontological ground for the self. In what follows I will critique this stance from a Heideggerian perspective, focusing primarily on Bromberg's criterion for health.

Having given much thought to their unique problems Bromberg suggests that "Health is the ability to be able to stand in the spaces between realities without losing any of them. This is what I believe self-acceptance means and what creativity is really all about" (Bromberg 1998: 186). But what does he mean by these terms: "stand," "spaces," "realities," and "losing"? Let's unpack this seemingly obvious sentence. "Realities" refers to the patient's representations of herself which she calls selves. These are not reality, but representations of her ontic qualities which are now treated as if they are her ontology or being and, in fact, have now replaced the reality of her Being. Of course, there is no space between representations. Therefore we cannot stand between them. In this slippery way, it's as if Bromberg "ontologizes" representations by referring to space between them and the patient's ability to stand between them. And by doing so, he loses any distinction between the patient's Being and her ontic qualities, between ontology as the ground of being and representations of ontic qualities which arise from this ground.

Then he calls this ability to "stand between the spaces between these realities without losing any one of them" self acceptance. Here he equates the collection of these representations with the self. While it becomes unclear which self is accepting all of these representations, a more troubling problem is apparent. Bromberg equates accepting *representations* of one's ontic dimensions with accepting the self!

From a Heideggerian perspective this position merely reflects the patient's ontical affliction. Relating to her false ontology (equating selves with her ontology) she has lost touch with a more primordial experience of Being. She is operating within a "deficient" mode of relatedness to herself. Her Being can now appear to her only in a mutilated non-dynamic form within the grip of her representations. Her Being has been, for her, reduced to the modalities of these selves. Rather than fully experience her felt sense of her bodily relation to the world, she reduces her bodyhood to a series of objects (selves) to be observed by a disembodied "I." Our task as therapists is to deepen the patient's relatedness to her own Being. Therefore, we need to diagnose her ontical affliction rather than operate within the limits of her vision. We need to diagnose, recognize, and make explicit how her way-of-being is distorting her capacity to see and relate to her Being. Her theory, in this case of multiple selves, restricts her vision of herself to the ontical realm, leaving her blind to the ontological realm, her Being. Inviting her to pay attention not to her thoughts and concepts, but to her feelings, her felt sense of her ontical distress, she will become open to her Being. "Feeling is that basic mode of *Dasein* by force of which and in accordance with which we are always already lifted beyond ourselves into being as a whole" (Heidegger 1979: 99). Since her affliction is ontical or "ego-logical," we need to help her listen to the bodily felt sense of her being, so that she can make contact with the body's more open dimension (Levin 1985: 53). For "we do not 'have' a body; rather, we *are* bodily" (Heidegger 1979: 99, original italics). Levin helps us to understand that through the body there is a pre-understanding of our relationship with Being, "an attunement darkly preserved in the primordial *body of feeling*" (Levin 1985: 54, original italics). By opening up to our bodying forth of this *under*standing, we are "*opening* into the clearing field of Being" (Levin 1985: 55, original italics).

To make this a little clearer, our bodily sense of self is ever changing in response to our openness to the world. As Sullivan pointed out, we may like a particular feeling and call it the self and dislike another feeling which threatens this "self" and call that the "not-me" as Sullivan proposed. We objectify these feeling states and call them a series of selves. But in doing so we forget that a feeling is not something we "have," nor is a feeling a "state." These modes of relating to ourselves are due to objectification. Feeling is an *activity*. *We* feel. We feel out others "and this feeling out constitutes our felt body as a 'field' . . . of awareness" (Wilberg 2003: 45).

In contrast to Bromberg's proposal, I would suggest that from a relational perspective, *self acceptance involves listening to my Being.* "You cannot heal a single human being, even with psychotherapy, if you do not first restore his relationship to Being" (Heidegger quoted in Wilberg 2004). According to Heidegger, we are always already gifted with a non-conceptual pre-understanding of our Being through bodily attunement. But distracted by our representations of the ontical dimensions we lack a developed awareness of our Being which could be integrated into the substance of our lives. By encouraging the patient to listen to her Being, we help her deepen her relatedness to her Being and Being as a whole. And by encouraging her to listen to her being, we must listen relationally through relatedness-to-being.

We listen to a patient, not her representations of herself. We listen to *her*, not to her mind. If listening is to be a *relational* practice, it cannot be merely a "skill" by which we decode meanings in the patient's words, nor a "skill" by which we help her form new representations of herself to relate to. We would merely be reinforcing what Buber (1965, 1970) referred to as "I–It" relations or what Heidegger refers to as objectification. We must not try to help her have a better "relationship" to her representations as Bromberg proposes. We are trying to help her listen to her Being. A non-relational listening is merely a "skill" by which we can objectify the patient according to a representational schema. In contrast, relational listening is a mode of Being – being-with-others (Wilberg 2004).

In his essay on "Language" Heidegger reminds us that "we should not re-present pain anthropologically as a sensation" (Heidegger 1975: 204). What he means here is that we should not simply re-present the pain, but be-with-the-person-in-pain in the wholeness of her experience that lets her be present as she is (Levin 1985: 88). Rather than help the patient re-present images of herself, we try to be-with her and help her listen to her own being, to be present to her primordial attunement: her bodying forth which is always already occurring beneath her words. And by helping her be present to her bodying forth through our own bodily presence she can open to a new dimension of the truth of her feeling and, thereby, make herself available for greater openness to her meaning. In essence, she must let go of her representations to become present to her Being.

Relational listening requires the therapist to be fully present listening to his own Being while listening to the patient's Being, who she is under the representations and words. And this presence as a relational listener means that I am not a separate person trying to "empathize" with the other. Rather I am a fully embodied presence. Only by listening with our full body and Being can we be fully there (Dasein) for the patient. Listening is a "bodily relational practice – a relational activity of our whole body and whole being and not just the instrumental professional use of our ears and mind" (Wilberg 2004: 2).

In contrast, Bromberg's model of self acceptance is non-relational. I am not relating to me, but to representations. I am not relating to your Being but to my representations of you. I am not accepting, listening to my being, but "relating" to representations. But self acceptance cannot take place on the cognitive level which Bromberg proposes. Rather, we *must relate to, listen to our Being*, the pre-reflective, bodying forth of our being, the logos of our Being. From a Heideggerian perspective, the patient with multiple personality disorder does not suffer from a pathological identity. She suffers from a forgetfulness of her Being!

We see in Bromberg's case examples, like much of the case material we read today, that listening is understood as a process by which therapist and patient make connections and represent relationships in a clearer way through words. In contrast, Wilberg proposes that our task in a listening dialogue is "not to represent their relationships in words but to actually *relate* in a deeper way" (Wilberg 2004: 49, original italics). Our goal is not "finding the words to say it," but helping her listen to her Being so that she finds a new way of being-in-the-world, relating to her Being and to the Being of others. Our goal is not conceptual but relational.

Behind a patient's words is her way of Being. In a sense, this shift in focus is apparent in relational clinicians such as Maroda (1991) and Ehrenberg (1992) who do not share the assumptions of the postmodernists. Maroda and Ehrenberg emphasize the importance of relating to the patient from the depth of our internal, bodily experience. Yet even here, in our concep-tualization of countertransference we find a non-relational element. We speak as if the patient projected something into us, as if we are separate containers into which alien contents may be placed. We speak and write as if we are not related to these contents. Yet, the health of any therapeutic relationship rests on a fundamental relational capacity: can I acknowledge the aspects of myself the patient embodies and expresses and can I acknowl-edge the aspects of the patient I embody and express. Can I acknowledge that I resonate with all these elements precisely because nothing human is alien to me, as the Roman poet Terence said? From Heidegger's perspective the objectification implicit in our concepts of countertransference relies on a false subject–object split. The body reverberates in response to the claim of Being. In our mutual bodily attunement we resonate with patients just like tuning forks. "Hearing the word of the other as the echo of an as-yet unheard and unfamiliar voice within us. It is that voice, *hidden* within 'gut feeling' which we must *heed*" (Wilberg 2004: 153, original italics). Being claims us through our bodily attunement. By consenting to work through our bodying forth of this being-with-the-patient we make contact with our mutual inwardnesses. For Heidegger, when I know you, I am situated in this relationship and this relationship vibrates through me (Heidegger 2001).

But even this phrasing does not quite capture what Heidegger is inviting us to notice. He keeps reminding us that perception is not merely a relation between a separate subject and object who exchange "objects" of perception or place these "objects" in each other through projection. As Heidegger keeps repeating in Being and Time, "*We* hear, not the ear." Being-with is a dynamic, non-linear relational field of two subjects in a continual state of mutual attunement on a bodily level. Our perceptions are not transferred between us. Rather they are themselves "expressions of this psychic field of interactivity". Perception is a not a subject–object relation but a "direct relation of beings, of an 'I' and a 'you'" (Wilberg 2004: 56).

In a relational listening we shift from a focus on the patient's words and representations to how she responds to the call of her own being – her way of listening to herself and to others (Wilberg 2004: 21). "[O]ntologically mood is a primordial kind of Being for Dasein, in which Dasein is disclosed to itself *prior to* all cognition and volition, and *beyond* their range of disclosure" (Heidegger 1962: 136). Our felt self emerges from mood, this disclosure of our Being which exists prior to our cognition and which surpasses anything our cognition can disclose. And by this listening I mean, how she listens to and *bears* the implicit, non-verbal, pre-reflective bodying forth of her Being. Our focus is not her words. Instead, we listen to hear whether she is listening to her Being in the process of *coming to speak* (Wilberg 2004: 90). We listen to hear if she is *relating* to her Being.

Now we can come back to Bromberg's idea that we must "stand between the spaces." Let us look at the word "stand." We cannot stand between representations. We stand on the earth. However, if we don't let ourselves experience "Being presencing as the grounding earth," we do not overcome the fate of a non-relational representational way of thinking (Levin 1985: 286). Heidegger referred to a "steadfast" hearing (*standhaltendes Horen*), a grounded and embodied type of listening. Whereas Bromberg would have us "stand" between the patient's representations, Heidegger urges us to stand underneath those representations – to stand *being ourselves*. In fact, to *embody* these previously disowned modes of conduct, with a more deeply felt sense of being their embodiment (Stern 1997). To stand in one's own embodied relationship to the world is *under*standing. Not to stand outside her representations but to stand in her own being. For, to adopt this *stand*point outside herself she locates herself not on the firm ground of Being but at the edge of an abyss

Understanding requires us to develop and deepen our always already existing capacity for openness-to-being. A relational thinking is not in relation to your concepts, but to your Being and my Being. A relational thinking arises out of our relatedness to our own being, to our pre-reflective, bodily, pre-understood potential for a continuous deepening of our experience and understanding of Being. A relational thinking "would open to the body, would listen, would shift into a more receptive attitude, an accepting attitude, an attitude whose spelling of graciousness the body would feel and find fulfilling" (Levin 1985: 41). We must learn to think not about our representations, but rather *through* and *with* the body, by *being-with* the body. We need to quiet the "ego-logical" mind and listen to the logos of the body: feeling which lifts us up beyond ourselves into Being as a whole (Heidegger 1979). All knowledge is relational. "Knowing is a relation in which we ourselves are related, and in which this relation vibrates through our basic comportment" (Heidegger quoted in Wilberg 2003: 91).

Relational thinking deepens our experience of the feeling field as a whole, our bodily attunement with ourselves and with others. Relational thinking must help us reclaim our felt sense of "being-open-to-Being as a way of being open, in our motility, to the grace of the field through whose clearing we move and pass" (Levin 1985: 104). We must shift from a field theory that was on the sociological level (Sullivan) to a field theory on the ontological level (Heidegger). No longer a field of subject/object but of openesses. No longer linear, but non-linear field dynamics. For Heidegger, our bodily attunement enables us to *feel* our relatedness to the field of Being as a whole. We are open to be "claimed" by Being so that it may reverberate through us and move us with its call.

Merleau-Ponty's perspective on embodiment can help to us to understand this "claim" of Being on the body. On the ontological level, we are talking about a relational field where we experience our bodily inherence in the field of Being as a whole (Levin 1985: 256). "In reality, there is neither me nor the other as positive subjectivities. There are . . . two openesses, two stages where something will take place" (Merleau-Ponty 1969: 263). Our "human existence in its most elemental dimensionality is a field of bodily awareness pervasively determined by interactions with other beings that conclusively demonstrate our interdependence and interpenetration" (Levin 1985: 256). Through feeling, our openness to Being, we experience our "intercorporeality." When I feel "touched" by what you say, you are also "touched" by my being which you have just "touched." The space of our bodily felt sense has "a *non-local* or field character – it is not bounded by the spatial dimensions of our own bodies viewed as localized objects within that space" (Wilberg 2003: 10, original italics). Therefore, our awareness is not, strictly speaking, localized within you or me, but rather it has its own kind of spatiality and field character. In fact, awareness is an event constituted by a field of emergence. Subjectivity is "the non-local or field dimension of experience as such – essentially irreducible to any locally experienced phenomena, any localized 'subject' or 'object'" (Wilberg 2003: 19). We are openings-for-Being "localized as bodies within the field of Being as a whole. "The boundary of the lived body is the horizon of being in which I dwell" (Heidegger quoted in Wilberg 2003: 37).

Let's come back to the patient with multiple selves. When I hear her, we must ask (as relational therapists), am I *hearing* her or am I hearing *her*? If there is no "I" as Bromberg asks, then I cannot hear *her*! There is no her to hear, only multiple representations. But then there can be no relational listening, where I am in relation to her Being and where I am in relation to my own. Yet as relational listeners, we must be continually listening to our own Being and from our own Being. There is a difference between listening as representing the other and listening as a wordless, pre-reflective, non-representational attunement out of which words emerge. Am I *open* to her? How am I moved by her? Am I receiving her into my Being?

And yet Bromberg is correct to question the existence of the "I." But his approach is mistaken, because it fails to understand the relationship between the ontic and the ontological. Heidegger noted that we do not "have" relationships. This way of thinking merely reflects objectification. Rather, we are relational beings. "To be is to relate – both to other human beings and to our own inner being (the inner You)" (Wilberg 2004: 136). I have the potential to relate from my innerness to yours. This Heidegger referred to as a Thou–Thou relationship (Heidegger 2001).

> Instead of always only speaking of the so called I-Thou relationship, one should speak of a Thou-Thou relationship instead. The reason for this is that an I-Thou is always only spoken of from my point of view, whereas in reality we have a mutual relationship here.
>
> (Heidegger 2001: 210)

We see here an interesting connection between Buber and Heidegger. Buber understood sicknesses of the soul as sicknesses of relationship – both to others and to one's self-being. Although Heidegger did not use the word "soul," he too thought that psychological illnesses could be understood also as a falling away from relatedness to one's being which led to deficient modes of being-with-others (Mills 1997). Thus, in being-with, as a whole person I am not, strictly speaking, an "I." I am a We. In our direct and unmediated Thou–Thou relation, this is not merely a relation between two persons as Buber proposed. Rather, you and I are relating to our own and each other's inner being. I can relate to you and your inner Being only if I am able to listen to my own inner Being. "Only when our personal self or 'I' links itself to this inner Thou and forms an intimate 'We', do we become whole human beings – able to listen and relate to others as whole human beings" (Wilberg 2004: 61).

Bromberg privileges epistemological categories (representations) over the ontological reality of Being. This is obvious when we discover that *I am supposed to find myself in the spaces between my representations of myself!* How is this possible? When the ontic qualities of personhood have been used to deny the ontology of our being, there is no source for an "I" except through consciousness of these representations. But then the illogic is revealed because both I and representations emerge at the same logical level: not possible.

According to Kant, a person cannot be reduced to the act of observation. My capacity to observe the world around me is a critical function of my inner life, but not all of it. Semyon Frank states:

> The "subject" as the formal bearer and source of the mental gaze is so to speak located *within* the subject as the bearer of the directly self-revealing life, but the two do not coincide: the subject in the second sense may be compared to a sphere rather than to a point.
>
> (Frank 1965: 18, original italics)

The pre-reflective subject is the prior ground, the precondition for the reflective subject (Frie 1997, 1999). Yet when we attend only to the capacity for self observation, we are selectively inattentive to the sense of oneself as the bearer of self-revealing life. And as the bearer of self-revealing life, I am my body. It is the absence of the body, the living reality of attunement to being-in-the-world, which helps us to understand why Sullivan and Bromberg lost sight of the ontological ground of our being.

As a concluding note on the concept of multiplicity, Bromberg and others have correctly noted how patients may use the idea of unity as a defense against recognizing the multiple ways of being we body forth in the world. Reifying each of these ways of being as a "self," they then correctly point out (within that frame of reference) that those multiple "selves" cannot be put together as one self. Yet the idea, feeling, and experience of unity continue to arise. Why? "If we want to understand more fully . . . the emergence of an ontological Self, then we must consider how the Selfhood of human being is defined by the wholeness it experiences through its openness-to-Being" (Levin 1985: 290). Feeling, our openness-to-being, provides a pre-understanding of the world and constitutes a pre-objective unity (Levin 1985: 297) of my being-in-the-world. Through our bodily attunement we experience our openness to Being as a whole. And it is through our sensibility (Heidegger uses the word Gemut) "that we first become acquainted with a *wholeness* of presence" (Levin 1985: 79). "This bodily felt sense of wholeness, hermeneutically disclosive of Being, is *necessary* for the unfolding of the Self as an *ontological* being" (Levin 1985: 291, original italics). For through listening to her Being she will experience the unity of feeling and Being.

What Bromberg proposes is that psychoanalysis helps change the patient's ability to observe her representations of herself. This, however, is a non-relational goal. Instead, I suggest that psychoanalysis has a relational goal: it helps *change the patient's relationship to her being.* The truth of our inter-pretations can only be measured by the depth and character of the patient's opening to being which results from her encounter with us and our interpretations. That is, the ontological truth of an interpretation is meas-ured by the patient's deepening relatedness to her inner Being and being-in-the-world.

Therefore, we always face a fundamental relational choice: to pursue a life moved by the truth of Being, moved by our embodiment or to be driven by an ontological anxiety, living in fear of the feelings, the bodying forth which threatens our conceptual and characterological rigidities and even the survival of our "ego-logical" way-of-being. Our choice is to deepen our relation to our innermost Being through our bodying forth or to choose a way-of-being which is deficient, the relation to representations of the ontical dimensions of Being.

References

Bromberg, P. (1998) *Standing in the Spaces: Essays on Clinical Process, Trauma, and Dissociation*, Hillsdale, NJ: Analytic Press.

Buber, M. (1957) 'The William Alanson White Lectures', *Psychiatry*, 20: 97–130.
—— (1965) *Between Man and Man*, New York: Macmillan.
—— (1970) *I and Thou*, trans. W. Kaufmann, New York: Charles Scribner's Sons.
Cohn, H. (2002) *Heidegger and the Roots of Existential Therapy*, London: Continuum.
Crowley, R. (1973) 'Sullivan's concepts of unique individuality', *Contemporary Psychoanalysis*, 9: 130–133.
Ehrenberg, D. (1992) *The Intimate Edge*, New York: Norton.
Frank, S. L. (1965) *Reality and Man*, trans. N. Duddington, London: Faber & Faber.
Frie, R. (1997) *Subjectivity and Intersubjectivity in Modern Philosophy and Psychoanalysis: A study of Sartre, Binswanger, Lacan, and Habermas*, Lanham, MD: Rowman & Littlefield.
—— (1999) 'Psychoanalysis and the linguistic turn', *Contemporary Psychoanalysis*, 35: 673–697.
Friedland, B. (1978) 'Toward a psychology of self', *Contemporary Psychoanalysis*, 14: 553–571.
Fromm, E. (1941) *Escape from Freedom*, New York: Avon Books.
Greenberg, J. and Mitchell, S. (1983) *Object Relations in Psychoanalytic Theory*, Cambridge, MA: Harvard University Press.
Heidegger, M. (1962) *Being and Time*, trans. J. Macquarrie and E. Robinson, Oxford: Blackwell.
—— (1975) *Poetry, Language, and Thought*, New York: Harper & Row.
—— (1979) *The Will to Power as Art, Nietzsche*, vol. 1, New York: Harper & Row.
—— (2001) *Zollikon Seminars: Protocols – Conversations – Letters*, edited M. Boss, trans. F. Mayr and R. Askay, Evanston, IL: Northwestern University Press.
Klenbort, I. (1978) 'Another look at Sullivan's concept of individuality', *Contemporary Psychoanalysis*, 14: 125–135.
Levin, D. (1985) *The Body's Recollection of Being: Phenomenological Psychology and the Deconstruction of Nihilism*, London: Routledge & Kegan Paul.
Lionells, M. (1999) 'Back to the future: Sullivan's anticipation of the post-modernist vision in psychoanalysis', paper presented at Advances in Relational and Interpersonal Psychotherapy, Harry Stack Sullivan Memorial Conference, Washington School of Psychiatry, Washington, DC.
Loewald, H. (1977) 'Reflections on the psychoanalytic process and its therapeutic potential', in *Papers on Psychoanalysis*, New Haven, CT: Yale University Press.
Maroda, K. (1991) *The Power of Countertransference*, New York: Jason Aronson.
—— (1999) *Seduction, Surrender, and Transformation: Emotional Engagement in the Analytic Process*, Hillsdale, NJ: Analytic Press.
Merleau-Ponty, M. (1969) *The Visible and the Invisible*, Evanston, IL: Northwestern University Press.
Mills, J. (1997) 'The False Dasein: from Heidegger to Sartre and psychoanalysis', *Journal of Phenomenological Psychology*, 28(1): 42–65.
Mitchell, S. (1993) *Hope and Dread in Psychoanalysis*, New York: Basic Books.
—— (2000) *Relationality*, Hillsdale, NJ: Analytic Press.
Moore, A. (1984) 'Unique individuality redeemed', *Contemporary Psychoanalysis*, 20: 1–32.
Mullahy, P. (1947) 'A theory of interpersonal relations and the evolution of

personality', in H. S. Sullivan, *Conceptions of Modern Psychiatry*, Washington, DC: William Alanson White Psychiatric Foundation.

Stern, D. (1997) *Unformulated Experience: From Dissociation to Imagination in Psychoanalysis*, Hillsdale, NJ: Analytic Press.

Sullivan, H. S. (1936–1937) 'A note on the implications of psychiatry, the study of interpersonal relations, for investigation in the social sciences', in (1971) *The Fusion of Psychiatry and the Social Sciences*, New York: Norton.

—— (1950) 'The illusion of personal individuality', in (1971) *The Fusion of Psychiatry and the Social Sciences*, New York: Norton.

Thompson, C. (1957) 'Concepts of the self in interpersonal theory', unpublished manuscript.

—— (1964) *Interpersonal Psychoanalysis*, New York: Basic Books.

Wilberg, P. (2003) *Heidegger, Medicine and 'Scientific Method'*, Eastbourne, UK: New Gnosis.

—— (2004) *The Therapist as Listener: Martin Heidegger and the Missing Dimension of Counseling and Psychotherapy Training*, Eastbourne, UK: New Gnosis.

Wolstein, B. (1971) 'Interpersonal relations without individuality', *Contemporary Psychoanalysis*, 7: 75–80.

Chapter 3

A strange convergence

Postmodern theory, infant research, and psychoanalysis

Judith Guss Teicholz

"I think there's a shared common ground all right, but that it's more like a quicksand" (Lahr 2007: 56). These are the words of Harold Pinter, perhaps a quintessential twentieth-century postmodernist, who went on to say, "Meaning which is resolved, parceled, labeled and ready for export is dead" (Lahr 2007: 56). Psychoanalysis today is pushed and pulled from within, between those who come closer to sharing the views evoked in Pinter's statements and those holding a more modernist view in which the potential for order, structure, meaning and shared understanding still prevails – a viewpoint exemplified by such cultural critics as Holland Cotter, in a review of drawings by Stuart Davies: "Without the defining, containing line, all is confusion; chaos prevails; the bottom falls out of life and art" (Cotter 2008). In this chapter I consider what these two views can say to each other. Can they somehow be put together, forging a psychoanalysis better suited to twenty-first-century psyches and to the challenges of life that individuals confront today? Or are they hopelessly irreconcilable?

Psychoanalysis and postmodern theory would seem at first glance to be singularly incompatible with each other. Psychoanalysis has historically used grand narratives or the universals of ancient myth to find meaning in the productions of the individual mind and to provide relief from psychic suffering. Postmodern theory, on the other hand, rejects both the existence of universals and the possibility of meaning.

More specifically, psychoanalytic self psychology suggests that psychic health lies in a continuous and cohesive sense of self whose "owner" is constantly integrating and making sense of the complexity and multiplicity of lived experience. The road to such cohesion and meaning-making is through the experience of being recognized, accepted and understood in intimate connection with another. Such understanding assumes common ground between individuals, on the basis of mutual empathy and the human condition. But postmodern theory posits a self ever in process – no more than an ongoing distillation of the individual's interactions with others – resulting in an experiential world so tenuous that there is no possibility for shared understanding.

Postmodern theory would thus seem to undermine the entire psycho-analytic project and even the project of forging a meaningful life – one filled with self-chosen commitments to love and work (Teicholz 1998, 1999). And yet certain aspects of the postmodern attitude have indeed infiltrated psychoanalytic discourse as well as practice, not always with negative results. I have elsewhere probed the postmodern project in psychoanalysis (Teicholz 1998, 1999) noting its marked limitations when applied to a healing endeavor. But I would here suggest that, while threatening the curative goals of psychoanalysis through its relentless questioning of self, meaning, and progress, postmodern theory can also have a liberating effect in certain ways. For instance in the very act of rejecting the universals of meaning, postmodern theory can open the door – and the analyst's mind – to the unique and evolving meanings attributed to ongoing experience by the individual patient. And in its rejection of a unitary and bounded self, postmodern theory recognizes the ever-present influence of context – particularly the context of relationship through which meaning is co-created. Postmodern theory can also free psychoanalysis from the notion of normal development as progressing through fixed stages to a pre-ordained, "genital" organization of the psyche. Looked at in these ways, the post-modern psychoanalytic attitude may offer a fine line – but a line neverthe-less – between nihilism and psychic freedom.

I am proposing that not postmodern theory proper but rather a modified postmodern attitude might have a liberating effect on psychoanalysis. Such an attitude rejects not meaning per se, but just any a priori meaning that predates individual and dyadic experience. It rejects not the self per se, but just the concept of a rigid, fixed, or bounded self, isolated from its context and relations with others. It rejects not understanding but only understand-ing derived from pre-established theory. It would embrace understanding co-created in the ongoing exchange between two individuals.

Admittedly postmodern ideas are inherently radical and do not readily lend themselves to moderation. And yet the postmodern negation of tradi-tion – especially of the foundational "truths" on the basis of which traditions are established – does leave room for postmodernists (and for others as well), to pick and choose among the elements of past theory and practice. This can be seen in postmodern architecture, for instance, when multiple design elements are used in a single building, taken from different periods of history. With this postmodern practice in mind, I argue for a "pick and choose" approach to postmodernism in psychoanalysis as well, in which selected elements of modern and postmodern theory might be brought together with compatible findings from scientific studies, to support a new view of the human mind and relationships. I am untroubled by the high probability that any such "integration" would be unacceptable to postmodern purists, should it ever come to their attention. My purpose is simply to draw attention to the seemingly overlapping and resonant elements from various sources, including postmodernism, that seem already to have influenced psychoanalysis in specific ways (Teicholz 2006a).

In examining these sources of influence I see an unexpected convergence between the postmodern project in psychoanalysis and recent empirical findings from infant–caregiver research, attachment theory, and cognitive neuroscience. The convergence between postmodern psychoanalysis and these diverse fields of research is strange because, from a postmodern viewpoint, there is no scientific truth "out there" beyond what can be mutually agreed upon through intersubjective negotiation. And yet, these two seemingly contradictory approaches to human experience – the scientific and post-scientific – seem to be moving toward each other as, paradoxically, certain of the research findings provide "evidence" for some of the central tenets of postmodern thinking. Perhaps the places where the elements of these contradictory approaches overlap are exactly at that fine point of psychic freedom before postmodernism crosses over into nihilism.

There has, of course, been a rich cross-fertilization among the fields of psychoanalysis, infant–caregiver research, and postmodern theory, making it difficult to tease out to what extent the research findings actually *support* postmodern thinking, versus in some way *reflecting* it. For instance, even while the empirical research from diverse fields of study yields findings that seem to justify certain postmodern attitudes, we have no way of assessing to what degree those very attitudes are influencing the kinds of scientific questions that get asked, or how the empirical "evidence" is interpreted. But in spite of these ambiguities, there is little question that both postmodern thought and infant–caregiver research have had a profound impact on contemporary psychoanalysis – especially on self psychological and relational theory – with, thus far, no attempt to integrate the apparently opposing approaches to the discovery or construction of realities.

I shall be writing as if there were clear distinctions among theoretical paradigms (especially between self psychology and relational psychoanalysis) – and as if each of these categories represented a monolithic viewpoint. But in fact, each of these theories exists in multiple versions. There are many conceptual points on which the theories overlap as well as many analysts (including this author) who feel comfortable across the paradigms. In psychoanalysis the postmodern attitude is for the most part represented in mild form and associated with a group of relational analysts who, when they acknowledge their postmodern leanings at all, designate themselves as only "moderate" postmoderns (Aron 1996; Mitchell 1997; Teicholz 1999).

In what follows I shall describe the postmodern attitude as it has infiltrated psychoanalysis and then describe a series of research findings that surprisingly seem to resonate with this attitude in spite of the incompatible worldviews between postmodern thought and any scientific endeavor. I shall discuss each research finding in terms of how well it fits with the contemporary self psychological and relational psychoanalytic viewpoints, and also suggest where each finding might fall on an (imaginary) postmodern continuum. My thesis is that – because both self psychology and relational psychoanalysis seem to have been influenced at the points where postmodern psychoanalytic thinking and infant research findings converge – the competing theories are moving closer together around a modified postmodern attitude that admits to the human necessity of coherence, attunement, and healing cycles of relational disruption and repair. This new (potentially integrative) model also embraces complexity within a systems view of the mind and human relationships. It sees "heightened affective moments" (Lachmann and Beebe 1996a) or "now moments" (Boston Change Process Study Group 1998) as holding curative potential and allows for recurrent periods of psychic destabilization within an overarching reach toward wholeness. This view further recognizes ongoing bidirectional influence in all human relationships creating a degree of unpredictability that may tilt toward chaos. But the same unpredictability makes room for the "something new" to emerge, which opens the potential for psychic change to occur in both partners to any dyad.

The postmodern attitude

The postmodern attitude is multifaceted and ambiguous (Protter 1996; Bader 1998; Fairfield 2001) but in all versions, it is argued that theories do not reflect objective realities as much as they reflect the subjective viewpoints of those who construct them. This belief – that no theory-maker can avoid being embedded in the phenomena about which he or she is theorizing – necessitates a radical questioning of all assumptions, exposing the ambiguity of knowledge and the illusive nature of "truth." It also suggests that in psychoanalysis, the patient's reality is (co)constructed through the treatment relationship (Hoffman 1991, 1992), rather than discovered through the analyst's objective observation and interpretation.

Arguments for the co-construction of reality, or constructivism, have emerged alike in self psychology and relational psychoanalysis whether the theories are self-defined as radically (Fairfield 2001), moderately (Aron 1996), or not at all postmodern. But this shared constructivism leads to different clinical emphases in self psychology and relational psychoanalysis. For instance acknowledgement of the co-construction of analytic experience for self psychologists entails an emphasis on the *analyst's* contribution to any hurts and misunderstandings that might occur between patient and analyst; whereas for relational analysts, recognition of the co-creation of experience leads to the analyst's search for and communication concerning how the patient contributes to his or her own disappointments and problems through repetitive patterns of relational behavior (Mitchell 1993, 1997; Teicholz 2006a).

Some of the other differences between self psychology and postmodern or relational psychoanalysis seem to be of emphasis rather than substance. For instance self psychology emphasizes the importance of a sense of continuity and coherence for feelings of well-being and adequate functioning in life. In seeming contrast, relational theory emphasizes a multiplicity of selves (Bromberg 1996; Mitchell 1997). However, Kohut (1984) also highlighted the complexity and multiplicity of experience – which, under optimal conditions, will "blossom" or "unfold" in the analytic relationship. He placed his emphasis on coherence because he recognized its essential role in an individual's capacity to pursue goals and participate in satisfying relationships and because he recognized the psyche's lifelong vulnerability to fragmentation (Teicholz 1999). Proponents of both paradigms believe it is multiplicity, but not fragmentation, that contributes to choices, complexity, and a sense of richness in individual lives. To achieve the enrichment of multiplicity rather than the depletion of fragmentation, multiplicity must be experienced within a context of psychic cohesion (Kohut 1984; Mitchell 1997). Contemporary self psychologists as well as relationalists refer to multiple-selves-in-relation-to-multiple-others (Mitchell 1997; Shane et al. 1997), both theories highlighting the multiplicity and complexity of psychic experience.

Kohut further recognized that trauma is inescapable in human life and that it leads to the splitting-off or dissociation of traumatic states, diminishing the sense of self and rendering it more fragmentation-prone or fragile (Kohut and Seitz 1963). Trauma and its consequent dissociation is similarly the focus of many relational and interpersonal theorists (Bromberg 1996; Mitchell 1997; Davies 2006), who think of it in a way not unlike Kohut. I therefore question how different the conceptual underpinnings of the theories truly are, even though practitioners working in accordance with the two paradigms work differently in the clinical setting believing that a different type of experience better facilitates healing and psychic growth.

But perhaps the most intractable disagreement between self psychologists and the relationalists – the moderate postmoderns – is around the topic of "difference" in human relationships. Relying on both Hegel (1952) and Winnicott (1971), Benjamin sees a lifelong struggle in all individuals between the desire for omnipotence and the need to recognize the "outside other" in order to be meaningfully recognized in turn (Benjamin 1995: 33). For Benjamin the outside other represents "difference." She applauds Kohut's emphasis on attunement and on the opening up of new channels of empathy between individuals. But she thinks self psychology tends to reduce relationships to their function of stabilizing the self, making too little of the "pleasure in mutuality between two subjects," or too little of the pleasure in enlargement of awareness of "others as animated by independent, though similar, feelings" (Benjamin 1995: 33). Thus Benjamin seems to fault Kohut for a dual failure: she suggests that he neither acknowledges how very painful the road to recognition of difference is, nor does he acknowledge how great is the pleasure, once mutual recognition has been finally achieved (and lost and achieved again). Meanwhile Benjamin herself fails to note that Kohut writes of joy in the achievement of mutual empathy (an achievement contingent on recognition, I would suggest). Nor does she acknowledge the complexity of Kohut's view of how the achievement of mutual empathy is made possible only by the individual's prior repeated experiences of being empathically understood. Nevertheless Benjamin's focus on recognition of difference has been taken up throughout the relational and interpersonal psychoanalytic literature, so that the analyst's expression and negotiation of difference has become almost synonymous with relational – or moderate postmodern – clinical practice, in contrast to self psychology's emphasis on attunement and resonance.

Certainly, I would say, that infants from birth onward recognize both similarity and difference between themselves and their caregivers. By this I mean that the human infant is "pre-wired" to respond to similarities: to gaze at human faces or their facsimiles, in keeping with attachment needs and the universality of facial features. At the same time infants are also born with curiosity concerning anything novel. If not distracted by undue discomfort or anxiety, infants will explore any new object to the full extent of their physical and psychic competence. But in argument with both the relational postmoderns and the Boston Change Process Study Group (1998) I have previously suggested that the infant's and small child's recognition of the other – as "different" and "outside" – is implicit only, limited to awareness of the other's caretaking interactions even though this awareness includes the uniqueness of how the caretaking is carried out, or the playfulness with which it is executed (Teicholz 2001). Only very gradually does interest in and recognition of the caregiver expand to include aspects of her subjectivity and activities outside the caretaking relationship. In other words, recognition of the caregiver as a differentiated and outside other is a later psychic achievement (Stern 1985; Ogden 1992a, 1992b). I will later discuss these contrasting viewpoints between self psychologists and relationalists in relation to the recent findings of infant–caregiver researchers.

What are some of the other features of the postmodern attitude in psychoanalysis? For postmodern analysts, there is an emphasis on process over structure in conceptualizing the mind, and on nonlinearity over linearity in conceptualizing development. There is a perception of multiplicity, complexity, or chaos of experience, rather than unity or organization. Postmodern theorists also tend to conceptualize apparent opposites in terms of dialectics and paradox, and they prefer theoretical pluralism over the claims of any single explanation. They reject the interrelated concepts of foundational knowledge; essences and universals; cause-and-effect relationships; grand or meta-narratives; and the notion of scientific progress (Teicholz 1999).

In the postmodern project, the self is seen as fluid and multiple, while identity of any kind – racial, ethnic, religious, gender, or sexual – is understood to be fraught with loss because it involves foreclosure of alternative possibilities (Barratt 1993, 1995; Butler 1995). Within psychoanalysis, postmodern questioning is directed equally toward Freud's tripartite structure of the mind and such later-emerging concepts as the "self" and "self-object." The concept of a unitary or bounded self gives way to a view of multiple-selves-in-relation-to-multiple-others (Benjamin 1998; Slavin and Kriegman 1992; Bromberg 1996; Mitchell 1997; Shane et al. 1997; Davies 1998; Fairfield 2001). And the terms self and selfobject are replaced by the terms "subjectivity" and "intersubjectivity," seen to connote greater fluidity of experience and to be less prone to reification (Stolorow et al. 1987; Ogden 1992a, 1992b). The analyst's subjectivity is acknowledged or even made central to the treatment process (Aron 1996), with analytic objectivity no longer the ideal.

We have noted that the postmodern attitude has been most closely associated with the relational paradigm in psychoanalysis (Aron 1996; Teicholz 1998, 1999). But Kohut (1971, 1977, 1982, 1984) repeatedly questioned Freud's ideal of scientific objectivity, going so far as to redefine the field in terms of what could be understood from a subjective vantage-point. This vantage-point he variously labeled "vicarious introspection" or "empathic immersion."

Kohut's focus on empathy has, in turn, been questioned by more "postmodern" or relational analysts (Aron 1992; Renik 1993; Mitchell 1997; Hoffman 1998) who refute any claim to "know" the patient's experience, even through subjective means. Relational analysts privilege interpersonal authenticity over empathy, often sharing their own experience with the patient (Aron 1991, 1992, 1996) because they assume the patient will interpret the analyst's subjectivity, whether or not the analyst deliberately brings it into the dialogue (Hoffman 1983). Beyond mutual interpretation, Jacobs speaks of mutual healing (Jacobs 2001), while Slavin and Kriegman (1992) insist that the analyst must join or even precede the patient in the process of change.

Mutual influence

Mutual influence, in itself, is not a value and not a prescription for a particular psychoanalytic attitude or intervention, but rather an ineluctable condition of human relating. Kohut's recognition of mutual influence was evident in his comments on transference/countertransference, in his goal of mutual empathy, and in his use of metaphors from quantum mechanics to evoke the indivisibility between observer and observed (Kohut 1984). In Stolorow et al.'s (1987) theory of intersubjectivity, mutual influence became the central principle. It has by now been "documented" in countless research studies of infants and their caregivers (Beebe and Lachmann 1988a, 1988b; Lachmann and Beebe 1996a; Beebe et al. 1997; Beebe 2005).

The new evidence for mutual influence undermines Freud's view of mind as a closed system and confirms the intersubjective (Stolorow et al. 1987) and relational (Aron 1996) views of co-constructed experience. It supports the term "co-transference" over the terms transference and countertransference, suggesting that the analyst – no less than the patient – brings constellations of unconscious affect, needs, and wishes to the analytic encounter.

Although mutual influence is accepted by both self psychologists and relational analysts, clinically each theory tends to highlight one direction-of-influence over the other (Teicholz 2006a). Self psychologists wonder how their own transferences are affecting their patients, while relational analysts focus on how their patients are affecting the analyst and often view their own *counter*transference as the *patient's* projection or as a clue to the *patient's* unconscious intent. Still, both self psychologists and relational analysts expect that in treatment there will be co-constructed enactments (Jacobs 2001) providing windows into the unconscious of both patient and analyst (Davies 2006). Most contemporary analysts also expect that they will sometimes have to negotiate their way out of enacted entanglements with their patients (Levenson 2005), while jointly examining the process.

This new focus on mutual influence undermines earlier notions of linear and fixed developmental stages. We now recognize that unique relational experience and the cultural milieu contribute to how constitutional "givens" are experienced and expressed. Replacing our earlier expectations of invariant developmental stages is a view of all dyadic experience as *emergent* from interaction and therefore as largely *un*predictable (Pickles 2006; Teicholz 2006b). Although each partner brings her own psychic history to the dyad and is the center of her own experience and initiative, there is always potential for something new to emerge as the influence flows between them.

In fact the "something new" has been raised to a position of curative factor in the work of the Boston Change Process Study Group (1998), a view that fits well with the recent emphasis on the analyst's improvisation (Ringstrom 2001; Kindler 2005), spontaneity (Aron 1996; Mitchell 1997; Hoffman 1998), and humor (Lachmann 2000; Newirth 2006) in both relational theory and contemporary self psychology. Meanwhile the recognition of nonlinear trajectories in psychic development, and of unpredictability in relational outcomes, has rendered nonlinear dynamic systems models (Lichtenberg et al. 1996), or chaos and complexity theories from biology and other sciences (Weisel-Barth 2006), as apt metaphors for the mind. Mutual influence, then, is a major finding from infant–caregiver research that seems to support a postmodern attitude in psychoanalysis, while bringing together previously disputed aspects of self psychology and relational theory.

Intersubjectivity in self psychology and relational theory

In most analytic paradigms the mind is now viewed as an open system under constant influence from its interaction with other systems. Reflecting this broad agreement, diverse intersubjective systems theories have emerged, including Dyadic Intersubjective Systems theory (Stolorow et al. 1987; Stolorow and Atwood 1992; Orange et al. 1997), nonlinear dynamic systems theory (Lichtenberg et al. 1992, 1996), or just plain intersubjectivity theory (Stern 1985; Ogden 1986, 1992b; Benjamin 1988, 1990) – with, however, the term "intersubjectivity" assigned different meanings in self psychology and relational psychoanalysis (Teicholz 2001).

"Intersubjectivity" is always about mutuality between individuals – about two-way exchanges of psychic activity. But in self psychology the term refers to mutual influence or regulation (Stolorow et al. 1987; Stolorow and Atwood 1992; Lachmann and Beebe 1996a, 1996b; Orange et al. 1997; Orange and Stolorow 1998) while in relational theory it refers to mutual recognition of mind, in self and other (Stern 1985; Benjamin 1988, 1990; Ogden 1992b). With each theory adhering to its own language and conceptual emphasis, the self psychologist's *attunement* is intended to facilitate self- and mutual *affect regulation* while the relational analyst's *expression of disjunctive subjectivity* is intended to facilitate mutual *recognition* of the unique psychological life of each party to the dyad – or recognition of difference.

Psychoanalytic attitudes toward empirical studies

Before presenting the actual research, I should mention that both self psychologists and postmodern theorists have questioned the value of infant caregiver research for psychoanalysis. Kohut rejected all modes of observation but the empathic for understanding the inner world. Goldberg eschewed theoretical constraints, wanting to rely exclusively on what could be learned in the authentic encounter between patient and analyst (Goldberg 1990). Relational analysts prefer the unique intersubjective negotiation of reality over any research findings, in part because in their view, the universals of science have historically been used to disenfranchise those who do not fit the empirically established "norms" of race, class, gender identification, or sexual orientation (Layton 1998; Fairfield 2001). All of these critiques struggle with the problem of using scientific research as a blueprint for an experiential process and a healing art. Still, if the research findings can be used, not as a instruction manual for psychoanalytic practice, but as a corroboration of hunches developed through empathic listening and engagement with individual patients, then they might serve to enhance the analyst's effectiveness. It also seems that the research is becoming increasingly nuanced, sophisticated, and relevant to an intersubjective psychoanalysis. And from diverse theoretical paradigms, analysts are exploring its implications and finding new support for their ideas. What follows is a selective overview of recent research that seems to resonate with both self psychology and relational theory.

Selected infant–caregiver research and cognitive neuroscience findings

We earlier noted that in self psychology, "affect regulation" is facilitated through mutual attunement (Beebe and Lachmann 1988a, 1988b) while in relational theory "recognition of mind" is pursued through expression and negotiation of difference (Benjamin 1988). Both emphases come into play in *marking* when it occurs in the interaction between infant and caregiver, as reported by Fonagy et al. (2002). In *marking*, the caregiver attunes herself to and actively *imitates* the infant's affect through facial, vocal, and postural expression. But the caregiver *marks* her mirroring by slight exaggeration, thus providing the infant with an experience of attunement along with a hint that the mirroring comes from an outside other. By both *matching* the infant's affective expression and at the same time *marking* herself as *different*, the caregiver manages to present both regulatory attunement and recognizing difference within a single interaction.

Another finding that seems to support the emphases in both self psychology and relational theory comes from a study of *affective tracking* between infant and caregiver. Beebe et al. (1997) report that *secure attachment* in infants is associated with *moderate affective tracking* in the mother–infant dyad. The *highest degree of tracking* is associated with the *least secure attachment*. Again these findings support both self psychological attunement *and* relational expression of difference – provided that the difference is not of such magnitude that it shatters the empathic bond. The correlation between secure attachment and only *moderate* degrees of attunement fits well with Kohut's notion of curative cycles of disruption and repair, in which manageable failures of attunement between patient and analyst give rise to mutual reparative efforts through which attunement is restored. In affective tracking as with marking, it seems that the dyadic expression of *small* degrees of difference can be growth-promoting, as long as they occur in the ongoing *context* of mutual attunement and regulation. I argue that sameness and difference work together throughout development to facilitate a sense of self that is felt as both unique and well-"fitted" with "like" others.

Other work that supports both self psychology's focus on "regulation" and relational theory's focus on "recognition" comes from Daniel Stern, who suggests a "core" or physical sense of self in the earliest months of life, in which the infant recognizes separate bodies but cannot yet grasp the psychological world (Stern 1985). At around nine months, a "subjective" sense of self emerges in which the infant first recognizes the *minds* of self and others, after which the two modes of experience coexist – a *pre-subjective*, core, or physical sense of self, alongside of a subjective or psychological self.

But – Stern (1985) says – as soon as the infant discovers that both he and his mother have unique psychological lives, he feels an increased need for bridges of empathic connection. The infant realizes that while two minds can enjoy sharing, they can also differ. And this first awareness of psychic difference leads to new anxieties about conflict, separation, and abandonment (Teicholz 2001). If the caregiver responds with increased attunement at this critical juncture, the infant goes on to be *curious* about the newly recognized, distinctive mind of the other. But without heightened attunement at this point, the infant's natural curiosity can be swamped by anxiety. Like Fonagy's marking or Beebe and Lachmann's tracking, then, Stern's finding of the move from a physical to a psychological sense of self and other suggests, once again, a role for both attunement *and* recognition-of-difference in development – and even suggests how the two kinds of experiences might relate to each other (see also Ogden 1992a, 1992b; Teicholz 2001).

While thus far, I have mentioned studies that seem to support the emphases in both self psychology and relational theories, there are several research findings that more specifically support the central tenets of self psychology and I believe, have persuaded many relational analysts of their "validity." (It may be another story that self psychology is often not "credited" with these ideas, by either relational analysts or the researchers themselves.)

For instance a basic need for attunement is evident in Sander's research findings of mutual "entrainment" in the bio-psychological rhythms between infant and caregiver – an attunement without words which he calls "rhythmicity" (Sander 2002). The curative potential of rhythmicity between patient and analyst has been explored by Knoblauch (2000, 2005a, 2005b), especially regarding experience not otherwise accessible because of its preverbal origins or traumatic intensity.

In addition to these research affirmations of Kohut's emphasis on attunement, his inseparable concepts of self and selfobject receive support from Beebe's (2005) finding that the infant's *self*-regulation remains prominent, even in the context of *mutual* regulation between infant and caregiver. And Kohut's view of the profound, lifelong impact of the early regulatory and structure-building relationship on the individual – again, the selfobject concept – receives support from Schore's (2003a, 2003b) neuroscience studies, suggesting that even brain structure and chemistry are shaped by early interactive experience. In Schore's words:

> Early failures in dyadic regulation . . . skew the developmental trajectory . . . [D]isruption of attachment bonds in infancy leads to regulatory

failure . . . [And] when the caretaker routinely does not participate in reparative functions that reestablish [affective regulation], the resulting psychobiological disequilibrium is expressed in a dysregulated and potentially toxic brain chemistry.

(Schore 2003: 33)

Schore's findings support Kohut's emphasis on both ongoing regulation and the rupture-and-repair process in the bond between parent and child – two of the three processes identified by Beebe and Lachmann (1994; Lachmann and Beebe 1996a) as principles of salience in psychic development.

Other neuroscience research findings support Kohut's notion of *coherence* as essential to a functional sense of self. Both Sander (2002) and Kandel (2005) suggest that the human mind self-assembles or self-organizes, moving in the direction of coherence when things go well. But Sander's (2002) findings equally support relational theory's emphasis on the multiplicity of experience, thus bringing together relational and self psychological views of a self that moves toward coherence in the face of the enormous complexity of its component experiences.

Still other research discoveries – such as the curative power of "now moments" (Boston Change Process Study Group 1998) or of "heightened affective moments" (Lachmann and Beebe 1996a) – support the current emphasis on improvisation, humor, and playfulness in both contemporary self psychology and relational theory, qualities also valued in postmodern thinking. These findings lead to a new recognition of multiple qualities of engagement contributing to psychic growth (Teicholz 2006a) – qualities such as authenticity, transparency, affective honesty, and spontaneity, as well as empathy.

In addition to embracing these multiple qualities of engagement, self psychologists now offer an expanded roster of *motivations* as well (Lichtenberg 1989). While radical postmodern theory rejects such universals, Lichtenberg's motivational systems theory, with its claim to five motivational systems, at least meets the postmodern requirement of pluralism. One of these motivations, "adversiveness" – or the need to fight against experiences that feel noxious or threatening to the self – brings self psychology closer to relational theory, with *its* emphasis on conflict. Lichtenberg, Lachmann, and Fosshage's nonlinear dynamic systems model of treatment (Lichtenberg et al. 1992, 1996; see also Lachmann 2000) also includes the concept of *perturbation* as a prelude to change. Their view of perturbation, as integral to the curative process, reflects the imperfectability of empathy and once again is compatible with Kohut's notion of curative cycles of disruption and repair.

But while always having recognized the growth-promoting potential of *manageable* disruptions and perturbations – and now making room for relational aversion, conflict, and confrontation – self psychology may still have to retain *empathy* as its *primary* quality of engagement in light of the recent discovery of "mirror neurons." Neuroscientists have found that the brain activity of one individual – while merely *observing* another individual in action – automatically mirrors the brain activity of the observed individual. Mirror neurons are active even in the brains of very young infants, suggesting that empathic perception and resonance are adapted responses, built into the very structure and function of our brains (Wolf et al. 2001; Kandel 2005; Decety and Jackson 2006).

The *autonomic* firing of neurons, in "sympathy" with the actions of others, seems to have parallels in the world of *purposeful* behavior as well. Trevarthen (2005) reports that "within hours of birth, babies imitate face expressions, hand gestures, shifts of the head . . . closing of the eyes and simple vocal sounds . . . [sometimes] with inter-modal sensory equivalence, and . . . matching gestures with different body parts" (Trevarthen 2005: 94). Detecting in these newborn activities the "cardinal features of . . . intentional behavior," Trevarthen concludes that "human imitation is generated by an innate interpersonal sensibility" (Trevarthen 2005: 94–95). But he adds that in every individual there is *also* an "inner autopoietic, self-making process" – once again supporting central tenets of both self psychology and relational theory (Trevarthen 2005: 95). Trevarthen sees the newborn's mimicry as reflecting a kind of proto-empathy, in which the infant seeks connection with and playful exploration of the relational world (see also Wolf et al. 2001).

The recognition of relational capacities at birth, as well as the interest in qualities of engagement between patient and analyst, reflects a new emphasis on the affective components of psychoanalytic cure (Teicholz 2006a). *Affect* is the connecting link among all qualities of engagement (Teicholz 2000), replacing drives as the primary human motivator. It is around affective experience that the sense of self is organized. But this organization can come about – and can remain open and flexible – only when affective experience is adequately regulated through the self–selfobject relationship (Kohut 1971; Stolorow et al. 1987; Lachmann 2000) operating primarily at an implicit, affective level.

Infant research suggests that the implicit/procedural (Boston Change Process Study Group 1998), subsymbolic (Bucci 2001), or enactive (Lyons-Ruth 1999) memory system developmentally precedes the symbolic, verbal, declarative, or reflective mode of psychic processing; but once both systems have developed, they operate side-by-side. While experience encoded in the two memory systems may in some instances be intertwined, the systems also remain for some purposes dissociable throughout life (Lyons-Ruth 1999).

With new recognition of these two memory systems, some authors now include, among their analytic goals, the "translation" of experiences from the implicit or subsymbolic system into the explicit, declarative, reflective, or symbolic realm – along with the more traditional goal of interpreting the dynamic unconscious. But Lyons-Ruth (1999) argues that the subsymbolic memory system is only partly or imperfectly "translatable" into the symbolic or declarative. She believes that implicit experience or procedural learning can be more directly transformed through new modes of affective and enacted experience in treatment, with or without an intervening process of verbalization. This is a view that fits well with the postmodern questioning of interpretation as the predominant pathway to psychic change in psychoanalysis, and fits as well with the new emphasis on qualities of engagement in the curative process – qualities that include empathy but also other modes of relating.

Other findings from Lyons-Ruth are less resonant with postmodern thinking. Granted, that even with the increasing egalitarian tilt of the analytic relationship, all but the most radical postmodernists recognize *some* asymmetry in the roles and responsibilities between patient and analyst. But Lyons-Ruth takes the asymmetry a step further in her notion of a functionally "disadvantaged partner" for whom the more "advantaged partner" provides psychic "scaffolding" (Lyons-Ruth 1999: 583).

While fitting poorly with the egalitarian postmodern attitude, the notion of a developmentally disadvantaged partner offers support for Kohut's emphasis on the selfobject function as *initially* moving from parent to child or from analyst to patient – albeit with selfobject *exchange* as the ultimate goal. But it is important to note that just because one partner transiently needs greater support than the other for certain areas of psychic functioning, this pocket of asymmetry in no way changes the mutuality and bidirectionality of influence in the dyad, whether they are interacting in a developmental or analytic setting. Among self psychologists, Beebe and Lachmann have pointed to *un*equal influence as well as to different roles and responsibilities *within* mutuality (Beebe and Lachmann 1988a, 1988b; Lachmann and Beebe 1996a, 1996b) – as have Aron and Mitchell among Relational theorists (Aron 1990, 1991, 1992, 1996; Mitchell 1997).

In addition to Lyons-Ruth's (1999) concept of scaffolding, Sander describes a growth-promoting quality of the infant–caregiver relationship which he calls "fittedness" (Sander 2002) – also explored in self psychology by Ornstein (1988) and Tolpin (2003). Highlighting the mutuality of the experience, the Boston Change Process Study Group refers to a step-by-step process of "fitting together" (Boston Change Process Study Group 2002: 1051).

Sander's research additionally points to a *recognition process* in fittedness, which he defines as "the experience of *specificity* in interaction and engagement" (Sander 2002: 13, original italics). The notion of specificity has been expanded in self psychology by Bacal and Herzog (2003). And without the specificity, *recognition* figures prominently in relational theory as well. But the relational emphasis is on the *child's* recognition of the mother as "outside other" (Benjamin 1988), while what is highlighted by both self psychologists and infant–caregiver researchers is the *mother's* recognition of the unique qualities and initiatives of the *child* (Sander 2002).

Benjamin explains the relational emphasis on the child's or the patient's recognition of "the other" with the notion that, in order to benefit from being recognized the one who is recognized must in turn recognize the recognizing other (Benjamin 1990). And more recently the Boston Change Process Study Group (1998) suggests that the infant *recognizes* the caregiver as an aspect of mutual *regulation* even before the attainment of intersubjective relatedness around nine months, previously identified as the earliest possible age for this developmental achievement (Stern 1985). These seeming contradictions may eventually be resolved by further refinement of how the different authors are using the term "recognition." Until then I would suggest that – to the extent this very early recognition-of-other exists – it is limited to the caretaking context and is more *im*plicit than *ex*plicit (Teicholz 2001). The earliest recognition does not entail any grasp of the unique psychological worlds of either self or other (Stern et al. 1998; Ogden 1992b). But recognition and attunement may indeed ultimately intertwine in development because, as an aspect of successful attunement or "fitting together," there seems to be new evidence for increasing *specificity* of "recognition" between the two partners (Sander 2002).

These several strands of research have influenced all psychoanalytic paradigms and have nudged into closer alignment their respective understandings of human development. I shall now turn my attention to changes that have come about in the analytic concept of "the unconscious," initially the defining concept of psychoanalysis.

Changing views of the unconcious in psychoanalysis

Long before the research described in this chapter – and long before the explicit postmodern turn in psychoanalysis – Kohut's notion (1971, 1977, 1984) of a self, constructed through selfobject experience, contributed to early changes in how we view "the unconscious." The forging of self or subjectivity through selfobject experience – much of which remains unconscious – results in what can only be viewed as an interactive unconscious, far removed from Freud's (1915) view of a closed system in which conscious and unconscious experiences are divided by a rigid repression barrier.

Both Freud and Kohut were interested in how the psyche keeps painful or threatening experience out of awareness, and both recognized that the human psyche has evolved multiple ways to accomplish this goal. But because Freud had thoroughly covered how individuals use repression to ward off instincts, Kohut undertook to explore how individuals use disavowal and splitting to ward off entire constellations of unbearable affects and self-states. Kohut and Seitz (1963) thought that splitting was a universal response to trauma; that trauma was inescapable; and that therefore splitting was a ubiquitous phenomenon of psychic life in which the individual alternates between incompatible self-states. The relational and postmodern views of trauma and splitting are quite similar to Kohut's.

Where Kohut *differed* from Freud about the unconscious, he thus uncannily anticipated the postmodern view, now validated by both infant–caregiver researchers and cognitive neuroscientists. Kohut spoke of "unconscious experience," rather than of "the unconscious," because he saw consciousness and unconsciousness not as psychic entities or locations but as qualities of experience subject to change over time in response to cues from the human environment. These views were decidedly postmodern.

Research and the unconscious

Today, not just self psychology but most analytic theories and research findings point to an interactive, intersubjective (Stolorow and Atwood 1992), dyadic (Boston Change Process Study Group 1998), two-person (Lyons-Ruth 1999), or relational (Likierman 2006; Tubert-Oklander 2006) unconscious, as well as to a far more fluid boundary between conscious and unconscious experience than previously believed.

While we still value Freud's notion of a dynamic unconscious, we distinguish it from other unconscious experience that we now realize is kept out of awareness not by dynamic forces but simply because it is "prereflective" (Stolorow and Atwood 1992), "subsymbolic" (Bucci 1997, 2001), "implicit/procedural" (Boston Change Process Study Group 1998), or "enactive" (Lyons-Ruth 1999). From birth onward, repetitive patterns of relational experience become generalized (Stern 1985) and are represented in the subsymbolic, implicit/procedural memory system, remaining non-conscious but powerfully informing affective experience and impelling behavior. These subsymbolic experiences are not necessarily more primitive than experience that is symbolized and in fact they often involve complex procedures for carrying out sensory-motor and affective-relational tasks such as athletic and artistic pursuits or "being with others" (Lyons-Ruth 1999: 582).

The earliest representations of "being with others" become patterned in accordance with specific qualities of infant–caretaker dialogue. Sander found that dialogue contributing to coherent and flexible ways of being with others has a quality of *specificity* in which the infant's unique initiatives are recognized and responded to, and a quality of *inclusiveness* in which the caregiver meaningfully responds to the whole spectrum of affects expressed by the child (Sander 2002). While Sander frames his research findings in terms of dyadic communication, his definitions of specificity and inclusiveness come close to what Kohut labels as empathic responsiveness, and to what Bacal and Herzog (2003) describe in their specificity theory.

New integrations

Looking at these research findings, we see that early development entails learning through repetitive patterns of interactive experience that may never become conscious. These patterns of experience – whether symbolically encoded or not – lead to procedural or enactive representations that inform expectations of relational transactions (Lyons-Ruth 1999). In treatment, powerful new relational experiences can create new representations that eventually crowd out older, less adaptive ones. Influenced by these findings, many self psychologists, relational, and postmodern analysts no longer think of themselves as merely making the unconscious conscious, but also as co-constructing new non-conscious experience with their patients. The analyst's empathy may play a vital role in these curative co-constructions, but so also may other qualities of relationship.

In these contemporary views of treatment, analyst and patient co-create news ways of being together, eventually changing what patients come to expect, how they access and express their affective experience, pursue their interests, and engage with significant others. The contributions to these changes can come from the (never-verbalized) enacted experience in the analytic relationship which – if powerful enough – shifts the patient's experience of self-and-other through implicit procedural learning. But changes can also come from, or be amplified by, the interpretive process in the explicit/verbal dialogue between patient and analyst – which, however, in most cases can make a difference only when preceded or accompanied by the direct experience of new patterns of relating.

Throughout, we have noted common ground in new conceptualizations of unconscious experience among postmodern, relational, and self psychological analysts. And yet the clinical approaches across these theories remain distinctive. The shared understanding – that the self is co-constructed through relational experience – does not seem to bring together the several competing views of how the analyst might best engage with the patient. Thus we hold to our separate paradigms.

Nevertheless there is increasing recognition across theories that there is much we can learn from each other, and much in *each* theory that is supported by scientific evidence. In fact the research findings have so influenced contemporary theorists that there is near-consensus concerning the curative power of attunement and repeated cycles of disruption and repair. There is also a widely shared view of the treatment relationship as a dyadic system characterized by bidirectional influence, no small part of which emanates from the analyst's subjectivity.

Admittedly, the very idea of making generalizations about what human beings need – and the search for such universals through empirical studies – is decidedly not postmodern. And yet such studies continue to emerge from diverse disciplines, with findings that confirm the fluidity and multiplicity of human experience, and its transmigration across self-other boundaries. We have evidence also that individuals strive for a sense of coherence in the face of daunting complexity and lifelong tendencies toward fragmentation. Additionally, most analysts now agree that in health, the striving toward feelings of integral wholeness coexists with an eagerness for new and enriching intersubjective, selfobject, and interpersonal experience – and therefore with periods of (creative) destabilization, or lifelong flux and change.

Some closing thoughts

I am proposing that modernist and postmodern trends in psychoanalytic theory temper each other so that our theory guides us as to human developmental needs but at the same time helps us to hold our theoretically based expectations quite lightly. At the same time the convergence of infant–caregiver, attachment, and neuroscience research findings with certain aspects of the postmodern attitude serves to temper the more abstract and stringent strains in postmodern theory and to focus our attention on their relevance for the relief of human suffering and the facilitation of psychic growth. Most of the defining notions of postmodernism – such as social constructivism, ambiguity, difference, and the dissolution of the subject – are not only supported, but also somehow modified, by the empirical findings under discussion here.

For example when it comes to the postmodern emphasis on difference, we have noted the subtleties of the recognitions that contribute to psychic growth, and also the way in which recognition of difference is optimally balanced, throughout healthy development, with resonance and recognition of similarity. Similarly – while all claims to a priori psychic dispositions, to certainty, and to the fixed subject are admittedly undermined by the evidence for ongoing mutual and bidirectional influence in dyadic experience – at the same time, the research lays out some parameters within which we are given some idea of what to expect. For instance, within a given dyad, nothing is from the start predictable but over time we can predict with somewhat greater certainty that when one partner behaves in a certain way, the other will respond in a way that has become characteristic for that dyad. Certain rhythms within the dyad will develop and also become characteristic. In other words, no two dyads are ever alike, but each dyad eventually develops its own unique (and therefore somewhat predictable) patterns of behavior and experience.

Most importantly, the very unpredictability of the dyad is exactly what leaves the doors open for psychic change. And change, after all, is the goal of psychoanalysis across all theories. The change process works for our patients because what an individual – repeatedly, over time – experiences, enacts, and elaborates verbally in one relationship can be carried over to the experience, actions and words in other relationships as well.

References

Aron, L. (1990) 'One-person and two-person psychologies and the method of psychoanalysis', *Psychoanalytic Psychology*, 7: 475–486.
—— (1991) 'The patient's experience of the analyst's subjectivity', *Psychoanalytic Dialogues*, 1: 29–51.
—— (1992) 'Interpretation as expression of the analyst's subjectivity', *Psychoanalytic Dialogues*, 2: 475–507.
—— (1996) *A Meeting of Minds*, Hillsdale, NJ: Analytic Press.
Bacal, H. and Herzog, B. (2003) 'Specificity theory and optimal responsiveness: an outline', *Psychoanalytic Psychology*, 20: 635–648.
Bader, M. (1998) 'Postmodern epistemology: the problem of validation and the retreat from therapeutics in psychoanalysis', *Psychoanalytic Dialogues*, 8: 1–32.
Barratt, B. (1993) *Psychoanalysis and the Postmodern Impulse: Knowing and Being since Freud's Psychology*, Baltimore, MD: Johns Hopkins University Press.
—— (1995) Review essay: 'Madness and Modernism: Insanity in the Light of Modern Art, Literature, and Thought, by Louis A. Sass, *Psychoanalytic Dialogues*, 5: 113–125.
Beebe, B. (2005) 'Mother-infant research informs mother-infant treatment', *Psychoanalytic Study of the Child*, 60: 7–46.
Beebe, B. and Lachmann, F. (1988a) 'Mother-infant mutual influence and precursors of psychic structure', in A. Goldberg (ed.) *Frontiers in Self Psychology: Progress in Self Psychology*, vol. 3, Hillsdale, NJ: Analytic Press.
—— (1988b) 'The contribution of mother-infant mutual influence to the origins of self and object representations', *Psychoanalytic Psychology*, 5: 305–337.
—— (1994) 'Representation and internalization in infancy: three principles of salience, *Psychoanalytic Psychology*, 11: 127–165.
Beebe, B., Lachmann, F. and Jaffe, J. (1997) 'Mother-infant interaction structures and pre-symbolic self and object-representations', *Psychoanalytic Dialogues*, 7: 133–182.
Benjamin, J. (1988) *Bonds of Love: Psychoanalysis, Feminism, and the Problem of Domination*, New York: Pantheon.
—— (1995) *Like Subjects, Love Objects: Essays on Recognition and Sexual Difference*, New Haven, CT: Yale University Press.
Boston Change Process Study Group (Stern, D., Sander, L., Nahum, J., Harrison, A., Lyons-Ruth, K. Morgan, A., Bruschweiler-Stern, N. and Tronick, E.) (1998) 'Noninterpretive mechanisms in psychoanalytic therapy: the "something more" than interpretation', *International Journal of Psychoanalysis*, 79: 903–922.
—— (Bruschweiler-Stern, N., Harrison, A., Lyons-Ruth, K., Morgan, A., Nahum, J., Sander, L., Stern, D. and Tronick, E.) (2002) 'Explicating the implicit: the local level and the microprocess of change in the analytic situation', *International Journal of Psychoanalysis*, 83: 1051–1062.
Bromberg, P. (1996) 'Standing in the spaces: the multiplicity of self and the psychoanalytic relationship', *Contemporary Psychoanalysis*, 32: 509–535.
Bucci, W. (1997) *Psychoanalytic and Cognitive Science: A Multiple Code Theory*, New York: Guilford.
—— (2001) 'Pathways of emotional communication', *Psychoanalytic Inquiry*, 21: 40–70.

Butler, J. (1995) 'Melancholy gender – refused identification', *Psychoanalytic Dialogues*, 5: 165–180.

Cotter, H. (2008) 'In grace notes, linear riffs on reality: art review', *New York Times*, January 4.

Davies, J. (1998) 'Multiple perspectives on multiplicity', *Psychoanalytic Dialogues*, 8: 195–206.

—— (2006) 'On the nature of the self: multiplicity, unconscious conflict and fantasy in relational psychoanalysis', paper presented at the Twenty-eighth Annual International Conference on the Psychology of the Self, Chicago, IL: October 27.

Decety, J. and Jackson, P. (2006) 'A social-neuroscience perspective on empathy', *Current Directions in Psychological Science*, 15: 54–58.

Fairfield, S. (2001) 'Analyzing multiplicity: a postmodern perspective on some current psychoanalytic theories of subjectivity', *Psychoanalytic Dialogues*, 11: 221–252.

Fonagy, P., Gergely, G., Jurist, E. and Target, M. (2002) *Affect Regulation, Mentalization, and the Development of the Self*, New York: The Other Press.

Freud, S. (1915) 'The unconscious', in *Standard Edition*, 14: 161–208, London: Hogarth Press.

Goldberg, A. (1990) *The Prisonhouse of Psychoanalysis*, Hillsdale, NJ: Analytic Press.

Hegel, G. (1952) *Phanomenologie des Geistes*, Hamburg: Felix Meiner.

Hoffman, I. (1983) 'The patient as interpreter of the analyst's experience', *Contemporary Psychoanalysis*, 19: 389–422.

—— (1991) 'Discussion: toward a social-constructivist view of the psychoanalytic situation', *Psychoanalytic Dialogues*, 1: 74–105.

—— (1992) 'Some practical implications of a social-constructivist view of the psychoanalytic situation', *Psychoanalytic Dialogues*, 2: 287–304.

—— (1998) *Ritual and Spontaneity in the Psychoanalytic Process: A Dialectical-Constructivist View*, Hillsdale, NJ: Analytic Press.

Jacobs, T. (2001) 'On unconscious communications and covert enactments', *Psychoanalytic Inquiry*, 21: 4–23.

Kandel, E. (2005) *Psychiatry, Psychoanalysis, and the New Biology of Mind*, Washington, DC: Psychiatry Publishing.

Kindler, A. (2005) 'Improvisation and spontaneity in psychoanalysis', unpublished paper presented at the Twenty-eighth International Conference on the Psychology of the Self, Baltimore, MD, October 22.

Knoblauch, S. (2000) *The Musical Edge of Psychoanalytic Dialogue*, Hillsdale, NJ: Analytic Press.

—— (2005a) Body rhythms and the unconscious: toward an expanding of clinical attention', *Psychoanalytic Dialogues*, 15: 807–828.

—— (2005b) 'What are we trying to do when we write about the psychoanalytic interaction? The relevance of theory and research to clinical responsiveness', *Psychoanalytic Dialogues*, 15: 883–896.

Kohut, H. (1971) *The Analysis of the Self*, New York: International Universities Press.

—— (1977) *The Restoration of the Self*, New York: International Universities Press.

—— (1982) 'Introspection, empathy, and the semi-circle of mental health', *International Journal of Psychoanalysis*, 63: 395–407.

—— (1984) *How Does Analysis Cure?*, edited A. Goldberg and P. Stepansky, Chicago, IL: University of Chicago Press.

Kohut, H. and Seitz, P. (1963) 'Concepts and theories of psychoanalysis', in P. Ornstein (ed.) *Search for the Self*, Vol. I, New York: International Universities Press, 1978.

Lachmann, F. (2000) *Transforming Aggression*, Northvale, NJ: Jason Aronson.

Lachmann, F. and Beebe, B. (1996a) 'Three principles of salience in the organization of the patient-analyst interaction', *Psychoanalytic Psychologist*, 13: 1–22.

—— (1996b) 'The contribution of self- and mutual regulation to therapeutic action: A case illustration', in A. Goldberg (ed.) *Basic Ideas Reconsidered: Progress in Self Psychology*, Vol. 12, Hillsdale, NJ: Analytic Press.

Lahr, J. (2007) 'Demolition man: Harold Pinter and "The Homecoming"', *The New Yorker*, December 24 and 31: 54–69.

Layton, L. (1998) *Who's That Girl? Who's That Boy? Clinical Practice Meets Postmodern Gender Theory*, Northvale, NJ: Jason Aronson.

Levenson, E. (2005) *The Fallacy of Understanding/The Ambiguity of Change*, Hillsdale, NJ: Analytic Press.

Lichtenberg, J. (1989) *Psychoanalysis and Motivation*, Hillsdale, NJ: Analytic Press.

Lichtenberg, J., Lachmann, F. and Fossghage, J. (1992) *Self and Motivational Systems*, Hillsdale, NJ: Analytic Press.

—— (1996) *The Clinical Exchange: Techniques Derived from Self and Motivational Systems*, Hillsdale, NJ: Analytic Press.

Likierman, M. (2006) 'Unconscious experience: relational perspectives', *Psychoanalytic Dialogues*, 16: 365–376.

Lyons-Ruth, K. (1999) 'Two-person unconscious: intersubjective dialogue, enactive relational representation, and the emergence of new forms of relational organization', *Psychoanalytic Quarterly*, 19: 576–617.

Mitchell, S. (1993) *Hope and Dread in Psychoanalysis*, New York: Basic Books.

—— (1997) *Influence and Autonomy in Psychoanalysis*, Hillsdale, NJ: Analytic Press.

Newirth, J. (2006) 'Jokes and their relation to the unconscious: humor as a fundamental emotional experience', *Psychoanalytic Dialogues*, 16: 557–571.

Ogden, T. (1986) *The Matrix of the Mind: Objects Relations and the Psychoanalytic Dialogue*, Northvale, NJ: Jason Aronson.

—— (1992a) 'The dialectically constituted/decentered subject of psychoanalysis, I: the Freudian subject', *International Journal of Psychoanalysis*, 73: 517–526.

—— (1992b) 'The dialectically constituted/decentered subject of psychoanalysis, II: the contributions of Klein and Winnicott', *International Journal of Psychoanalysis*, 73: 613–626.

Orange, D. and Stolorow, R. (1998) 'Self-disclosure from the perspective of intersubjectivity theory', *Psychoanalytic Inquiry*, 18: 530–537.

Orange, D., Atwood, G. and Stolorow, R. (1997) *Working Intersubjectively: Contextualism in Psychoanalytic Practice*, Hillsdale, NJ: Analytic Press.

Ornstein, A. (1988) 'Optimal responsiveness and the theory of cure', in A. Goldberg (ed.) *Learning from Kohut: Progress in Self Psychology*, Vol. 4, Hillsdale, NJ: Analytic Press.

Pickles, J. (2006) 'A systems sensibility: commentary on Judith Teicholz's "Qualities of engagement and the analyst's theory"', *International Journal of Psychoanalytic Self Psychology*, 1: 301–316.

Protter, B. (1996) 'Classical, modern, and postmodern psychoanalysis: epistemic transformations', *Psychoanalytic Dialogues*, 6: 533–562.

Renik, O. (1993) 'Analytic interaction: conceptualizing technique in the light of the analyst's irreducible subjectivity', *Psychoanalytic Quarterly*, 62: 553–571.

Ringstrom, P. (2001) 'Cultivating the improvisational in psychoanalysis', *Psychoanalytic Dialogues*, 11: 727–754.

Sander, L. (2002) 'Thinking differently: principles of process in living systems and the specificity of being known', *Psychoanalytic Dialogues*, 12: 11–42.

Schore, A. (2003a) *Affect Regulation and the Repair of the Self*, New York: Norton.

—— (2003b) *Affect Dysregulation and Disorders of the Self*, New York: Norton.

Shane, M., Shane, E. and Gales, M. (1997) *Intimate Attachments: Toward a New Self Psychology*, New York: Guilford.

Slavin, M. and Kriegman, D. (1992) *The Adaptive Design of the Human Psyche: Psychoanalysis, Evolutionary Biology, and the Therapeutic Process*, New York: Guilford.

Stern, D. N. (1985) *The Interpersonal World of the Infant*, New York: Basic Books.

Stern, D. N., Sander, L., Nahum, J., Harrison, A., Lyons-Ruth, K., Morgan, A., Bruschweiler-Stern, N. and Tronick, E. (1998) 'Noninterpretive mechanisms in psychoanalytic therapy: the "something more" than interpretation', *International Journal of Psychoanalysis*, 79: 903–922.

Stolorow, R. and Atwood, G. (1992) *Contexts of Being*, Hillsdale, NJ: Analytic Press.

Stolorow, R., Brandchaft, B. and Atwood, G. (1987) *Psychoanalytic Treatment: An Intersubjective Approach*, Hillsdale, NJ: Analytic Press.

Teicholz, J. (1998) 'Self and relationship: Kohut, Loewald, and the postmoderns', in A. Goldberg (ed.) *The World of Self Psychology: Progress in Self Psychology*, Vol. 14, Hillsdale, NJ: Analytic Press.

—— (1999) *Kohut, Loewald, and the Postmoderns: A Comparative Study of Self and Relationship*, Hillsdale, NJ: Analytic Press.

—— (2000) 'The analyst's empathy, subjectivity, and authenticity: affect as the common denominator', in A. Goldberg (ed.) *How Responsive Should We Be? Progress in Self Psychology*, Vol. 16, Hillsdale, NJ: Analytic Press.

—— (2001) 'The many meanings of intersubjectivity and their implications for analyst self-expression and self-disclosure', in A. Goldberg (ed.) *The Narcissistic Patient Revisited: Progress in Self Psychology*, Vol. 17, Hillsdale, NJ: Analytic Press.

—— (2006a) 'Qualities of engagement and the analyst's theory', *International Journal of Psychoanalytic Self Psychology*, 1: 47–77.

—— (2006b) 'Negative identifications, messy complexity, and windows of hope: response to Pickles' discussion of "Qualities of engagement and the analyst's theory"', *International Journal of Psychoanalytic Self Psychology*, 1: 435–444.

Tolpin, M. (2003) 'Doing psychoanalysis of normal development: forward edge transferences', in A. Goldberg (ed.) *Progress in Self Psychology*, Vol. 19, Hillsdale, NJ: Analytic Press.

Trevarthen, C. (2005) 'First things first: infants make good use of the sympathetic rhythm of imitation, without reason or language', *Journal of Child Psychotherapy*, 31: 91–113.

Tubert-Oklander, J. (2006) 'On the inherent relationality of the unconscious: reply to commentary', *Psychoanalytic Dialogues*, 16: 227–239.

Weisel-Barth, J. (2006) 'Thinking and writing about complexity theory in the clinical setting', *International Journal of Psychoanalytic Self Psychology*, 1: 365–388.

Winnicott, D. (1971) 'The use of an object and relating through identification', in *Playing and Reality*, New York: Basic Books.

Wolf, N., Gales, M., Shane, E. and Shane, M. (2001) 'The developmental trajectory from amodal perception to empathy and communication: the role of mirror neurons in this process', *Psychoanalytic Inquiry*, 21: 94–112.

Chapter 4

Primary process of deconstruction

Towards a Derridian psychotherapy

Heward Wilkinson

> We need another language that does not exist (outside poetry) – a language that is steeped in temporal dynamics.
>
> (Daniel Stern)

This evocative statement by Daniel Stern (2004: 173) suggests that poetry can provide a paradigm not only for understanding psychotherapy, but also that psychotherapy itself is a kind of poetry. I believe that poetry provides a means to understand Derrida, and correlatively to make sense of Derrida's relevance to psychotherapy. Although Derrida's abstractness has led to much confusion and misunderstanding, I shall seek to show that Derrida's insights are similar to and, indeed, expand on Stern's. In this chapter, I shall focus above all on Derrida's profound insight into the *particular existence* with which psychoanalysis or psychotherapy concerns itself.

Poetry provides a working paradigm for psychotherapy. The final sentence of P. B. Shelley's *Defence of Poetry* (Shelley 1840/2004) reads: "Poets are the unacknowledged legislators of the World." Shelley's expansive conception of poetry would undoubtedly include the reality that the literature of religion and philosophy were originally one and the same with poetry. Despite the fact that in our technocratic, modern culture, poetry has become marginalized, it remains a fertile source.

The bridging of poetry, philosophy, and psychotherapy is vividly illustrated in William Wordsworth's *The Prelude*, R. M. Rilke's *Duino Elegies*, and T. S. Eliot's *Four Quartets*. The philosophies of Friedrich Nietzsche and the later Martin Heidegger both draw extensively on poetry. In the history of psychoanalysis, Freud and Jung each make use of poetry. Freud's insights are indebted to Greek and Shakespearean tragedy. As Lionel Trilling (1967: 89) points out, Freud's theory of primary process in dreams (Freud 1900/1991) is implicitly a theory of poetic creation. Similarly, Jung's key work, *Symbols of Transformation* (Jung 1956) draws from such diverse sources as Lord Byron, *The Book of Job*, Henry Wadsworth Longfellow, Richard Wagner, Nietzsche, *The Epic of Gilgamesh*, the

Upanisads, and Friedrich Hölderlin. More recently, Stern has extended this cross-pollination of psychoanalysis and poetry to develop his radical insights into the psychotherapeutic process (Stern 2004).

Poetry likewise gives us a means of access to Derrida. I shall begin by exploring Derridean categories by way of a poem by William Blake entitled "The Sick Rose" (Blake 1977). Blake's poem has elements that resonate profoundly with a psychoanalytic perspective. Indeed, I view psychoanalysis as located between poetry and literary analysis. In order to use Blake's poem to illuminate a Derridian framework, I delineate six major themes in Derrida's work, which I then intertwine with evocation of elements in Blake's poem. These themes include:

1 *Writing* (before the letter) and the primacy of *text* (in an extended sense)
2 *Context*, cross-referentiality, and indeterminacy (*dissemination*)
3 *Différance*, with an '*a*'
4 *Deferral*, novelty, and temporality
5 *Core deconstructive concepts*, which unfurl the significance of what Derrida means by *writing* – these are concepts which entwine or straddle ideal and real, the *a priori* and the individual, such as *différance* itself, iterability, *parergon*, and *hymen*, supplementarity, and *metaphor* (cf. Derrida, 1971/1982)
6 *Enactment* and performativity.[1]

The last of these themes, *enactment* and performativity, take on increasing importance in Derrida's development, particularly as the ethical preoccupation with persons and with the Other becomes more pronounced.[2] Indeed, given Derrida's sustained encounter with Levinas' work,[3] I would argue that his concern with ethics was never absent.

My use of the term "enactment" compares and contrasts with the common usage of enactment in psychoanalysis, especially relational psychoanalysis. In the broadest sense, enactment in psychoanalysis means something like the repetitional *re*-enactment of restrictive patterns derived commonly from childhood and childhood traumatizations. Enactment can be particularly manifest in transference-countertransference processes. Hoffman (2007), for example, writes that:

> The oscillation that took place during these times is best understood through a brief review of Heinrich Racker's elaboration of the concept of countertransference. Racker (1968), an Argentinian psychoanalyst, theorized that there are two kinds of countertransferences which emerge in treatment. The first is a complementary countertransference. Here, the analyst is nudged into the role of a significant other in the person's life, experiencing *and potentially enacting* that person's feelings

and behaviors. The second kind of countertransference is concordant. The patient assumes the role of a significant other, and the analyst is made to feel what the patient had to go through at some point in her life. *Often, the most difficult and painful enactments are of this type.* For healing to occur, the analyst must bear the experience of pain that the patient felt, that is, he/she must become a "faithful high priest".

(Hoffman 2007: 77–78, my italics)

The relationship between *enactment* in Hoffman's sense, and *enactment* in my sense, parallels the relationship between normal philosophical pejorative references to "writing," and Derrida's deconstruction/expansion of it into a much wider paradigm. The psychoanalytic use of enactment goes with concepts like "acting out" and "acting in," and enactments are regarded, however benignly, as transcendable and exorcizable. By contrast with this more limited negative definition, I will suggest that enactment is a *toto caelo* reality, which is absolutely ubiquitous, quite uneliminable, and creatively at the heart of the work. In my concept, *enactivity* creates space for the realigning of *enactments* in the standard psychoanalytic sense.

From the perspective of the poetic paradigm, *enactment* and *performativity* give us a vantage point from which we can attain an appreciation of Derrida's insights into psychotherapy. In addition, by adding poetry to the list of deconstructive concepts, we can better elucidate Derrida. Drawing on an example from Stern (2004), I will then suggest that such concepts as "empathic attunement" and "projective identification" be understood as core deconstructive concepts. Finally, I discuss two clinical vignettes, real and fictional, to convey the application of my analysis to *praxis*.

William Blake and six Derridian concepts

Blake's (1977) bardic poetry, with its precise, yet suggestive and musical resonances, and extraordinary rhythmic force, gives us innumerable wonderful and graphic examples of enactment. Its extraordinary density lends itself to elucidation of the Derridean framework, which is itself such a dense and saturated framework. In the space I have, I can only allude marginally to the range of such an analysis.

The Sick Rose

O Rose, thou art sick!
The invisible worm
That flies in the night,
In the howling storm,

Has found out thy bed
Of crimson joy:

And his dark secret love
Does thy life destroy.

I now examine the six elements I am attributing to Derrida in the light of structural elements and motifs we can identify in Blake's poem.

1 Writing (before the letter) and the primacy of text (in an extended sense)

What Derrida means by "writing" is that there is an inherent aspect of language, which he dubs "iterability" (Derrida 1988), which transcends the conception of utterance and speech as simply *events*, as constituted in an immediate present. This aspect is inherently *cross-referencing*, and *this* notion of writing is contrasted with "writing" conceived as a derivative, secondarily referential, affair, one dependent on the primacy of speech. Poetry embodies something like his concept in the permanence of the totality of *form and forms*, which give it an indefinitely re-repeatable character, and enable it to be read and connected even with worlds of awareness never contemplated by the author, as classically illustrated by Shelley's *Ozymandias* (Shelley 1818/1999):

And on the pedestal, these words appear:
My name is Ozymandias, King of Kings,
Look on my Works, ye Mighty, and despair!
Nothing beside remains. Round the decay
Of that colossal Wreck, boundless and bare
The lone and level sands stretch far away.

Now, in the Blake poem there is very clear cross-referencing to Shakespeare's *King Lear*. For instance, in the lines

That flies in the night
In the howling storm

the combination of the allusion to "storm" with the potent word "howling", which evokes Lear's repetition of the word "howl" in his final entry with Cordelia dead in his arms, along with other elements I cannot adduce in the space I have, makes the cross-reference virtually certain, making a major contribution to the potent undercurrents of the poem. It also makes it a powerful implicit comment upon the play! All this illustrates the characteristic of "writing" as iterability.

Again, we may call upon the way in which the poem straddles the epochs, first of the courtly love idealization of "the Rose" (Lewis 1935/1977), and then that in which the ideal has collapsed (in Shakespeare already), in favour of a conception in which love has become inherently corrupted ("his dark secret love"). This second epoch looks onward to Wagner, Baudelaire, Proust, Freud, and Klein. The abysmal faultline of tragedy is evoked, in the poem, in a way which will prevent us ever again looking on human love as innocent. Blake, in this regard, even reminds us of Melanie Klein's pessimism, and her invocation of a primary splitting (Klein 1946/1987). And thus, also, we who have a psychoanalytically informed consciousness, cannot retrospectively eliminate from *our* perspective the later dimension of psychoanalytic awareness, and go back to *not* seeing Blake partly through a psychoanalytic lens.

2 Context, cross-referentiality, and indeterminacy (dissemination)

This aspect of cross-referencing, then, leads us on to vividly invoking Freud's (1900/1991) concept of *over-determination* of meaning, as revealed in the analysis of the Blake poem. Given the lack of space, it is not possible to dwell on the question of the criteria of literary and hermeneutic attributions, but there is a gradient of criteria of relevance which is what makes such analysis non-relativistic. The infinite possibilities of cross-connection, in both the real and the ideal, the total field, are what Derrida (1976: 158) means by the slogan, *there is nothing outside the text* ("il n'y a de hors-texte"). That is, the relevance of the implicit range of meanings relates out *to the totality of historic existence*, in indissoluble interrelation with the indefinitely large cross-connections of meaning as such. It does not reduce world to text but, as it were, expands text to include world; text fades into context. Textual cross-referencing becomes contextual and "in-world" (Heidegger 1967) overdetermination.

3 Différance, with an 'a'

Derrida's (1968/1982) argument, in *Différance*, which critics such as Peter Dews (1987: 32–33, 36–37) and Alisdair MacIntyre (2006) find back-handedly absolutistic, is that the intervals, or between-modes, of otherness, which differentiate positively different elements or things, are *not themselves perceivable as such.* Yet at the same time they are foundational for all which *is* perceivable, all that is perception and presence, enable all recognition of meaning, all identifiability of what is. This apparently means that Derrida privileges discontinuity over continuity and sameness, and it often reads, and is read, that way (cf. Dews 1987).

But the deeper implication can be put as follows: suppose, for instance, I spot a bird against the background of a bush. Now, a bird is both different from a bush, yet not *absolutely* unlike a bush (there is no absolute unlikeness); they are both alive, for instance, and part of a total ecology, which in turn is what enables me to recognize the bird in its context.

So there is a sense in which *both* sameness and difference are manifestations of something more primary, which we could crudely or awkwardly label, for instance, *recognitionality*. Now, this recognitionality is what Derrida is calling *différance*. And the elusive thing Derrida is saying, is that we cannot derive this from any item, or collection of items, as such, in the field of awareness and being. Rather, it is the whole, the *gestalt* as a whole. Clumsily, again, it is the *comparativity* of the elements of the whole. It is intentional, it transcends or surpasses any of the items in awareness towards the sense of the whole.

To support this interpretation, referring to the differing/deferring ambiguity, Derrida (1967/1973) writes:

> In the one case "to differ" signifies non identity; in the other case it signifies the order of the same. Yet there must be a *common* though entirely differant (*différante*) root within the sphere that relates these two movements of differing to one another. We provisionally give the name of *différance* to this *sameness* which is not *identical*: by the silent writing of its *a* it has the desired advantage of referring to differing, *both* as spacing/temporalizing and as the movement that structures every dissociation.
>
> (Derrida 1967/1973: 129–130)

Derrida concludes that this aspect or manifestation of existence is ineffable, in a sense, not nameable or objectively describable *as such*, but this does question-beggingly assume that being a *res*, an item, as such, *is* the paradigm of describable existence. Oddly, he simply inverts what he is opposing, rather than deconstructing it. In his defence, it is certainly true that there is an irreducibly metaphoric aspect to the understanding of this, for instance, in appeal to the metaphor of musical intervals or silences, and this metaphoricity is inherently mind-discerned, but, precisely by his previous argument, about text (section 2), it is also inherently "worldly".

So this in the end leads on to the articulation of his case for *the primacy of writing and text*, and to the general argument that *all forms of symbolism partake of iterability/re-iterability* (Derrida 1988; there is no difference marked by the "re-", for Derrida; this is also what he means by "architrace", 1968/1982). His argument for all this then is:

> The différance which establishes phonemes and lets them be heard *remains in and of itself inaudible*, in every sense of the word.
>
> (Derrida 1968/1982: 5, my italics)

> An interval must separate the present from what it is not in order for the present to be itself, but this interval which constitutes it as present must, by the same token, divide the present in and of itself, thereby also dividing, along with the present, everything that is thought on the basis of the present, that is, our metaphysical language, every being, and singularly substance or the subject.
>
> (Derrida 1968/1982: 13)

On this basis of "primary writing", "archi-trace", etc., Derrida is sometimes accused of *denying* immediacy, presence, encounter, and so on, whereas it is rather that, at the deepest level, he seeks to *ground* them in this totality which is beyond sameness and difference. At this point, I simply recall how far psychotherapeutic work, like that of poets and musicians, essentially depends upon the inchoate, the silent, the intervallic, intersections of sensory modalities, intersections between verbal and non-verbal, etc. Stern (2004) labels this the realm of the "sloppy". In connection with this, how frequent metaphors of ballet and choreography are in Stern! Hence, the issues we are struggling with in Derrida and the philosophic tradition are profoundly relevant to psychotherapy.

4 Deferral, novelty, and temporality

This element is one aspect of *différance* for Derrida. Temporality, whether in Augustine, Husserl, Heidegger, Derrida, Freud (cf. Derrida 1978b), and Stern (2004), is *trans-momentary*; in the poem this is, for instance, evoked in the shift, where there is a marked musical pause and "breath", between the line about the storm, and the beginning of the second stanza: "Has found out thy bed . . ." Innumerable such poetic instances of the transtemporal could be adduced; indeed it is inherent in poetry. Once we grasp this we go on to realize our *whole experience* is trans-momentary, deferred, poetic, of its essence. In my concept, this implies that *experience itself* is inherently enactment.

5 Core deconstructive concepts

These unfurl the significance of what Derrida means by *writing* (cf. Derrida 1971/1982): Poesis or poetic movement, in the light of Blake's poem, now itself appears as a deconstructive concept, because it inherently overrides the distinction between objectivity and subjectivity. For instance,

Has found out thy bed

is inextricably both metaphor (subjective), and concrete factual description (objective). As in the greatest moments in Shakespeare and Keats, without the concrete factuality of the description, the metaphoricity would hang in the air. Poesis both is *there*, public, analysable, yet not apprehensible except existentially. Later we shall find that such concepts as "empathic attunement" – which appeals irreducibly to experience, yet can still be both described and researched – also occupy this space.

6 Enactment *and performativity*

While enactment is not Derrida's term, but mine (cf. Leavis 1952/1962: 110–111, endnote i), Derrida does adopt *performativity* from Austin (1962). The following threefold concept of enactment – embracing both ethics and poetics/aesthetics – seeks to capture that towards which the concept of action and will, implicit in the poem *as* poem, tends:

A. the intentionality or meaning of action, and of words as action, is *irreducible*, that is, the intentionality of any of my actions cannot be eliminated reductively, which is *not* to say no causal analysis is possible at all;

B. *qua* action, in so far as it is an action, any action or enactment or performative is *beyond knowledge*, or, rather, more accurately, it is other, *it is neither knowing nor not knowing*;

C. but *in so far as*, by A, *it is irreducible meaning*, it can be epitomised, it is iterable, it has a teleology, it can be known (it is not ineffable), and it can be appraised.

Enactment is inclusive, and truly *mimetic* (cf. Aristotle, trans. 1997), in that, at the level of primary experience, we can only *evoke it*, and to evoke it is indispensable in that, in part, it *is* how we characterize it.

Interpretations, though indefinitely extendable, are nevertheless governed by implicit criteria, only to be challenged in terms of deeper or better implicit criteria. The great Shakespeare producer, Peter Brook, states this poignantly:

Now if one takes [Shakespeare's] thirty-seven plays with all the radar lines of the different viewpoints of the different characters, one comes out with a field of incredible density and complexity; and eventually one goes a step further, and one finds that what happened . . . is some thing quite different from any other author's work. It's not Shakespeare's view of the world, it's something which actually resembles reality. A sign of this is that any single word, line, character or event has not only a large number of interpretations, but an unlimited number. Which is the characteristic of reality.

(Brook 1977: 114–115)

Brook's statement aptly describes the mode of deconstruction as enactment, which is not, however, relativistic. I shall now put these concepts to work in considering a pertinent passage from Stern (2004).

Present moments

Stern's work is crucial to the development of the concept of psychotherapy as enactment. His "implicit knowledge", "moments of meeting", "present moments", "sloppy process", and "temporal dynamics" are all enactments in my sense of the term (cf. Wilkinson 2003a). Stern touches the heart of this in making his implicit/explicit distinction more fundamental than the conscious/unconscious distinction. The example I examine from Stern's work is an ordinary human situation that can equally be applied to psychotherapy process, yet is vivid, paradigmatic and takes the form of poetic communication.

Stern is writing not merely about *narrated* and *shared* feeling processes (which he designates "shared feeling voyages": Stern 2004: 172), but about *experienced*, and hence *enacted*, lived experience. He wrestles to elucidate this experience linguistically. It is significant that Stern is riding on a wave of metaphor (he too loves Blake, and the passage ends with Blake's very Derridean – "nothing outside the text" – "world in a grain of sand"):

> During a shared feeling voyage (which is the moment of meeting) two people traverse together a feeling-landscape as it unfolds in real time. Recall that the present moment can be a rich, emotional lived story. During this several-second journey, the participants ride the crest of the present instant as it crosses the span of the present moment, from its horizon of the past to its horizon of the future. As they move, they pass through an emotional narrative landscape with its hills and valleys of vitality affects, along its river of intentionality (which runs throughout), and over its peak of dramatic crisis. It is a voyage taken as the present unfolds. A passing subjective landscape is created and makes up a world in a grain of sand.
>
> (Stern 2004: 172)

A limit on the scope of Stern's analysis is implicit, in its being clear that any metaphoric physical evocation of temporal dynamics simply *presumes* the temporality it seeks to clarify. Therefore, if the analysis is indeed to *elucidate* temporality, it has to be a metaphor *used in certain way*, as Heidegger (1967), for instance, does. Stern continues:

> Because this voyage is participated in with someone, during an act of affective intersubjectivity, the two people have taken the voyage together. Although this shared voyage lasts only for the seconds of a

moment of meeting, that is enough. It has been lived-through-together. The participants have created a shared private world. And having entered that world, they find that when they leave it, their relationship is changed. There has been a discontinuous leap. The border between order and chaos has been redrawn. Coherence and complexity have been enlarged. They have created an expanded intersubjective field that opens up new possibilities of being-with-one-another. They are changed and they are linked differently for having changed one another.

(Stern 2004: 172–173)

Stern resorts to the language of chaos and catastrophic change, in my view, partly because he is embarrassed by the risk of accounting for intersubjectivity in purely personal, phenomenological, non-physical, terms, which would take the matter out of the realm of neurological investigation, and into the realm of the phenomenological temporal intersubjective a priori. He asks:

Why is a shared feeling voyage so different from just listening to a friend or patient narrate episodes of their life story? There, too, one gets immersed in the other's experience through empathic understanding. The difference is this. In a shared feeling voyage, the experience is shared as it originally unfolds. There is no remove in time. It is direct – not transmitted and reformulated by words. It is cocreated by both partners and lived originally by both.

(Stern 2004: 173)

Stern continues:

Shared feeling voyages are so simple and natural yet very hard to explain or even talk about. *We need another language that does not exist (outside poetry) – a language that is steeped in temporal dynamics.* This is paradoxical because because these experiences provide the nodal moments in our life. Shared feeling voyages are one of life's most startling yet normal events, capable of altering our world step by step or in one leap.

(Stern 2004: 173, my italics)

Stern is writing about what I am calling *enactment*. As anyone who reads his remarkable book may know, he moves his dialectic forward by way of generating antitheses. These antitheses, like Freud's own use of them, continually dissolve and reshape themselves (cf. Wilkinson 2003a). Here Stern is playing with the antitheses of the *implicit* and the *explicit*, and the *non-verbal* and the *verbal*, the latter as foils to the former. These antitheses readily ally themselves with his concern for the neuroscientific level, mirror neurons and perhaps, not surprisingly, there is a very strong pull towards the concrete.

The temptation,[4] to contrast elements which are *absolutely immediate*, with ones which are secondary, verbal, and "after the event" is strong. I believe that this pull towards a *concrete* characterization of enactment is what leads Stern into the conceptual trap of momentarily equating *the enacted* with *the non-verbal*:

> In a shared feeling voyage, the experience is shared as it originally unfolds. There is no remove in time. It is direct – not transmitted and reformulated by words. It is cocreated by both partners and lived originally by both.
>
> (Stern 2004: 173)

From a Derridean point of view, this equation presumes the direct, the immediate, the "pure expression", the metaphysics of presence. For Stern, "It is direct – not transmitted and reformulated by words" (Stern 2004: 173).

Instead, as we have now seen by way of the distinctions I have drawn, *the enacted can equally be verbal, reflexively invoking the quasi-permanence of language and writing*, and yet still be an enactment, and indeed always is enactment. And Stern immediately illustrates this, affording us opportunity for a modest deconstruction, by the spelling out of his latent paradigms. Stern *narrates and evokes* an enactment. In other words, to make sense of what this is about, *he himself resorts to poetic process*. And in resorting to poetic process, he also enacts the distinction I am drawing.

Here, in parallel with what has been said already, we must pause to more sharply distinguish two aspects of the characterization process. First, there is a dimension of the evocation of a poetic process which consists in an epitomization, and at the same time a reproduction of it. Although literal total reproduction is a logically contradictory conception, poetic reproduction participates in that deferral, that quasi-permanencing aspect, iterability, of the poetic process of events which makes them *universals*, in the Platonic sense. I awkwardly label this process *enactive-reproductive epitomization*. Second, the relevant aspect is the *descriptive* task which involves *process-characterizing* conceptualizations, which may well also involve poetic coinage (*mimesis* and *diegesis*: Aristotle, trans. 1997).[5] This would include both *evocative characterization*, which Stern's passage mainly illustrates and *technical characterization*. The immensely subtle struggle, to both formulate and enact at this level, is indeed Derridean territory, as it is the territory of psychotherapy.

All these are illustrated, positively or negatively, in the graphic transition Stern now makes. Here Stern, in however sober academic terminology, is

actually describing a *seduction*, with all the viscerally physical intersubjective potency a seduction involves. Despite his academic mask, he actually
manages to characterize this seduction quite evocatively; in other words,
Stern is also functioning as a poet, in evoking one of the great subjects
of poetry.

A seduction is peculiarly central to Stern's purpose because of the
profound level of intersubjectivity achieved in deep erotic encounter. In
Stern's almost coyly academic evocation, with a quotation from the writing
of a peer ("Kendon"), of the process of "intention movements", leading up
to the "moment of meeting" of holding hands, it may occur to us that,
erotically, *he is also paralleling and cross-referencing the process of foreplay
in sexual intercourse*, the consummation which is overtly omitted from the
account, but surely implied. How dare I suggest such a thing? Well, to the
extent that it is valid (and it only has to be *possible*, irrespective of Stern's
own intention), it illustrates the inherent textuality and metaphoricity of
the evoked field of mnemic resonance and instinct, which I have described
as poetic.

Throughout, Stern's analysis is bedevilled by the power of the objecthood
or objectivity paradigm. His instinct is to feel that an event must have
occurred in the spatio-temporal physical realm, or an analogue of it, to
really have happened. By contrast, an enactment, in my sense, never *simply*
happens; that is its peculiarity. I am claiming Stern evokes an enactment in
the full iterable sense, with all the cross-referencing that involves. Hence he
strongly desires to emphasize the non-verbal and the implicit, and the
neurological. Yet Stern cannot help invoking an element of irreducible
intersubjectivity and cross-reference. The passage, for those who want the
full context, runs from page 173 to page 176 (Stern 2004); I can only quote
highlights here.

Stern (2004: 173) alludes to the difficulty in grasping the concept of
shared feeling voyage because of the exclusion of explicit content. But this
does not entail the exclusion of *implicit metaphoric meaning and cross-
referencing*. And it is only "difficult to think of two people cocreating their
joint experience in an intersubjective matrix" (Stern 2004: 173) because *it
cannot be done* within the framework of the objecthood paradigm, for
which there is no intrinsic connection between what happens in me and
what happens in you. This is indeed why I believe the analogues of intersubjectivity belong with the core deconstructive concepts.

In the narrative of the skaters, the significance of Stern's (2004: 174)
parenthesis – "(Note that each is also participating neurologically and
experientially in the bodily feeling centred in the other. And each of them
knows, at moments, that the other knows what it feels like to be him or
her.)" – is the blurring of the differentiation between the *physical material
body* and the *experienced phenomenological body*, which opens the way to
either a neurological reduction or to thoroughgoing psychophysical

parallelism, without heading further towards mysticism than that. But the neurological reference in this example is *an inference for us* here, however direct it may be "in itself". This is a characteristic instance of how Stern elides this difference, and does not tackle the dualistic issue.

Stern turns to describe the skaters pausing to have a drink and evokes their changed intimacy. He now leans boldly towards a "mystical" or "telepathic" strand when he says, unequivocally,

> They have directly experienced something of the other's experience. They have vicariously been inside the other's body and mind, through a series of shared feeling voyages. They have created an implicit inter-subjective field that endures as part of their short history together.
>
> (Stern 2004: 174)

If taken at all literally, this passage seems a far cry from Stern's earlier *The Motherhood Constellation* (1995: 42) with its blunt repudiation of the mystical and telepathic elements in projective identification, not to mention from the neurological references of the previous paragraph. But something like attunement, it now becomes clear here, belongs with those irreducible core deconstructive concepts I have mentioned.

What seems to me Stern's overemphasis on the *non-semantic dimension* of the implicit, which enables him to relegate, what he thinks of as the *verbal unconscious* dimension, to the realm of the repressed (the Freudian unconscious), also enables him to posit that this will all eventually be assimilated by the neurological accounts. Stern continues the story:

> What will our skaters say? They will talk across the table and share meanings. And while they talk, the explicit domain of their relationship will start to expand. Whatever is said will be against the background of the implicit relationship that was expanded before, through the shared feeling voyages they had on the ice. Once they start talking, they will also act along with the words – small movements of face, hands, head, posture. The explicit then becomes the background for the implicit, momentarily. The expansion of the implicit and explicit domains play leapfrog with each other, building a shared history – a relationship.
>
> (Stern 2004: 174–175)

If their implicit and explicit shared intersubjective field has altered enough that they mutually feel that they like one another, enough to want to go further in exploring the relationship, what might happen? They will engage in a sequence of intention movements. Kendon (1990) described intention movements exchanged between people to test the waters of their motivations towards each other. They consist of split-second, incomplete, very partial fullness of display, abbreviated movements that belong to the behavioural sequence leading to the communication of an intention or motivation. (They are the physical-behavioral analogs of intersubjective orienting.)

(Stern 2004: 175)

Our skaters will now engage in a series of intention movements. Short head movements forward, stopped after several centimetres, slight mouth openings, looks at the other's lips and then their eyes, back and forth, leaning forward, and so on, will take place. This choreography of intention movements passes outside of consciousness but is clearly captured as "vibes". These vibes are short-circuited shared feeling voyages and deliver a sense of what is happening. An evolving pattern develops as the sequence of intensity, proximity, and fullness of display, of their intention movements progresses. These relational moves are enacted out of consciousness, leading up to the moment of meeting – their hands move to meet.

(Stern 2004: 175)

Here, too, a notion of readiness is needed, because suddenly the full act is executed in a leap. The present moment surfaces quickly like a whale breaching the water's surface. There is not an incessant, agonizing progression up to the final act.

(Stern 2004: 175–176)

The above account can only make limited sense if we remain blind to temporal dynamics and fail to see them as the tissue of lived experience.

(Stern 2004: 176)

Here, now, is the very striking exemplification of a poetic shift in the emergence of a metaphor (from the earlier "leap", and the "ocean" of the waves of temporal dynamic), namely in the movement from: "Here, too, a notion of readiness is needed, because suddenly the full act is executed in a leap" (Stern 2004: 175). In the repetition of the language of leap, there is a hint of the leaps which the skaters have just been involved in. But in a Shakespearean shift, a piece of genuine poetry, the characterization suddenly emerges from its dormancy within the image of leap, emerging into full concreteness, in a fully developed and very graphic metaphor: "The present moment surfaces quickly like a whale breaching the water's surface" (Stern 2004: 175–176). Now, the event of the hand-contact, is *the present moment*, in Stern's terms, and into the metaphysical or the conceptual, that is, into the poetic, in our terms, and writing, in Derrida's.

The resonance of penetration which I earlier invoked is not at all gainsaid by this, and the summoning up of an enactment at this moment is corroborative; the resort to metaphor, in this instance, is sudden and has

the startling quality of true metaphor and, as such, enacts both the enactment and the conceptuality it is evoking. In this evocative character of
double metaphoric enactment, Stern comes as near as is possible for him, to
evoking the temporality of enactment.[6]

Thus Stern himself *enacts*, as vividly as he can without saying it, the
character of an enactment. He thus realizes his own precept in the most
vivid possible way: "We need another language that does not exist (outside
poetry) – a language that is steeped in temporal dynamics" (Stern 2004:
173). In the combination of the conceptual-metaphysical with the concrete
in this particular enactment, we also have the element of *literal impossibility*
so readily available in poetic expression, and therefore the impossibility of
any "direct" expression of it. In my view, therefore, Stern has implied the
element of *evocative characterization*. And discovering such moments is
indeed the work of deconstruction, as a variant hermeneutic principle.

The scope of enactment

The power and generalizing capability of a fundamental principle, *if it
genuinely is the relevant generic principle we are looking for*, is huge. The
scope of enactment as a hermeneutic and analytically clarificatory principle
is therefore vast. This principle of practical reason (the rationality of action,
Kant 1788/1997) *makes sense* of how many, caught within, and seeking a
"beyond" of, a cognitivist understanding, have again and again been
compelled to invoke a dimension of ineffability – the neo-Platonists,
Augustine and the medieval mystics, Nietzsche, Freud, and Bergson, the
Wittgenstein of the *Tractatus* (Wittgenstein 1921/2001) and, in part (cf.
Dews 1987; MacIntyre 2006), the earlier Derrida (1968/1982) of *Différance*.

Not only does enactment apply to the whole range of literature and
psychotherapy, but also if the understanding I have developed is correct, it
makes sense of a vast movement over the millennia in philosophy and
theology in the West. Enactment moves away from logos-based or logo-
centric understandings of philosophy and the world, including empiricism
and rationalism, of the philosophies since Descartes. At the same time,
since, as a principle of action or practical reason, it does not challenge the
domain of rationality as a comprehensive principle, in the way the inef-
fabilist trend does; the principle of enactment, as Derrida's work ultimately
indicates (see Derrida 1994, 1997, 2000/2006), resolves the dilemma.

Derrida's poetic-enactive understanding appears throughout his work; in
particular, in *Politics of Friendship* (Derrida 1997), after celebrating a
fabulous and stunning sentence of Nietzsche's, he summarizes as follows:

> By way of economy – and in order, in a single word, to formalise the
> absolute economy of the feint, this generation by joint and simul-
> taneous grafting of the performative and of the reportive, without a

body of its own – let us call the event of such sentences, the "logic" of this chance occurrence, its "genetics", its "rhetoric", its "historical record", its "politics", etc., *teleiopoetic*. *Teleiopoiós* qualifies, in a great number of contexts and semantic orders, that which *renders* absolute, perfect, completed, accomplished, finished, that which *brings* to an end. But permit us to play too with the other *tele*, the one that speaks to distance and the far removed, for what is indeed in question here is a poetics of distance at one remove, and of an absolute acceleration in the spanning of space by the very structure of the sentence (it begins at the end, it is initiated with the signature of the other).

This is enactment.

The reach of the positive concept of enactment or *teleiopoesis* also explains Derrida's perhaps excessively laboured exposure of Lacan's decontextualizing of Poe's (1844/1982) dramatization in *The Purloined Letter* (Derrida 1987, chapter, *Le Facteur de la Verité*). Derrida argued previously (Derrida 1987: 371–372) that Freud, in his use of Aristophanes' myth of *eros*, in *Beyond the Pleasure Principle*, is theorizing *totally without regard to the enactive context of the setting* in which the theory is enunciated. In avoiding the significance of its reference to Aristophanes (the enemy, the betrayer, the satirist, the Other to Plato's Socrates), *Freud's avoidance itself has huge enactive significance*. This is extended to Lacan also.[7]

The enactive implication, then, is that the analyst cannot avoid being wholly implicated in the analysis he or she seeks to objectify. Clearly that has to apply, not only to Lacan, but also to the waspish intent of Derrida in relation to Lacan, and indeed to Derrida's entire "mimesis" of Freud (and the "mimesis" of deconstruction in general), in work after work, obsessively.

A simple principle, enactment's basic application to psychotherapy and poetry is fairly easily grasped, but its scope – both in theory of psychotherapy, and in literary, theological, and philosophical understandings – is vast and complex. Enactment enables a thorough revaluation of *descriptive* understandings of both the world, and of relevant spheres of discourse. At the same time it embraces both ethics and aesthetics as a *unified sphere of evaluative enquiries* (cf. Wilkinson 2003a, 2009).

It also sheds light on psychoanalysis, on para-analytic approaches such as Gestalt and psychodrama, and also on the alchemical development of Jung's psychology. We can, for example, view transference as enactment (e.g., Joseph 1989), as the inherent medium of the work or "opus", of the process of transformation in the work,[8] *without* attempting to try to reduce it *to some other system of knowledge*, be it developmental theory, libido theory, or contact theory in Gestalt (Perls et al. 1951/1994) and in Reich (cf. Totton 1998). We can also, non-reductively, do justice to the understanding of frame and context, of which Erving Goffman (1974/1986) wrote so profoundly, as not extraneous to, but inherent in, the full apprehension of transference/countertransference. Thus transference/countertransference emerges as part of a multifaceted whole which is, in a broad sense, *always transferential, since enactivity is the realm of the work and its process.*

In what follows, I sketch all too briefly some more concrete terms of *praxis* of what a Derridian psychotherapy might look like.

Derridian psychotherapy: who writes whom?

Taking psychoanalysis as point of reference, I outline some features of a possible Derridian psychotherapy. First, our understanding of *frame* opens out. We cannot absolutely privilege certain paradigms of neutrality; they are only apparently neutral. The *intersection* of frame and process is profound, and is constantly being enacted and re-enacted. How we *reflexively address the process* as such is what counts. Acting out – or acting in – is an altered concept and it is half dissolved. It cannot be absolutized, so is replaced by a more pragmatic spectrum of tolerability and containment.

In a Derridian psychotherapy, interpretation would be fine, but not paramount; the rule of thumb would be to honour the client's sense of justice by negotiating around interpretation – such a powerful form of intervention, comparable to touch – if at all possible. Personhood and mutuality in the process become crucial – but in very specific, historically contextual, forms, not as contextless absolutes, and with an awareness of multiplicity and self-synthesis as a process. There will be a massively increased emphasis on *context* in the work, in general. There will be, as a corollary, a de facto *pluralism* of method – based on taste and individuality, not just of the client but the therapist also, thus *integrative* – but not predetermined in its mode. The relational base is important but not a shibboleth either, especially for those with elements of autism in their nature whose "relationship with relationship" may be different.

Therapeutic work will be experimental in certain aspects, made up as we go along. Drama, play, humour, enactive elements in general, take on more central roles. There will be a strong emphasis on countertransference – but in a broadened sense (Searles 1999 being nearest to mapping this). Therapeutic goals will be as open as possible, determined substantially by the client – again, on a basis of contractual justice.

I end with two examples, first a brief vignette of live work, and then a partially or quasi-fictional example of how this might work at the countertransference level. Countertransference is understood as enactment, evoking the other aspect of enactment in *mimesis.*

First example

I have a client who, like me, regards Dostoievsky as the *ne pus ultra* of novelists, and as perhaps the single human being who has most endured the sight and feeling of the terribleness and sheer brutal horror of human existence. My client does idealize him, and me, and his tendency to idealization is linked to his predicament. This is the background to what transpired. In the course of conversation which had touched upon creativity and dramatic art and experience, including Shakespeare, we reached Dostoievsky, and he remarked, very earnestly and shyly, with a pause in the middle, as if whispering a secret: "But I have realized that in Dostoievsky – there are some cracks . . ." I chuckled and paused, and then said, "But, – you know, – no one's perfect."

We both fell about laughing. What was the joke? Very hard to explain! Something about the extreme contrast between Dostoievsky's supreme greatness and the hyperbolic perfectionism that would find fault *even with him* – and, in a sense, thus, even with life itself! Such a moment is impossible to capture (even for myself in retrospect), virtually impossible to explain, because it depends on the ramifications and idiosyncrasy of persons, and context, depends on *enactivity*. In its accessing universal themes, and in its participation in language, in iterability, the enactment transcends the moment, as a poem transcends the moment. But this embraces also "real life enactivity", as, for instance, Boswell's dramatic evocations of Johnson's *actual real-time conversations* transcend the moment (Boswell 1791/1998; Wilkinson 2005).

Second example

A nearly silent session with a silent client . . .
Enactments at the level of countertransference . . .
I imagine something vaguely erotic . . .
I then experience a sense of paralysis and frozenness . . .
Against that background I consider my erotic image . . .
It is as if it is excluded by the frozenness of what I suddenly recognize as shame . . .
Images of shrivelling and frozen breaking up with such a hard frost come to me . . .
I share with my client an image of the perma-frost . . .
She nods assent – recognizing this completely as a conveying of the atmosphere . . .
After scanning the element of risk in saying this, I say I can imagine the spring that is to come . . .
I see the ghost of a smile on her face and her colour changes but she remains silent . . .
I am certain she has sensed the erotic connotations and I feel a connection and a warming . . .
Now I can hear the thunder of the melting waters beneath the ice . . .
I share my image with her . . .

She smiles again . . .
I am aware I am beginning to write a poem in my mind . . .
Her silence has not been broken . . .
But the spring poem has begun to be written . . .
I think of Tolstoy's *Anna Karenina* and the Russian spring . . .
A Russian winter lay across Tolstoy's own soul . . .
Tolstoy tried to shout down his eros . . .
In her silence her eros is free to unfold . . .
I think of Cordelia, Lear on his "wheel of fire" of shame . . .
And Tolstoy's hatred of *King Lear* . . .

Winston Smith's wonderfully Blakean dream in Orwell's *Nineteen Eighty-Four* . . . In which he evokes the old England (he awakes with the word "Shakespeare" on his lips) in a dream of a place which he calls the "Golden Country", and in which there appears the promiscuous anti-Party "girl with dark hair" who, in a magnificent gesture, tears off her clothes and flings them aside disdainfully. A gesture which, at a stroke, annihilates all that "The Party", and all that goes with it, stands for . . . "That too was a gesture belonging to the ancient time."

And I think of the affirmation of desire in Blake's *Ah Sunflower!*
My client looks at me dewy eyed – and sighs deeply and contentedly . . .
Without a word, she has welcomed her eros . . .
No more need be said . . .
The session ends.

I am able to process my images to the point where I can offer her part of one of them – the perma-frost. My relationship with her is such that I know, normally, what she will comfortably receive from me, and this is one such. I then risk mentioning the spring to come – and again she receives this. The third image I share is of the thundering melt-waters beneath the ice. For a third time she receives.[9] Then, because she has received my comments and images, I am free to become aware of the poetic flow of my thoughts, and I simply allow them to unfold, and of their own sequence they pass from the Tolstoyan winter in relation to eros to the Shakespearean and Blakean spring and awakening. The flow engages us both at the embodied level without the need of words, but expressed in her dewy-eyed sigh of welcome – which of course is, at the subtlest level, erotic arousal and satisfaction. For the moment, she has passed beyond shame.

These connections of the poem have come up just here; even though the pathway was familiar, but unexpected was the passage into the recognition of Tolstoy's own shame and shouting down of his own eros, and the greater creativity (and eros) of Shakespeare's Cordelia. The shame of eros is as equally present in Blake as the release of eros. The range of cross-connections is so vast it is not possible except as an enactment, and as writing.

This, then, might be a little of how one – broadly *integrative* – version of a Derridian psychotherapy might look.

Notes

1 Enactment *in this extended sense* is not Derrida's term, but mine via F. R. Leavis (e.g. Leavis 1952/1962: 110–111). When I say "mine" or "my" in what follows, it is with this proviso. The speech act term "performativity" Derrida modifies from J. L. Austin (1962).
2 For example Derrida 1994, 1997, 2000/2006; cf. Critchley 1992/1999, Critchley, 2000/2006.
3 From *Violence and Metaphysics*, by far the longest essay in his *Writing and Difference* from 1967 (Derrida 1978a) onwards.
4 Compare a similar system of assumptions when Wittgenstein in §244/5 of *Philosophical Investigations* (Wittgenstein, 1953/1967) writes:

> How do words refer to sensations? – There doesn't seem to be any problem here; don't we talk about sensations every day, and give them names? But how is the connection between the name and the thing named set up? This question is the same as: how does a human being learn the meaning of the names of sensations? – of the word "pain" for example? Here is one possibility: words are connected with the primitive, the natural, expressions of the sensation and used in their place. A child has hurt himself and he cries; and then adults talk to him and teach him exclamations and, later, sentences. They teach the child new pain behaviour.
>
> So you are saying that the word "pain" really means crying? – On the contrary: the verbal expression of pain replaces crying and does not describe it.

5 I am most grateful to Alice Lombardo Maher for drawing my attention to this prototype of the distinction in Aristotle.
6 This all relates to my account of what previously I called "phenomenological causality" (Wilkinson 1998, 1999).
7 Notoriously, Derrida (1987: 413–496) in *The Postcard* repeats this argument in relation to Lacan's analysis of E. A. Poe's *The Purloined Letter* (cf. Forrester 1991, for an account creatively sympathetic to both parties; Dews 1987 aligns himself fairly vigorously with Lacan), and urges that Lacan's restriction of the enactment concept *also* is an enactment, as is betrayed by Lacan's *Dessein/Destin* slip.
8 Darlene Bregman-Ehrenberg, in a remarkable book, comes closest to this conception in recent psychoanalysis (Bregman-Ehrenberg 1992, Wilkinson 2003b).
9 And then the cock crowed! The signifiers multiply – as they do in enactments. I realized only afterwards that this composition had echoed Peter's three denials in John's Gospel – which turns my thoughts also to the resurrection of the flesh in D. H. Lawrence's *The Man who Died*. I also realized I was walking in the footprints of Derrida's account (1987: 295–296), in *The Postcard*, of Freud's, this time, *four dismissals*, of any "beyond" of the Pleasure Principle in Chapter 2 of *Beyond the Pleasure Principle* (Freud 1920/1984).

References

Aristotle (trans. 1997) *The Poetics Part I*, trans. S. H. Butcher, New York: Dover.
Austin, J. L. (1962) *How To Do Things with Words*, Oxford: Oxford University Press.
Blake, W. (1977) *Complete Poems of William Blake*, London: Penguin.
Boswell, J. (1791/1998) *Life of Johnson*, Oxford: Oxford University Press.
Bregman-Ehrenberg, D. (1992) *The Intimate Edge: Extending the Reach of Psychoanalysis*, New York: Norton.
Brook, P. (1977) 'Interview with Peter Brook', in R. Berry, *On Directing Shakespeare*, London: Croom Helm.
Critchley, S. (1992/1999) *The Ethics of Deconstruction: Derrida and Levinas*, Oxford: Blackwell.
Derrida, J. (2000/2006) *Frankfurt Impromptu: Remarks on Derrida and Habermas*, in *The Derrida-Habermas Reader*, edited L. Thomassen, Edinburgh: Edinburgh University Press.
—— (1967/1973) *Preliminary Remarks* to *Différance*, in *Speech and Phenomena and Other Essays on Husserl's Theory of Signs*, Evanston, IL: Northwestern University Press.
—— (1968/1982) *Différance*, in *Margins of Philosophy*, London: Prentice Hall.
—— (1971/1982) *White Mythology: Metaphor in the Text of Philosophy*, in *Margins of Philosophy*, London: Prentice Hall.
—— (1976) *Of Grammatology*, trans. G. C. Spivak, Baltimore, MD: Johns Hopkins University Press.
—— (1978a) *Violence and Metaphysics*, in *Writing and Difference*, London: Routledge.
—— (1978b) *Freud and the Scene of Writing*, in *Writing and Difference*, London: Routledge.
—— (1987) *The Postcard: From Socrates to Freud*, Chicago, IL: University of Chicago Press.
—— (1988) *Limited Inc.*, Evanston, IL: Northwestern University Press.
—— (1994) *Specters of Marx*, London: Routledge.
—— (1997) *Politics of Friendship*, London: Verso.
—— (2000/2006) *Performative Powerlessness: A Response to Simon Critchley*, in *The Derrida-Habermas Reader*, edited L. Thomassen, Edinburgh: Edinburgh University Press.
Dews, P. (1987) *Logics of Disintegration: Post-Structuralist Thought and the Claims of Critical Theory*, London: Verso.
Forrester, J. (1991) *The Seductions of Psychoanalysis: Freud, Lacan, and Derrida, Cambridge Studies in French*, Cambridge: Cambridge University Press.
Freud, S. (1900/1991) *The Interpretation of Dreams*, London: Penguin.
—— (1920/1984) *Beyond the Pleasure Principle*, in *Papers on Metapsychology*, London: Penguin.
Goffman, E. (1974/1986) *Frame Analysis: An Essay on the Organisation of Experience*, Boston, MA: Northeastern University Press.
Heidegger, M. (1967) *Being and Time*, trans. J. Macquarrie and E. Robinson, Oxford: Blackwell.

Hoffman, M. (2007) 'From libido to love: relational psychoanalysis and the redemption of sexuality', *Journal of Psychology and Theology*, 35(1): 74–82.

Joseph, B. (1989) *Psychic Equilibrium and Psychic Change: Selected Papers*, London: Routledge.

Jung, C. G. (1956) *Symbols of Transformation*, London: Routledge.

Kant, I. (1788/1997) *Critique of Practical Reason*, edited and trans. M. J. Gregor, Cambridge: Cambridge University Press.

Kendon, A. (1990) *Conducting Interaction*, Cambridge: Cambridge University Press.

Klein, M. (1946/1987) *Notes on Some Schizoid Mechanisms*, in *The Selected Melanie Klein*, edited J. Mitchell, New York: Harper.

Leavis, F. R. (1952/1962) *The Common Pursuit*, London: Chatto & Windus.

Lewis, C. S. (1935/1977) *The Allegory of Love: A Study in Mediaeval Tradition*, London: Oxford University Press.

MacIntyre, A. (2006) *The Tasks of Philosophy: Selected Essays*, Cambridge: Cambridge University Press.

Perls, F., Hefferline, R. and Goodman, P. (1951/1994) *Gestalt Therapy: Excitement and Growth in the Human Personality*, Gouldsboro, ME: Gestalt Journal Press.

Poe, E. A. (1844/1982) *The Purloined Letter*, in *The Complete Tales and Poems of Edgar Allan Poe*, London: Penguin.

Racker, H. (1968) *Transference and Counter-transference*, London: Hogarth Press.

Searles, H. F. (1999) *Selected Papers on Countertransference and Related Subjects*, Madison, CT: International Universities Press.

Shelley, P. B. (1818/1999) *Ozymandias*, in *The Complete Poetry of Percy Bysshe Shelley*, edited D. H. Reiman and N. Fraistat, Baltimore, MD: Johns Hopkins University Press.

—— (1840/2004) *A Defence of Poetry and Other Essays*, Whitefish, MT: Kessinger.

Stern, D. N. (1995) *The Motherhood Constellation: A Unified View of Parent-Infant Psychotherapy*, London: Karnac.

—— (2004) *The Present Moment: In Psychotherapy and Everyday Life*, New York: Norton.

Totton, N. (1998) *The Water in the Glass: Body and Mind in Psychoanalysis*, London: Rebus Press.

Trilling, L. (1967) *Beyond Culture: Essays on Literature and Learning*, London: Penguin.

Wilkinson, H. (1998) 'Phenomenological causality and why we avoid examining the nature of causality in psychotherapy: a dialogue', *International Journal of Psychotherapy*, 3(2): 165–182.

—— (1999) 'Schizophrenic process, the emergence of consciousness in recent history, and phenomenological causality: the significance for psychotherapy of Julian Jaynes', *International Journal of Psychotherapy*, 4(1): 49–66.

—— (2003a) 'The Shadow of Freud: Is Daniel Stern still a psychoanalyst? The creative tension between the present and the past in psychoanalytic and existential psychotherapies, in Daniel Stern's The Present Moment, and his humanistic-existential partners in dialogue': review article on Daniel Stern's 'The Present Moment: In Psychotherapy and Everyday Life' and 'Creative License: The Art of Gestalt Therapy', M. Spaniolo Lobb and N. Amendt-Lyon, Eds, *International Journal of Psychotherapy*, 8(3): 235–254.

—— (2003b) 'Impossible meeting: "too strange to each other for misunderstanding": review article on Darlene Bregman-Ehrenberg's *The Intimate Edge*', *International Journal of Psychotherapy*, 8(1): 65–72.

—— (2005) *Episodes and Scenes*, Submission for Metanoia Institute Doctorate, available at http://hewardwilkinson.co.uk/EpisodesandScenes.pdf

—— (2009) *The Muse as Therapist: A New Poetic Paradigm for Psychotherapy*, London: Karnac.

Wittgenstein, L. (1921/2001) *Tractatus-Logico-Philosophicus*, London: Routledge.

—— (1953/1967) *Philosophical Investigations*, Oxford: Blackwell.

Part II

Psychoanalysis beyond postmodernism

Chapter 5

Toward the art of the living dialogue

Between constructivism and hermeneutics in psychoanalytic thinking

Donna Orange

There is nothing outside of the text.

(Jacques Derrida)

By hermeneutics I understand the ability to listen to the other in the belief that he could be right.

(Hans-Georg Gadamer)

In the last session before my travels, my patient, long informed about my planned absence, now asks where I am going. "One month in Europe?" she exclaims, "I don't believe you will return." I had already been working with this patient for six years, and, although she had expressed concern for my safety when flying in the past, she had apparently not reacted to this trip until now. Nor had she apparently believed in the past that I would decide not to return.

This incident raises both theoretical and practical questions for me as a big-tent relational psychoanalyst. In constructivist-theoretical terms, would it be right to say that this whole incident was constructed? Did patient, analyst, or the two of us construct my trip, my way of telling her, her dire expectations, or what? Are the meanings we later find together constructed or coconstructed? If I think of myself as a constructivist or postmodernist, how might I respond to the patient? Or (in hermeneutic terms), could we hear the patient's statement as a question addressed to the dialogic other, perhaps commenting on something only half-perceived, perhaps a question or request for reassurance? Could this be an emotionally loaded fragment of participation in a joint and dialogic search for understanding? If my thinking is more hermeneutic and phenomenological, will there be a differ-ence – "a difference that makes a difference," as William James might have said (James 1907/1975)?

To address such questions, let us briefly describe the appeal construc-tivism and hermeneutics hold for contemporary relational psychoanalysis, and next take a short excursion through some disputes in twentieth-century continental philosophy. Thinkers like Richard Rorty (1991) have grouped together neopragmatism, deconstruction, social constructionism, and hermeneutics as forms of postmodern ironic skepticism. Although comparing and contrasting these ideas to show their family resemblances and their distinctive voices would be an enticing task for me, space does not permit. I will, however, make as clear a distinction as possible between postmodern deconstructionism and hermeneutic thinking, so that we may see a possible way between the extremes of traditional psychoanalytic objectivism and the currently popular constructivism found in much relational psychoanalytic theorizing. I believe there are more than two choices. For me, though I respect and hold important the concerns of constructivists, I believe philosophical hermeneutics offers a third possibility more faithful to the spirit and practice of relational psychoanalysis. Even more, I believe that dialogue between constructivists and hermeneuts could be extremely fruitful for relational psychoanalysis. The question is, however, as we shall see, whether genuine dialogue is possible at all.

Psychoanalytic constructivism and psychoanalytic hermeneutics

Contemporary psychoanalytic constructivism, it seems to me, tends to take three principal forms. First there is the refined, carefully delineated critical or dialectical constructivism of Hoffman (1991, 1998) and others (Beebe and Lachmann 2002), according to which meanings are interactively built up in the psychoanalytic process. Hoffman's early account emphasized the clinical shift occurring in relational psychoanalysis:

> A different step is required, one that has to do specifically with the kind of knowledge that the participants are thought to have of themselves and of each other. The paradigm changes, in my view, only when the idea of the analyst's personal involvement is wedded to a constructivist or perspectivist epistemological position. Only in effecting that integration is the idea of the analyst's participation in the process taken fully into account. By this I mean, very specifically, that the personal participation of the analyst in the process is considered to have a continuous effect on what he or she understands about himself or herself and about the patient in the interaction.
>
> (Hoffman 1991: 136)

At the time, I objected that perspectivism was not equivalent to constructivism in the Berger and Luckmann (1967) sense upon which Hoffman relied (Orange 1992). At the same time I agreed entirely with the clinical sensibility he was articulating, and was therefore interested to see his constructivism develop during the 1990s. Though I still have some reservations that will become apparent in my discussion of paradox and dialectic below, I suspect that little difference remains now between his "dialectical constructivism" (Hoffman 1998) and my perspectival hermeneutics.

A second form, even more influential, has entered relational psychoanalysis through gender studies and French feminism. This influence in relational psychoanalysis links it to the deconstructionism of Derrida, Foucault, and Lyotard, and places it within "postmodernism" as defined by Lyotard:

> I define postmodern as incredulity toward metanarratives. This incredulity is undoubtedly a product of progress in the sciences; but that progress in turn presupposes it. To the obsolescence of the meta-narrative apparatus of legitimation corresponds most notably, the crisis of metaphysical philosophy and of the university institution which in part relied on it. The narrative function is losing its functors, its great hero, its great voyages, its great goal.
>
> (Lyotard 1984: xxiv)

Among the grand narratives refused by postmodern psychoanalysis are the Freudian, the Kleinian, the Jungian, and the Kohutian. Although it is possible that relational psychoanalysis may be creating a new set of dogmas, for the present let us consider its allegiance to the major emphases of postmodern deconstructionism and of Hoffman-like participatory constructionism.

In addition to the critical and thoughtful uses of "constructivism" by leading relational theorists, there is the informal use of the expression "co-constructed" in professional conversation to refer to things, situations, ideas, feelings, impasses, "enactments", and so on, a usage that philosopher Ian Hacking has elegantly addressed in *The Social Construction of What?* (Hacking 1999). In an ironic tone suggesting a *reductio ad absurdum*, Hacking challenges this catchall constructivism, but at the same time outlines a range of purposes that constructivism can serve. Of these the most interesting here are the "unmasking" challenge to presumed universals, and the illumination of what he calls "the looping effect of human kinds". By this latter he means the tendency of names or categories (like "child abuse" or "women refugees") to interact with their cultural contexts to take on reality and to become epidemics.[1] To call a concept "constructed", Hacking suggests, is to suggest that it is neither necessary nor universal, but that it could be, or could have been, otherwise. Both critical constructivism – including Hoffman's participatory constructivism and the even more pervasive deconstructive spirit – and what I am calling catchall constructivism share this critical spirit, so important to challenging authoritarian approaches to psychoanalysis, including all the diagnostic and metapsychological ideas it has sometimes contained. In this way postmodern constructivism shares the spirit and heritage of the "deconstructionism" so prominent in late-twentieth-century literary theory (Derrida 1978; Culler 1982). In the words of Alfred Margulies:

> Apart from its trendy (and annoying) appeal as a devastating way of positioning arguments (postmodernism as dogma and intellectual weapon), postmodernism is, quite simply, our historical Situation, a Zeitgeist in which we find ourselves. The ironic overarching theories that are now before us are ones that undo – deconstruct – overarching understanding. Privileging (and often reveling in) ambiguity and indeterminacy, these arguments, powerful and compelling, cannot be shrugged off. And so now we are all – like it or not – postmodern existentialists, searching for connections and meaning, trying to find our way.
>
> (Margulies 1999: 704)

In psychoanalysis, the constructivisms have further advantages. They call attention to the power of the analyst's participation in shaping the patient's experience of the psychoanalytic situation, of herself, and of the analyst, including the analyst's experience of the patient (Hoffman 1983). They keep the analyst aware of the multiplicity of possible meanings, and thus help combat tendencies to premature foreclosure. Over time, constructivist attitudes may support the patient in developing a sense of the ways he or she contributes to the making of the relational situations in which previously she just seemed to find herself. Psychoanalytic constructivism also tends to replace the authoritarian, all-knowing tone of traditional psychoanalysis with a greater respect for the patient's point of view (although still less, in my view, than does a hermeneutic sensibility). In the end, the constructivist hope is that in the course of the shared critical project of a psychoanalysis, the patient becomes freer from past constructions, and more flexibly and creatively engaged with others.

In addition, postmodern attitudes – what philosopher Richard Bernstein (1992) calls "the rage against reason" – have called into question the psychoanalytic faith in insight and awareness. In Morris Eagle's (2003) view, "one major factor contributing to the new view in psychoanalysis is a disillusionment with the traditional ideas that making the unconscious conscious, insight, and learning the truth about oneself are crucial to therapeutic change" (Eagle 2003: 413). Instead, Eagle observes that Stephen Mitchell claimed that "There are no clearly discernible processes corresponding to the phrase 'in the patient's mind' for either the patient or the analyst to be right or wrong about" (Mitchell 1998: 16). Instead, as I have also noted (Orange 1995), we find "versions" of lives (Shafer 1992), fictions (Geha 1993), narrative truths (Spence 1982), and constructions and coconstructions (Renik 1998). Mitchell "interpretively constructs" the other's mind (Mitchell 1998: 16). Eagle summarizes: "legitimate questions regarding the therapeutic efficacy of insight and self-knowledge are transformed into claims that there are no truths about the mind to be learned or discovered" (Eagle 2003: 415). The pendulum has swung.

Hermeneutics, like constructivism, comes to psychoanalysis in more than one flavor. For Stern (1991) and for my own work (Orange 1995; Orange et al. 1997; Orange and Stolorow 2002; Stolorow et al. 2002), the hermeneutic tradition, especially including the work of Hans-Georg Gadamer (1975/1991) on the context-embedded, historically conscious and dialogic nature of understanding, has been most important. For others, hermeneutics has informally provided a way to distinguish psychoanalysis from the natural sciences, and to claim for it its own kind of validity. In this usage, it has often become a synonym for postmodernism, for constructivism, for relativism, for skepticism, and for a refusal of tradition. People say rather interchangeably that psychoanalysis is a hermeneutic discipline, or that everything is constructed (or co-constructed).

It would require a long historical journey from Schleiermacher, through Dilthey and Heidegger, to Gadamer, to show that the leading hermeneutic thinkers have not understood hermeneutics as a deconstructive process,[2] but rather as resituating and reconceptualizing the processes of interpretation as dialogic attempts to understand. There has been a progression from the understanding of texts within their historical contexts, through the *Einfuehlung* (or empathic attempt to enter the mind of the author in Dilthey), through the phenomenology of Husserl and Heidegger, to the Gadamerian dialogic interplay from which understanding of whatever is under discussion can emerge. In Gadamer's words:

> We say that we "conduct" a conversation, but the more genuine a conversation is, the less its conduct lies within the will of either partner. Thus a genuine conversation is never the one that we wanted to conduct. Rather, it is generally more correct to say that we fall into conversation, or even that we become involved in it. The way one word follows another, with the conversation taking its own twists and reaching its own conclusion, may well be conducted in some way, but the partners conversing are far less the leaders of it than the led. No one knows in advance what will "come out" of a conversation. Understanding or its failure is like an event that happens to us.
> (Gadamer 1975/1991: 383)

It seems that the Nietzschean critique of the Western worship of reason ultimately took two paths. One led through the later Heidegger toward the French tradition of deconstruction – the constructivism in American psychoanalysis belongs principally to this tradition – and the other through the hermeneutics of the early Heidegger into the work of Gadamer, whose various roots in the German hermeneutic tradition and in Greek philosophy shaped his encounter with Heidegger's thought. Let us consider the respective emphases of each, as well as some common misunderstandings.

Derridian deconstruction and Gadamerian hermeneutics

The similarities between the two points of view we are discussing are probably plain enough: both reject naive realism and take Kant's critique as their epistemological starting point. Both are concerned with the text and with what assumptions the reader brings to the text. Both are engaged in "a common quest for liberation" (Risser 1989). Both resist authoritarian know-it-all approaches to interpretation. Each of these similarities, though, hides important differences, contrasts that include more isolated or more contextual readings of text, strong skepticism or moderate realism, dismissiveness or engagement.

These differences, however, are even more complex. Perhaps the easiest way to contextualize and to delineate the differences between constructivism and hermeneutics as resources for psychoanalysis is to compare and contrast them in the works of their best-known philosophical sources, Jacques Derrida (1930–2004) and Hans-Georg Gadamer (1900–2002).[3] Let us consider several contrasting themes in their work in no particular order, and then return to reflect on the usefulness of both approaches for psychoanalysis.

First to consider, perhaps, is the relation of both thinkers to the work of Heidegger. Gadamer, immersed in Plato and inspired by Heidegger's early work, developed his own dialogic philosophy of universal hermeneutics, domesticating Heidegger's language without losing its "worlding" quality and its temporality-consciousness. He never, however, followed Heidegger into his post-*Sein und Zeit* rejection of technology and democracy, or into his embrace of mysticism, or as some might say, mystification. Derrida, on the contrary, is the student of the later Heidegger, the Heidegger whose questioning concerns the forgetfulness of being (*die Seinsvergessenheit*) more than it does the early being as temporality. This Heidegger no longer asks so much what it means to be at all (*die Seinsfrage*) as he challenges humanism, with all the assumptions he believed humanism implies.

These two relations to Heidegger become visible, for example, when we consider the two relations to history and tradition. For Derrida and most deconstructionists, rupture and disruption are primary. His encounter with a text, his reading, Derrida tells us, is

> marked by an erasure which allows what it obliterates to be read, violently inscribing within the text that which attempted to govern it

from without, I try to respect as rigorously as possible the internal, regulated play of philosophemes or epistememes by making the slide – without mistreating them – to the point of their nonpertinence, their exhaustion, their closure.

(Derrida 1981: 6)

Discontinuity is the most important feature of a text. The work of the critic or philosopher is to uproot and dislodge, to call into question the assumed realities and essences. To "deconstruct" philosophy, Derrida explains,

would be to think – in the most faithful, interior way – the structured genealogy of philosophy's concepts, but at the same time to determine – from a certain exterior that is unqualifiable or unnamable by philosophy – what this history has been able to dissimulate or forbid, making itself into a history by means of this somewhere motivated repression.

(Derrida 1981: 6)

Like Wittgenstein, Derrida thus makes himself a psychoanalyst of philosophy, asking himself what philosophy has systematically repressed. Though Derrida does not, like Descartes, settle on a foundation or reinstate the essences, he relentlessly deconstructs the text.

When Derrida asks what the focus on essence represses, his answer is "*differance*". By this change in spelling he means to indicate that philosophy has ignored or repressed not only what differs, what escapes its names and categories, but also the ways in which this naming violates:

The structure of violence is complex, and its possibility – writing – is no less so . . . To name, to give names that I will on occasion be forbidden to pronounce, such is the originary violence of language which consists in inscribing within a difference, in classifying, in suspending the vocative absolute. To think the unique *within* the system, to inscribe it there, such is the gesture of the arche-writing: arche-violence, loss of the proper, of absolute proximity, of self-presence, in truth the loss of what has never taken place of the self-presence which has never been given but only dreamed of and always already split, repeated, incapable of appearing to itself except in its own disappearance.

(Derrida 1976: 112, original italics)

We can see, thus, that naming and categorizing are, for Derrida, the important structures to be deconstructed. Every name, as in Freud's *On Negation* (Freud 1925) hides its opposite as well as everything else that it excludes. To unmask what names conceal – otherness (alterity) and differences – relentless deconstruction of the text is indispensable.[4] To summarize,

"Derrida's deconstructionism is provocative, if not subversive, in questioning the self-evidence, logic and non-judgmental character of dichotomies we live by, such as legitimate/illegitimate, rational/irrational, fact/fiction, or observation/imagination" (Rawlings 1999: 1).

For Gadamer, on the other hand, as for the younger Heidegger, temporality and embeddedness in history and culture are foregrounded and inescapable. Heidegger's ground-breaking work, *Sein und Zeit* (*Being and Time*) (Heidegger 1927/1962), emerged from his attempt to rearticulate Aristotle's concretely situated *phronesis* (practical wisdom) and to recognize the inescapable temporal situatedness of human being (*Dasein*). It would be almost correct to say that the younger Heidegger conceived being *as* temporality, to be as to be in time (*zeitlich*). Gadamer's dialogic philosophy has been developed more from a very long conversation with the Greeks, especially with Plato (Gadamer 1980). For Gadamer, tradition is the condition for the possibility of understanding or interpreting anything. To understand a text or a person is to understand how that text or person developed within living contexts, cultures, or traditions. Rootedness is primary and inevitable. As the hermeneutic dialogue always brings into play the background of prejudice and tradition that all participants bring to the conversation, Gadamer saw this background as the condition for the possibility of understanding anything:

> It is not so much our judgments as it is our prejudices that constitute our being . . . the concept of prejudice did not originally have the meaning we have attached to it. Prejudices are not necessarily unjustified and erroneous, so that they inevitably distort the truth. In fact the historicity of our existence entails that prejudices, in the literal sense of the word, constitute the initial directedness of our whole ability to experience. Prejudices are biases of our openness to the world. They are simply conditions whereby we experience something – whereby what we encounter says something to us. This formulation certainly does not mean that we are enclosed within a wall of prejudices and only let through narrow portals those things that can produce a pass that says, "nothing new will be said here." Instead we welcome just that guest who promises something new to our curiosity.
>
> (Gadamer 1976: 9)

We are always embedded in history, in *wirkungsgeschichtliches Bewusstsein* (historically effective/effected consciousness),[5] in temporality and relatedness. We can understand only from within the interplay of traditions from which we cannot entirely extricate ourselves.

Disengagement, on the contrary, seems to be the primary ethic in deconstructionism. This is not a simple matter, but appears to mean extricating ourselves from essentialist interpretations, from received meanings, and instead noticing all the "markings" of the text that presume structures (contemporary French philosophy is often also called poststructuralist in reference to its critique of French structuralists Saussure and Lévi-Strauss). These structures often involve race, class, gender, and other forms of domination–subjection relationships. Disengagement from such structures forms an important aspect of the postmodern, deconstructionist project.

The parallel aspect of the hermeneutic project, I think, is praxis. Both Gadamer and Juergen Habermas – a relentless critic of the deconstructionist project – see the hermeneutic dialogue as a form of practice that is indispensable to being human. They appeal to the Aristotelian conception of *phronesis* (practical wisdom) that is not a set of rules, but an art of living wisely with others. Praxis, in their view, means we are "always already" engaged in an uncertain and complex world, engaged by means of an ever more inclusive dialogue. In effect, some might say, the deconstructivist disengagement from structures that exclude and nullify has the same result. To me, it is unclear whether the critical distance of the disengaged deconstructionist (witness the increasing and often-noted disengagement of intellectuals and professors in favor of "theory") is really also a form of critical praxis, or whether this difference in emphasis really makes a difference, in general and for psychoanalysis. Does psychoanalytic constructivism incline us to be more or less profoundly and intimately engaged (Ehrenberg 1992)? Do we sometimes imply that that the patient's experience is to be taken less seriously than is the view of the expert analyst who can see everything as constructed?

This brings us to another way of framing this contrast: critique versus dialogue. Critique, the central emphasis of the Derridians, can have a detached quality that was easy to see in the recent film, *Derrida*, in which he avoided eye contact or even any obvious engagement with his interlocutors. Possibly the idea is that more engagement with the other, a person or a text, undermines critique by destroying the necessary distance. Dialogue, probably the word and idea most used by Gadamer, on the contrary, is embodied in his many conversations and interviews available in books and on videotape. He appears intensely interested in what the other is saying, and responds to that, usually by placing the question or critique in a larger conceptual and historical context. In his obituaries, Gadamer was often called the "philosopher of *Verstaendigung*", that is, of a dialogic process of reaching an understanding together.

In 1981, Gadamer was invited to Paris for a symposium with Derrida. Because he knew of Derrida's interest in Nietzsche, Gadamer prepared a substantial lecture, "Text and Interpretation" (Gadamer 1989) in which he showed how differently he and Derrida read Nietzsche. Derrida responded dismissively, simply asking, in three pages, whether the good will that Gadamer's dialogic hermeneutics presupposes is just a return to the same old metaphysics. He did not respond to anything Gadamer had said, nor did he present his own ideas. Gadamer was admittedly disappointed, and some years later explained:

> what we are dealing with here is a conversation in which, unfortunately, Derrida is not allowing himself to get involved. Why he cannot do this I do not know. I think he suspects that the readiness to reach an understanding and the will to reach an understanding, which are the presuppositions of every conversation, magically reintroduce the transcendental signified in into the event of posing and answering questions. I certainly don't want this. The "dialectic of the world," . . . is based on the freedom of each partner, which I have never disputed but on the contrary have particularly emphasized. Conversation is the game of language, and readiness for conversation is only the entrance door into this game.
>
> (Gadamer et al. 2001: 68)

(Fortunately this refusal is not the end of the story, as we shall see.)

But Gadamer's passionate interest, even faith, in the dialogic process leads us to additional important and related contrasts. Gadamer often said that the precondition for dialogue was a trust in the good will of the other. Derrida, on the contrary, seems to believe, not only that this good will should never be trusted, but even that we will be blinded by our desire to trust the other.[6] Knowing that the meaning of any communication or text is ultimately undecidable, he believes this trustful dialogue is bound to mislead us. Instead, remaining faithful to the Derridean idea of undecidability – keeping all questions open, perhaps – we can still highlight and admire the artistry of the text. There is no need to ask it for more than that. Gadamer, on the other hand, retains what many might call an "essentialist" interest in the idea of truth. His magnum opus, *Truth and Method (Wahrheit und Methode)* (Gadamer 1975/1991), resolutely refuses a reliance on method in favor of dialogue as the route to understanding. Gadamer did not, however, reject the search for truth that has been the shared vocation of Western philosophers since the pre-Socratics; rather he reconceptualized both truth and the search for it. Truth became the provisional, traditionembedded understanding that emerges in and from dialogue. Truth is not a set of context-and-interpretation-free facts.

The emphasis on undecidability in Derridian deconstructionism, as in psychoanalytic constructivism, often involves an appeal to paradox. "Oh my friends, there are no friends," began Derrida's book on friendship (Derrida 2006: 1), citing Aristotle. Or again, "Monsters cannot be announced. One cannot say: 'here are our monsters', without immediately turning the monsters into pets" (Derrida 1989: 80). That every statement and idea somehow implies its opposite often seems to mean not only that there are no essences, but that texts are forever elusive, and that the best we can do is to shrug our individual and collective shoulders.

Paradox, dialectic, postmodernism, and relational psychoanalysis

> A man couldn't cover himself with dust by rolling in a paradox, could he?
> (H. G. Wells, *The Time Machine*)

Current psychoanalytic discourse is replete with talk of paradox and of dialectic, an unacknowledged but strong link to Derridian undecidability. I will instead suggest that, without returning to rationalism, a moderate or hermeneutic approach can preserve otherness while still valuing dialogue. In the years since Winnicott (1971), in his effort to recognize and articulate the transitional and potential character of relational experience,[7] urged the acceptance of paradox, psychoanalytic writing has often suggested that oppositions be renamed paradoxes. Further, we are enjoined to adopt a hands-off policy toward these paradoxes, even a reverence for them. Examples of this view appear in Ghent (1992), Pizer (1992), Dimen (1994), and Aron (1996).

A similar strategy appears in Blatt and Blass (1990), Ghent (1989), and Hoffman (1998) where we are encouraged to understand that notions such as attachment and separation, interpersonal and intrapsychic, one-person and two-person psychologies, psychoanalytic discipline and expressive participation, are dialectical opposites, i.e. paradoxical, and to assume that no further resolution is possible or even desirable. By "dialectic" Hoffman says he means "interdependence and interweaving" (Hoffman 1998) of apparent duality and polarity. "I think dialectic has the advantage . . . of implying an interactive dynamic between opposites, whereas paradox seems more static. In any case, I intend the connotation of tension, not resolution" (Hoffman 1998: 200). Ogden, on the contrary, explicitly embracing the Hegelian version, defines dialectic as "a process in which each of two opposing concepts creates, informs, preserves, and negates the other, each standing in a dynamic (ever-changing) relationship with the other" (Ogden 1986: 208). A dialectic, for these thinkers, seems to mean a generation and juxtaposition of opposites, or at least of ambiguities, to be tolerated, even embraced, in a postmodern spirit.

For one steeped in the tradition of Western philosophy,[8] this injunction to accept paradoxes or dialectical oppositions and to ask no more questions is disconcerting. In colloquial usage, *paradox* is a seemingly contradictory or absurd statement. When something seems conceptually odd to us, we shrug our shoulders and call it a paradox. To logicians, from the time of Zeno of Elea on, however, a paradox is an indication that something is seriously wrong with the system of thought that generates the paradox. Dialectic is the art of getting someone to see that the received theory ends in an absurdity, i.e. in a paradox. In the words of the *Cambridge Dictionary of Philosophy*, paradox is

a seemingly sound piece of reasoning based on seemingly true assumptions that leads to a contradiction (or other false conclusion). A paradox
reveals that either the principles of reasoning or the assumptions on
which it based are faulty. It is said to be solved when the mistaken
principles or assumptions are clearly identified and rejected.

(Audi 1995: 558)

The appearance of paradox calls not for acceptance, not for wry humor –
"No, it's not incoherence, it's just paradox" – (I am told that computer
programmers like to refer to bugs as "anomalies"), nor for throwing up
hands.[9] No, paradox means there is hard thinking yet to be done, or
emotional disintegration not yet understood. Similarly, since Socrates dialectic has meant a process of moving beyond apparent oppositions to
deeper and more general understanding. With all respect to the memory of
Winnicott, and to the work of the other thinkers mentioned above, I
suggest that a facile appeal to paradox and dialectic usually means we have
not yet considered carefully enough. More attentive consideration often
reveals that the two poles of the "paradox" or "dialectic" are less contradictory than they seem.

On the other hand, however, let us consider some of the useful functions
the appeals to paradox and dialectic may be meant to serve in psychoanalytic discourse. They may, in some instances, be intended to recognize
and respect complexity that ought not to be rationalized or reduced away.
The psychoanalytic community has seen the effect of Occam's razor (the
principle of parsimony) used indiscriminately. We know that it is dangerous
and that it can reduce away important realms of human experience. Drive
theories are obvious examples, but there others more current: self theory,
enactment theory, neuroisms, and so on.

Another function of paradox-and-dialectic talk may be epistemological.
It can be a shorthand for understanding and describing a critical perspec-
tivalism – perhaps even a perspectival realism (Orange 1995) – that does
not degenerate into relativistic constructivism or into solipsism. It can invite
us to change perspective, to switch gestalts, and to respect the view from
where the other sits even when we cannot see it from our own position. It
may also intend to take into account the impact of the observer on the
observed. I think, however, that these epistemological points are better
made directly, because both ideas – paradox and dialectic – contain within
themselves a Hegelian pull toward mutual inclusion and further resolution.
Such inclusion and resolution undoes the intended "let it be," the refusal to
allow complexity and diversity to disappear into a too-simple unity.

A third use of the notion of paradox is to call attention to mutual
implication and to "co-construction." Discussions of narcissism sometimes
point out that self-love and love of the other require each other. The reader
is created by the writer and vice versa. Patient and analyst cocreate the

analytic situation. As important as these ideas are, as indispensable to current psychoanalytic thinking, they are not paradoxes or dialectics to be left alone. In some instances – writer and reader – they are logical relations of mutual implication, and probably best so described. In others – the real and the imaginary, for example – the dialectic is again the locus of the conversation in search of understanding. It may be useful to distinguish between logical relations between concepts and ideas and personal relationships between people which involve ironies.

A fourth function of paradox-and-dialectic talk may be an attempt to retain the idea of conflict in psychoanalysis. Both attachment and individuation, for example, are fundamental aspects of human life. Neither should be explained away. But they are, in the experience of most people, often in conflict. To content ourselves theoretically with the idea that they represent irreducible paradox or dialectic, however, is to give up on the job of thinking. Why must individuality be conceived, even if sometimes so experienced, as antithetical to relatedness? Why must relatedness, when secure attachment has been so firmly linked empirically to independent exploration, be understood as paradoxically juxtaposed with individuality? We could ask a similar set of questions about conflicts between ideals and impulses. The point is that paradox and dialectical opposition constitute invitations to, even demands for, further theoretical reflection and/or clinical exploration.

The fifth, and least palatable, possibility for explaining the current rage for paradox and dialectic, is a desire to escape theoretical choices and to keep peace. It is easiest to say, "We are both right." We will have both one-person and two-person psychologies, without considering whether there is something wrong with the underlying philosophy of mind that generates this "paradox" or "dialectic." We will have both real and not-real, as in Winnicott, without considering whether some slippage in language or concept creates the paradox that we then are supposed to respect.

I must caution that I am not urging disrespect for each other's experience. Instead I am suggesting that the language of paradox and dialectic is theoretical language and bears examination and questioning. It invites, like all theory, reflection on its origins in the developmental/relational experience of the theorist (Peirce 1931–1935).

How would a contextualist hermeneut approach dialectical opposites and paradoxes? Let us consider the approach of Mikhail Bakhtin, the Russian philosopher. Bakhtin (1981) was fascinated with otherness, alterity, *heteroglossia* (his word for the rich and diverse community of languages). He saw difference not as problematic, but as interesting, as invitation to dialogue and process. Difference and opposition were not to be accepted and left alone, but engaged and understood within larger systems of reference. Self and other were correlative terms. Neither had meaning outside an intersubjective field or system of reference, but derived reality from that system, from the heteroglossia. Bakhtin was not a Hegelian, that is, he did not believe that differences would be swallowed up in the Absolute or the whole. Neither, however, was he willing to see difference as irreducible plurality. On the contrary, difference constitutes an invitation to dialogic communication.

Gadamer's hermeneutic conversation is a similar idea. For him, dialectic means dialogue. The participants' initial points of view, always already full of historically effective and effected consciousness (*Wirkungsgeschichtliches Bewusstsein*) are not to be left alone, but put at risk in dialogue for the sake of the growth of understanding. Paradoxes are questions at play in the conversation.[10]

Deconstruction and hermeneutics as clinical philosophies

As we have seen, psychoanalytic constructivism, including its reliance on paradox and dialectic, has performed an important service by replacing more authoritarian attitudes with a more open and egalitarian relational psychoanalysis. For me, however, there can be important clinical problems with the constructivist program. If "realities" (Modell 1991) or meanings are viewed as constructed, and thus to be deconstructed, there can be a tendency to invalidation that is particularly problematic when a patient already has a fragile grasp on a sense of reality, a strong inclination to distrust her or his own perceptions, or when the intersubjective fields of childhood or analysis require that important aspects of personal and shared experience remain unknown (Stolorow et al. 2000). A patient, for example, who was not allowed or able to name the madness or violence of a parent, and thus lives a massively confused and dissociated life, can sometimes, with a postmodernist analyst, become more and more lost. Like the devaluation of perception involved in many classical transference interpretations, the otherwise healthy skepticism of the constructivist may leave the patient with a profoundly disorganizing self distrust. Perhaps, like classical analysis, constructivist analysis is safe enough for the relatively healthy patient. For the more disturbed, I think constructivist skepticism needs to be tempered with a strong dose of a hermeneutic passion for understanding based on an epistemology of perspectival realism (Orange 1995), and tempered with what Peirce (1931–1935) called "a contrite fallibilism." Fallibilism is the recognition that we may always be mistaken, especially in our tending to take our own point of view as the whole truth.

Another concern, about which I have written before, is that the emphasis on coconstruction in contemporary relational psychoanalysis tends to privilege the here-and-now or the momentary (Orange 1995: 419). Though Eagle is arguing for enduring structures of mind, and I for a developmental emphasis, we both find in postmodern deconstructivist psychoanalysis a tendency to imagine what Jacobson has described as "a temporally flat-tened self embedded solely in its contemporary relational world" (Jacobson 1997: 82). The hermeneutic attitude, to which I am more inclined, may not meet Eagle's concern for the loss of the real and enduring in "new view" psychoanalysis (Eagle et al. 2001), but it does emphasize understanding the patient and the analytic pair in multiple historical contexts. Continuity and fluidity are equally important to a psychoanalytic hermeneut.

Let us now consider what else a hermeneutic sensibility contributes to psychoanalysis. Perhaps most important, well recognized by Stern, Hoffman, and many other relational psychoanalysts, is that the analyst is never, never separate from the reality under consideration, that is, the patient's trouble. Not only do we always understand through our own situated emotional history, and our theories, but also our situated engagement shapes and participates in this "reality under consideration," that is, the patient's trouble. The trouble immediately becomes not only your trouble or my trouble (never absent from the processes of understanding) but also *our* trouble. A hermeneutic approach to understanding thus fits perfectly with most relational approaches to psychoanalysis, including our intersubjective systems work (Atwood and Stolorow 1984; Orange et al. 1997; Stolorow et al. 2002).

Hermeneutics also fits easily with a descriptive phenomenology in psycho-analysis that avoids diagnostic labeling and reductionistic categories.[11] Its attention to fore-understanding, preconceptions – in Gadamer, prejudices – keeps us close to our patient's experience. Before we leap to call the patient borderline, manipulative, sadistic, or projectively identifying, we can ask ourselves why we need to use such labels, and instead attempt to understand with the patient whatever experience is in question – yours, mine, and ours – past, present, and future. We will, in a fallibilistic spirit, be slow to foreclose possibilities of understanding; ready to hold our own perceptions and opinions, and theoretical language lightly; and prepared to allow the inquiry to rest when the patient says the understanding is good enough for now. In other words, we work as engaged partners in the joint search for under-standing, but not as the authority who says that bedrock (Freudian/Kleinian drives, the patient's aggression, or *the* meaning of a "delusion" or a symp-tom or a dream) has been reached.

Another advantage of a hermeneutic sensibility in psychoanalytic work, and one that often provides a useful focus, is the old hermeneutic advice to take what is most difficult to understand – in a dream, in a patient's self-description or story, in a particular patient–analyst interaction – as the centerpiece of inquiry. Whatever understanding of this focus can be found, it can often help us to understand other parts of the picture. Often what emerges from such a shared conversation is a relatively clear, though previously perhaps unsuspected, articulation of the most basic emotional convictions (in intersubjective systems theory called "organizing principles", in Gadamer, the "binding expectations" (Grondin and Weinsheimer 2003) that structure a person's psychological world, or lifeworld.

A very common example appears with a patient who, despite apparent professional and social success, feels depressed and fearfully alone, at the moments of greatest success. For the patient and for us together, the other pieces of the life story seem to interpret themselves rather easily – perhaps too easily. This puzzling disparity, though less frequently experienced than the more daily troubles, is the hardest to understand. So, assuming that the patient agrees, we make this puzzle the center of our inquiry.[12] After much musing together, much playing with possibly related factors, many trips to the mental recycling bin, we may find a strong shared sense (is this the same as "we construct that"?) that this patient has long deeply felt that getting public attention would mean losing whatever attachments were most important to her, and that thus she would be completely, desperately, and irredeemably alone. Or perhaps if she ever outshone the family's designated star or genius, that is, if she emerged momentarily from her assigned Cinderella role, she would lose whatever relational world she had. Or perhaps we find that, having grown up with less intelligent or less successful parents, this person has always felt any success as a sign that she is not really even human, or doesn't belong to these people, or anywhere. There are, of course, many other possibilities. The point is that the hermeneutic task is to search together, taking as the central question whatever is most puzzling or surprising, for an understanding that allows us to then organize our understanding of everything else that we consider together (working through). There is no claim here that the lifeworld we (analyst and patient) seek to understand is fully created by us, nor that it fully pre-exists (a "pre-existing condition") our attempt to understand it. Usually, in my experience, the sense is more of discovery of the unexpected (aha, so that was/is the trouble!), more a Gestalt-shift, than of the satisfaction one takes in a new creation. (In fact, this sense probably in part explains my preference for hermeneutics over constructivism.) "Every experience worthy of the name thwarts an expectation" (Gadamer 1975/1991: 356).

This last aspect, the Gestalt-shift that Gadamer calls a fusion of horizons, addresses the problem of the therapeutic efficacy of psychoanalysis. As suggested in our recent work on a horizonal metaphor for unconsciousness (Stolorow et al. 2000), it may be that the relational experience of the recontextualization and reorganization of emotional experience (the finding together in the context of emotional engagement, often of an experience of good-enough attachment, of unsuspected emotional organizing convictions), becomes profoundly healing and opens new lifeworld possibilities. Understanding emerges from the dialogic world within which we play with possible meanings ("truth-as-possible-understanding": Frank 1992), while the process itself both de-rigidifies our overly structured expectancies and creates the space for emergent possibility. Thus, the daily experience of psychoanalytic work: the struggles to understand, the misunderstandings that are necessary to understanding, the spreading of life changes beyond the areas explicitly discussed in the analysis or therapy, all make sense in hermeneutic terms.

Yes, the process of understanding is creative, but not *ex nihilo*. Understanding is a different process from the processes of construction and deconstruction. As the French tradition has clearly seen, what is constructed can always be deconstructed, seen as arbitrary or as less than inevitable, and perhaps to be taken with a grain of salt. And yes, the processes of understanding in psychoanalysis commonly lead us to see as questionable what we had always regarded as certain and inevitable – for example, our own worthlessness or unimportance to others. Not only these background convictions, but also the meanings we "discover" together, could in principle be otherwise. Nevertheless, the ideas of understanding and interpretation suggest that there is something there to be understood, and that this makes its own claims on us who seek to understand. A 16-year-old patient's serious suicide attempt, together with her view that it was a desperate attempt to call her parents' attention to the impact of eight years of incest by an older sibling, is not well described as construction. It cries out for understanding within some community, for an understanding witness that allows its meanings to emerge in dialogue. When a therapist had finally told the parents what their daughter had been unable to say to them, and the father's only words were, "Where shall we go for lunch?" the suicide attempt followed. We could say that this family had co-constructed a system in which it seemed unsafe to the patient to ask for protection. Or we could say that she and her (later) analyst had constructed this whole story, and we would in one sense not be wrong. But such construction-talk, in my view, tends to distance clinicians from the outrages our patients have suffered, and thus protects us from feeling with them. We become a milder version of the invalidating father in this story.

Similarly, George Atwood tells a story from his years of inpatient work with those diagnosed as schizophrenic. The patient and her therapist were walking on the hospital grounds one day when she pointed out that behind a nearby tree, a ghost lurked. In the clinical case conference, he was told that he should take the patient over to the tree, walk her around it, and say, "Look, no ghost!" Instead, he had looked thoughtfully at the patient and said, "I believe in ghosts," and proceeded to engage her in a conversation about this particular ghost and its place in her world and in the world they were inhabiting together.

A psychoanalytic constructivist might protest that holding the ghost as a co-construction is not equivalent to the no-ghost response of the naive realist; instead, it treats the ghost as a kind of intermediate reality that can be deconstructed or analyzed. My clinical concern and attitude is to take what my patient says seriously (not necessarily literally), and to try to make sense of it together. If I meet my patient's terror and confusion with a deconstructive distancing attitude it seems to me I may have abandoned my patient. I have instead preferred what Ricoeur (1970) called the "hermeneutics of suspicion" that he associated with Marx and Freud. To me it seems that choosing undergoing-the-situation (Gadamer 1975/1991) with the patient in the search for understanding is required for a compassionate psychoanalysis.

I have suggested (Orange 2006) that a relational psychoanalysis that is complexity-and-context-sensitive will be a psychoanalysis of compassion. I am attempting to articulate a sensibility that relational constructivists and hermeneuts would presumably hold in common, but that for me expresses itself best in hermeneutic terms. Compassion, a word that appears rarely in psychoanalytic literature,[13] is a word with resonances that come from its use in many discourses or language-games. In everyday English, compassion often connotes pity or sympathy, and thus, for psychoanalysts, could further connote the being-nice-to-patients often disparagingly attributed to self psychology. For relational psychoanalysis, however, including intersubjective systems theory and some contemporary versions of self psychology, the meanings could be rich enough to earn compassion a place in respectable theoretical and clinical discourse. Most analysts continue to refer to analysands as patients (*patior*: to suffer, undergo), whether or not we are aware of the Latin origin: a patient is one who suffers, one who bears what feels unbearable. Compassion, then, is etymologically, a suffering-with, a bearing together.

Compassion is not technique, and much less is it a rule of technique. I would say instead that it is both process and attitude. As process, compassion is roughly equivalent to what I have called emotional understanding, the dialogic process of undergoing the situation with the other (Gadamer 1975/1991: 323), and coming-to-an-understanding (*Verstaendigung*). We make sense together (Buirski and Haglund 2001) of the patient's emotional predicament within the relational system that we experience together, and gradually this shared world changes by means of a personal reorganization of experience (of both participants). A compassionate attitude, which may not, at times, seem gentle or nice – indeed it may occasionally challenge or contradict or introduce alternative perspectives – enables hitherto unknown and impossible forms of experiencing. Implicit and explicit forms of participation in the patient's suffering create a world of compassion that introduces new experiential possibilities. This participation, however, is a way of *being*-with, not a formula for *doing* psychoanalysis. Where there was indifference, humiliation, rejection, shattering loss, and the like, compassionate psychoanalytic understanding does not simply replace or heal by intentionally providing new experience. Instead, treating a person as endlessly worth understanding, his or her suffering as worth feeling together, an attitude of compassion implicitly affirms the human worth of the patient. Instead of being preoccupied with the question of the patient's recognition of the analyst as a subject, the psychoanalytic relationship can accord to the patient, often for the first time, the dignity of being treated as the subject of one's own experience (the reciprocity may come later).

It seems to me that there may be an important difference in spirit between this engaged understanding and the distance required to see everything that occurs in life and in analysis as constructed. At the same time it is clear that many theoretically constructivist analysts are also in practice compassionate in the sense I am trying to describe. Both constructivists and meaning-oriented hermeneuts see many patients who, because of their previous experience in life and in treatment, come to us expecting to be classified, judged, treated with rigidity, or exploited. If, however, the analyst or therapist is not too intent on naming pathologies and defenses, with deconstructing, or with being right, but instead relentlessly seeks to understand and accompany the sufferer, an implicitly interpretive system emerges. For me, close and compassionate listening is itself an important form of interpretation, dissolving the interpretation/gratification duality, and fully deserves to be considered psychoanalytic. It says to the other: "You are worth hearing and understanding." This listening includes attention to the ways the patient's experiential world has created suffering for the patient as well as for others in the patient's life. Without leaving the patient's side or becoming judgmental, we can understand how one could come to be so hurtful to oneself and to others. We can understand the simultaneous two-sided experience – so often dissociated – of being both hurt and hurtful. Recognizing context and complexity prevents reduction and judgmental attitudes, and enables compassionate understanding.

This may be a good moment to highlight a concept of accompanying the other that I believe important to fill out a hermeneutic or dialogic concept of psychoanalytic compassion. Years ago, as mentioned above, I wrote and spoke of witnessing to outrageous mistreatment as an important aspect of the psychoanalytic profession. In recent years I have become more aware of the importance of simple accompanying that some would contrast with proper "analytic" work, and might disparage as "supportive" psychotherapy. Whether my patient suffers from an incurable, painful, and debilitating disease, or from terminal cancer, or has lost a family member in the World Trade Center, I must not look for ways to see my patients as constructing or even contributing to their suffering and thus join those who tell them just to accept it or get over it. There is no way to fix the situation or to "cure" the patient, so I must accept my own powerlessness to help. I must simply stay close to their experience, sorrowing and grieving and raging with my patients, even if this means that my practice feels very heavy to me. Even when – and it always is – the story is very complex, a willingness to walk together into the deepest circles of the patient's experiential hell characterizes the *attitude* of compassion or emotional availability (Orange 1995) that the process of psychoanalytic understanding requires. This psychoanalytic compassion, I repeat for emphasis, is not reducible to moral masochism on the part of the analyst, nor is it to be contrasted with properly psychoanalytic work, usually seen as explicitly interpretive. It is, instead, an implicitly interpretive process of giving lived meaning and dignity to a shattered person's life by enabling integration of the pain as opposed to dissociation or fragmentation. A compassionate attitude says to every patient: your suffering is human suffering, and when the bell tolls for you, it also tolls for me (Orange 2006).

Thus I believe that as much as we can learn from psychoanalytic constructivism, that a dialogic hermeneutics of compassion better expresses and encourages the vocational sense that most of bring to our psychoanalytic thinking and work. Hermeneutics preserves the psychoanalytic emphasis on interpretation and the relational emphasis on engaged understanding. Its fallibilistic openness to the other conserves, in addition, the constructivist and deconstructionist critical spirit.

However we may conceive what escapes and limits our capacity to know or understand – as the Real, as some form of transcendence, as the Peircean Second which occurs and cannot be thought away, or even – banish the thought – as hard facts, I believe that Stern is right, especially in noting the connection of this "impossible" quality with trauma, and as well in as implying that not everything is constructed, or even co-constructed. While I often say that there are no uninterpreted facts, this does not mean that we can understand everything. So the discussion among psychoanalytic deconstructionists and hermeneuts will, I predict, continue for some time. Where Eagle sees de-linking postmodernism and relational psychoanalysis as crucially important, I view dialogue within relational psychoanalysis about its various philosophical assumptions as potentially much more fruitful.

Postscript

When Gadamer died in 2002, twenty-one years after his 1981 encounter with Derrida in Paris, Derrida spoke publicly of Gadamer for the first time: "Wie Recht er hatte! Mein Cicerone Hans-Georg Gadamer" (How right he was! My great Cicero Hans-Georg Gadamer) (Derrida 2002). Meanwhile, conversation had resumed (Grondin and Weinsheimer 2003). The two had met in Paris in 1988 and 1993 (also with Paul Ricoeur), in Capri in 1994 (also with Gianni Vattimo), and Derrida seems also to have visited Gadamer in Heidelberg during the last years when Gadamer could no longer travel much, but still enjoyed conversation enormously. What had happened?

The answers are unclear, but still interesting. By Derrida's account, they always spoke French, and it seems that Gadamer's French was much better than Derrida's German. Gadamer said that Derrida "was always very friendly with me face to face" (Gadamer 2001: 62). Although we know little of Gadamer's experience with Derrida beyond the 1981 disappointment and frustration, he went on to contrast their styles:

> The difference between Derrida and me, I think, is that I myself would like to reach an understanding with him in which we can talk with one another . . . dialogue is not his strength. His strength is in the artful spinning of a yarn further and further, with unexpected new aspects and surprising reversals.
>
> (Gadamar: 2001: 62)

From Derrida, by contrast, we have extensive comments written for a *Festrede* (honoring speech) given in Heidelberg a year after Gadamer's death and a year before his own. The *Frankfurter Allgemeine Zeitung* reported that Derrida read his first sentence in German to honor Gadamer. Here are a few excerpts, with the caution that Derrida's language is idiosyncratic in his own French, and I am translating him from German:

> Can I express fittingly and truthfully before you my admiration for Hans-Georg Gadamer, admiration that for so long has arisen from respect and affection and is mixed with a dark and very old melancholy . . . Already at our first meeting in Paris 1981 I fell into this melancholy, different then and yet the same. Our discussion could probably only begin with a remarkable interruption, that was not exactly a misunder- standing, but rather a kind of speechlessness, an inhibition of the undecideds . . . There I stood, with my mouth open, speechless. I scarcely spoke with him, and what I said then, scarcely had to do with him. And yet I was sure, that from then on we shared something in a remarkable, but inner, way . . . If I speak here of dialogue, I use a word that remains admittedly strange in my way of speaking . . . This word remains strange to me like a foreign language, whose use demands a careful and circumspect translation. But then if it is a matter of saying what "inner dialogue" means, I'm happy that I have allowed Gadamer to speak in me.
>
> (Derrida and Gadamer 2004: 7–9)

Derrida went on to say that there was something uncanny about this story, that an encounter that initially failed so badly should have become, for him at least, such a great success, and attributed this in part to the emphasis that Gadamer in his later years placed on problems of translation as limitations on understanding (perhaps he learned this in part from his attempts to communicate with Derrida!).

Derrida continued: "My inner dialogue with Gadamer, with Gadamer himself, with the living, still always-living Gadamer, if I may speak so, has never since our first meeting in Paris been interrupted" (Derrida and Gadamer 2004: 12–13).

I end with this story in hopes that problems of translation between constructivist-talking and meaning-talking relational psychoanalysts will likewise become an unbroken dialogue.

Notes

1 A striking application of Hacking's concept can be found in the December 2000 *Atlantic Monthly* article on voluntary amputation, showing that this looping-kind creation is a tendency accelerated by the internet.

> The phenomenon of healthy people deliberately amputating one or more of their limbs with or without the help of a physician is not as rare as one might think. By regarding such a phenomenon as a psychiatric diagnosis, treating it and listing it in psychiatric diagnostic manuals, psychiatrists may be unwittingly colluding with broader cultural forces to contribute to the spread of a mental disorder.

According to this article by Elliott (1998), Hacking (1998) has also devoted a whole book to multiple personality disorder as a looping kind.
2 Heidegger, of course, claimed the history of philosophy needed *"Destruktion"* (destructuring, in the sense of identifying the assumed structures of being that prevented philosophers from considering the question of the meaning of being itself (*die Seinsfrage*)).
3 Of course there are other important sources, notably Lyotard and Foucault on the deconstruction side, Habermas and Ricoeur on the hermeneutics side.
4 A text, for Derrida, as also for Gadamer, is more than words written on a page. Because Derrida has written and emphasized that "there is nothing outside of the text" (Derrida 1976), some accuse him of exalting the isolated text and of decontextualizing it. Here is his own clarification:

> the concept of text or context which guides me embraces and does not exclude the world, reality, history . . . the text is not the book, it is not confined in a volume itself confined to the library. It does not suspend reference – to history, the world to reality, to being, and especially not to the other, since they always appear in an experience, hence in a movement of interpretation which contextualizes them according to a network of differences.
> (Derrida 1988: 137)

5 J. Grondin translates w*irkungsgeschichtliches Bewusstsein* as "a consciousness of being affected by history" (Grondin and Weinsheimer 2003: 8).
6 Possibly this attitude resembles the "hermeneutics of suspicion" that Paul Ricoeur attributes to Marx, Nietzsche, and Freud. According to Ricoeur, this is

> a method of interpretation which assumes that the literal or surface-level meaning of a text is an effort to conceal the political interests which are served by the text. The purpose of interpretation is to strip off the concealment, unmasking those interests.
> (Ricoeur 1970: 27).

7   I am drawing attention to the paradox involved in the use by the infant of what I have called the transitional object. My contribution is to ask for a paradox to be accepted and tolerated and respected, and for it not to be resolved. By flight to split-off intellectual functioning it is possible to resolve the paradox, but the price of this is the loss of the value of the paradox itself.
(Winnicott 1971: xii)

And, "The resolution of paradox leads to a defense organization which in the adult one can encounter as true and false self organization" (Winnicott 1971: 14). Did Winnicott mean to suggest that all philosophical and logical inquiry is the product of false-self organization?

8   Taoists too accept opposition, but understand it as part of the total Tao. Buddhists embrace paradox (the *koan*) as a discipline on the way to enlightenment. Hegel's strategy was similar: thesis and antithesis would be resolved by *Aufhebung*, or lifting up to a higher level of generality. Hegel, however, was more indebted to the Eleatic tradition than to Plato in one important sense: "The reason we call Hegel's procedure dialectic is not that it can be said to be originate in dialogue but that it is based in thinking in contradictions" (Gadamer 1980: 93).

9   "A man couldn't cover himself with dust by rolling in a paradox, could he?" (Wells 1895/2002: 22).

10   "Dialectic is the art of having a conversation, and that includes the art of having a conversation with oneself and fervently seeing an understanding of oneself. It is the art of thinking. But this means the art of seriously questioning what one really means when one thinks or says this or that. In doing so, one sets out on a journey, or better is already on the journey.
(Gadamer 1997: 33–34).

11   We noted above that deconstructionists also tend to see naming as a form of violence.

12   An old hermeneutic maxim suggests that whatever aspect of the text seems most strange should be taken as the key to understanding the whole. Similarly, George Atwood has taught me to pay close attention to the most puzzling, the most "psychotic" thing that a patient says.

13   Heinz Kohut was concerned carefully to distinguish empathy from compassion, noting that empathic modes of perception could be used cruelly. In his last work, however, Kohut (1984) began to ask why feelings of compassion seemed to expand his capacity for empathy. I tend to think of empathy as a larger capacity to understand another emotional experience from within an intersubjective field (Orange 1995). Compassion, in my view, is that part of empathy that makes willing and able to descend into and to explore the Dantean realms of suffering with the other.

References

Aron, L. (1996) *A Meeting of Minds: Mutuality in Psychoanalysis*, Hillsdale, NJ: Analytic Press.

Atwood, G. and Stolorow, R. (1984) *Structures of Subjectivity: Explorations in Psychoanalytic Phenomenology*, Hillsdale, NJ: Analytic Press.

—— (1993) *Faces in a Cloud: Intersubjectivity in Personality Theory*, Northvale, NJ: Jason Aronson.

Audi, R. (ed.) (1995) *The Cambridge Dictionary of Philosophy*, Cambridge: Cambridge University Press.

Bakhtin, M. (1981) *The Dialogic Imagination*, Austin, TX: University of Texas Press.

Beebe, B. and Lachmann, F. (2002) *Infant Research and Adult Treatment: Co-constructing Interactions*, Hillsdale, NJ: Analytic Press.

Berger, P. and Lachmann, T. (1967) *The Social Construction of Reality: A Treatise in the Sociology of Knowledge*, New York: Anchor.

Bernstein, R. (1992) *The New Constellation: The Ethical-Political Horizons of Modernity/Postmodernity*, Cambridge, MA: MIT Press.

Blatt, S. J. and Blass, R. B. (1990) 'Attachment and separateness: a dialectic model of the products and processes of development throughout the life cycle', *Psychoanalytic Study of the Child*, 45: 107–128.

Buirski, P. and Haglund, P. (2001) *Making Sense Together: The Intersubjective Approach to Psychotherapy*, Northvale, NJ: Jason Aronson.

Culler, J. (1982) *On Deconstruction*, Ithaca, NY: Cornell University Press.

Derrida, J. (1976) *Of Grammatology*, Baltimore, MD: Johns Hopkins University Press.

—— (1978) *Writing and Difference*, Chicago, IL: University of Chicago Press.

—— (1981) *Positions*, Chicago, IL: University of Chicago Press.

—— (1988) *Limited Inc.*, Evanston, IL: Northwestern University Press.

—— (1989) 'Some statements and truisms about neologisms, newisms, postisms, parasitisms, and other small seismisms', in D. Carroll (ed.) *The States of Theory*, New York: Columbia University Press.

—— (2002) 'Wie Recht er hatte! Mein Cicerone Hans-Georg Gadamer', *Frankfurter Allgemeine Zeitung*, March 28.

—— (2006) *The Politics of Friendship*, trans. G. Collins, London: Verso.

Derrida, J. and Gadamer, H.-G. (2004) *Der Ununterbrochene Dialog*, Frankfurt am Main: Suhrkamp.

Dimen, M. (1994) 'Money, love and hate: contradiction and paradox in psychoanalysis', *Psychoanalytic Dialogues*, 4(1): 69–100.

Eagle, M. (2003) 'The postmodern turn in psychoanalysis: a critique', *Psychoanalytic Psychology*, 20: 411–424.

Eagle, M., Wolitzky, D. and Wakefield, J. (2001) 'The analyst's knowledge and authority: a critique of the New View in psychoanalysis', *Journal of the American Psychoanalytic Association*, 49: 457–488.

Ehrenberg, D. (1992) *The Intimate Edge: Extending the Reach of Psychoanalytic Interaction*, New York: Norton.

Elliott, C. (2000) 'A new way to be mad', *Atlantic Monthly*, 286: 72–86.

Frank, M. (1992) *Stil in der Philosophie*, Stuttgart: Reclam.

Freud, S. (1925) 'On negation' in *Standard Edition*, 19: 235–239, London: Hogarth Press.

Gadamer, H.-G. (1975/1991) *Truth and Method*, New York: Crossroads.

—— (1976) 'The universality of the hermeneutical problem', in D. Linge (ed.) *Hans-Georg Gadamer: Philosophical Hermeneutics*, Berkeley, CA: University of California Press.

—— (1980) *Dialogue and Dialectic: Eight Hermeneutical Studies on Plato*, New Haven, CT: Yale University Press.

—— (1989) 'Text and interpretation', in D. Michelfelder and R. Palmer (eds) *Dialogue and Deconstruction: The Gadamer-Derrida Encounter*, Albany, NY: State University of New York Press.

—— (1997) 'Reflections on my philosophical journey', in L. Hahn (ed.) *The Philosophy of Hans-Georg Gadamer*, Chicago, IL: Open Court.

—— (2001) *Gadamer in Conversation: Reflections and Commentary*, New Haven, CT: Yale University Press.

Gadamer, H.-G., Palmer, R. E. and Dutt, C. (2001) *Gadamer in Conversation: Reflections and Commentary*, New Haven, CT: Yale University Press.

Geha, R. (1993) 'Transferred fictions', *Psychoanalytic Dialogues*, 3: 209–244.

Ghent, E. (1989) 'Credo: the dialectics of one-person and two-person psychologies', *Contemporary Psychoanalysis*, 25(2): 169–211.

—— (1992) 'Paradox and process', *Psychoanalytic Dialogues*, 2: 135–159.

Grondin, J. and Weinsheimer, J. (2003) *Hans-Georg Gadamer: A Biography*, New Haven, CT: Yale University Press.

Hacking, I. (1998) *Rewriting the Soul*, Princeton, NJ: Princeton University Press.

—— (1999) *The Social Construction of What?*, Cambridge, MA: Harvard University Press.

Heidegger, M. (1927/1962) *Being and Time (Sein und Zeit)*, London: SCM Press.

Hoffman, I. (1983) 'The patient as interpreter of the analyst's experience', *Contemporary Psychoanalysis*, 19: 389–422.

—— (1991) 'Discussion: toward a social-constructivist view of the psychoanalytic situation', *Psychoanaltic Dialogues*, 1: 74–105.

—— (1998) *Ritual and Spontaneity in the Psychoanalytic Process: A Dialectical-Constructivist View*, Hillsdale, NJ: Analytic Press.

Jacobson, L. (1997) 'The soul of psychoanalysis in the modern world: reflections on the work of Christopher Bollas', *Psychoanalytic Dialogues*, 7: 81–115.

James, W. (1907/1975) *Pragmatism*, Cambridge, MA: Harvard University Press.

Kohut, H. (1984) *How Does Analysis Cure?*, Chicago, IL: University of Chicago Press.

Lyotard, J.-F. (1984) *The Postmodern Condition: A Report on Knowledge*, Manchester: Manchester University Press.

Margulies, A. (1999) 'A review essay on ritual and spontaneity in the psychoanalytic process: a dialectical-constructivist view', *Contemporary Psychoanalysis*, 35: 699–712.

Mitchell, S. (1998) 'The analyst's knowledge and authority', *Psychoanalytic Quarterly*, 67: 1–31.

Modell, A. (1991) 'A confusion of tongues or whose reality is it?', *Psychoanalytic Quarterly*, 60: 227–244.

Ogden, T. (1986) *The Matrix of the Mind*, Northvale, NJ: Jason Aronson.

Orange, D. (1992) 'Commentary on Irwin Hoffman's "Discussion: toward a social-constructivist view of the psychoanalytic situation"', *Psychoanalytic Dialogues*, 2(4): 561–566.

—— (1995) *Emotional Understanding: Studies in Psychoanalytic Epistemology*, New York: Guilford.

—— (2006) 'For whom the bell tolls: complexity, context, and compassion in psychoanalysis', *International Journal of Psychoanalytic Self Psychology*, 1: 5–21.

Orange, D. and Stolorow, R. (2002) 'Perspectival realism and intersubjective systems: reflections on meaning, truth, and reality', *Intersubjectivity in Psychoanalysis*, Northvale, NJ: Jason Aronson.

Orange, D., Atwood, G. and Stolorow, R. (1997) *Working Intersubjectively: Contextualism in Psychoanalytic Practice*, Hillsdale, NJ: Analytic Press.

Peirce, C. (1931–1935) *The Collected Papers of Charles Sanders Peirce*, Cambridge, MA: Harvard University Press.

Pizer, S. A. (1992) 'The negotiation of paradox in the analytic process', *Psychoanalytic Dialogues*, 2(2): 215–240.

Rawlings, J. (1999) *Jacques Derrida*, Stanford, CA: Stanford University.

Renik, O. (ed.) (1998) *Knowledge and Authority in the Psychoanalytic Relationship*, Northvale, NJ: Jason Aronson.

Ricoeur, P. (1970) *Freud and Philosophy: An Essay on Interpretation*, New Haven, CT: Yale University Press.

Risser, J. (1989) 'The two faces of Socrates: Gadamer/Derrida', in D. Michelfelder and R. Palmer (eds) *Dialogue and Deconstruction: The Gadamer-Derrida Encounter*, Albany, NY: State University of New York Press.

Rorty, R. (1991) *Objectivity, Relativism and Truth: Philosophical Papers*, Vol. 1, Cambridge: Cambridge University Press.

Shafer, R. (1992) *Retelling a Life: Narration and Dialogue in Psychoanalysis*, New York: Basic Books.

Spence, D. (1982) *Narrative Truth and Historical Truth*, New York: Norton.

Stern, D. (1991) 'A philosophy for the embedded analyst: Gadamer's hermeneutics and the social paradigm of psychoanalysis', *Contemporary Psychoanalysis*, 27: 51–58.

Stolorow, R., Orange, D. and Atwood, G. (2000) 'World horizons: a post-Cartesian alternative to the Freudian unconscious', *Contemporary Psychoanalysis*, 37: 43–61.

Stolorow, R., Atwood, G. and Orange, D. (2002) *Worlds of Experience; Interweaving Philosophical and Clinical Dimensions in Psychoanalysis*, New York: Basic Books.

Wells, H. (1895/2002) *The Time Machine*, New York: Penguin.

Winnicott, D. (1971) *Playing and Reality*, London: Tavistock.

Chapter 6

Trauma and human existence

The mutual enrichment of Heidegger's existential analytic and a psychoanalytic understanding of trauma

Robert D. Stolorow

During a sixteen-year period after having the experience of a traumatic loss, I strove, in a series of articles culminating in a book (Stolorow 2007), to grasp and conceptualize the essence of emotional trauma. Two interweaving central themes crystallized in the course of this work. One pertains to the context-embeddedness of emotional life in general and of the experience of emotional trauma in particular. The other pertains to the recognition that the possibility of emotional trauma is built into the basic constitution of human existence. In this chapter I first explicate these two themes and show how Heidegger's (1927) existential analytic can provide a philosophical grounding for them. Next I propose a synthesis of the two themes – trauma's contextuality and its existentiality – from a perspective that I believe can encompass them both. Lastly I show how this broader perspective on trauma can enrich aspects of Heidegger's existential analytic that concern "Being-with" (*Mitsein*), the existential structure underpinning relationality. Although Heidegger's philosophy may in some respects be regarded as a forerunner of postmodern thought, this enriched conception of *Mitsein* will be shown to extend his existential analytic far beyond the moral relativism characteristic of postmodernism.

The contextuality of emotional trauma

It is a central tenet of intersubjective-systems theory, the psychoanalytic perspective that my collaborators and I have been developing over the course of more than three decades (Stolorow et al. 2002), that a shift in psychoanalytic thinking from the primacy of drive to the primacy of affectivity moves psychoanalysis toward a phenomenological contextualism and a central focus on dynamic intersubjective fields. Unlike instinctual drives, which originate deep within the interior of a Cartesian isolated mind, affectivity – that is, subjective emotional experience – is something that from birth onward is regulated, or misregulated, within ongoing relational systems. Emotional experience is grasped as being inseparable from the intersubjective contexts of attunement and malattunement in which it is felt (Socarides and Stolorow 1984–1985). Therefore, locating affectivity at its center automatically entails a radical contextualization of virtually all aspects of human psychological life.

Traditional Freudian theory is pervaded by the Cartesian "myth of the isolated mind" (Stolorow and Atwood 1992). Descartes' (1641) philosophy bifurcated the subjective world into inner and outer regions, severed both mind from body and cognition from affect, reified and absolutized the resulting divisions, and pictured the mind as an objective entity that takes its place among other objects, a "thinking thing" that has an inside with contents and that looks out on an external world from which it is essentially estranged. The Freudian psyche is fundamentally a Cartesian mind, although one greatly expanded to include a vast unconscious domain. It is a container of contents (instinctual energies, wishes, etc.), a thinking *thing* that, precisely because it is a thing, is ontologically decontextualized, fundamentally separated from its world. Affectivity, by contrast, is always a feature of broader contextual wholes.

The radical contextualization achieved by emphasizing the primacy of affectivity is nowhere more clearly seen than in the understanding of developmental trauma. From an intersubjective-systems perspective, such trauma is viewed not, as Freud (1926) would have it, as an instinctual flooding of an ill-equipped Cartesian container, but as an experience of unbearable affect. Furthermore, the intolerability of affect states can be grasped only in terms of the relational systems in which they are felt. Developmental trauma originates within a formative intersubjective context whose central feature is malattunement to painful affect – a breakdown of the child–caregiver system of mutual regulation. This leads to the child's loss of affect-integrating capacity and thereby to an unbearable, overwhelmed, disorganized state. Painful or frightening affect becomes lastingly traumatic when it cannot find a relational home in which it can be held and integrated.

Within philosophy, perhaps the most important challenge to Descartes' metaphysical dualism was mounted by Heidegger, whose existential analytic holds great promise in providing philosophical grounding for psychoanalytic contextualism. Descartes' metaphysics divided the finite world into two distinct basic substances – res cogitans and res extensa, thinking substances (minds) with no extension in space and extended substances (bodies and other material things) that do not think. This metaphysical dualism concretized the idea of a complete separation between mind and world, between subject and object. Descartes' vision can be characterized as a decontextualization of both mind and world. Mind, the "thinking thing," is isolated from the world in which it dwells, just as the world is purged of all human significance or "worldhood" (Heidegger 1927). Both mind and world are stripped of all contextuality with respect to one another, as they are beheld in their bare thinghood, their pure presence-at-hand, as Heidegger would say. The ontological gap between mind and world, between subject and object, is bridged only in a relationship of thinking, in which the "worldless subject" somehow forms ideas that more or less accurately represent or correspond to transcendent (i.e., mind-independent) objects in an "unworlded world."

In his existential analytic, Heidegger sought to refind the unity of our Being,[1] split asunder in the Cartesian bifurcation. Thus, what he called the "destruction" of traditional metaphysics was a clearing away of the latter's concealments and disguises, in order to unveil the primordial contextual whole that it had been covering up.

Heidegger's contextualism is formally indicated in the early pages of *Being and Time*, in his designation of the human being as *Dasein*, to-be-there or to-be-situated, a term that already points to the unity of the human kind of Being and its context. This initially indicated contextualization is fleshed out as he pursues his aim of "lay[ing] bare a fundamental structure in Dasein: Being-in-the-world" (Heidegger 1927: 65), also described as Dasein's "basic state" (constitution) or "constitutive state" (78). The hyphens unifying the expression *Being-in-the-world* indicate that the traditional ontological gap between our Being and our world is to be definitively closed and that, in their indissoluble unity, our Being and our world "primordially and constantly" (65) contextualize one another.[2] Heidegger's existential analytic unveils the basic structure of our Being as a rich contextual whole, in which human Being is saturated with the world in which we dwell, just as the world we inhabit is drenched in human meanings and purposes. In light of this fundamental contextualization, Heidegger's consideration of affectivity is especially noteworthy.

Heidegger's term for the existential ground of affectivity (feelings and moods) is *Befindlichkeit*, a characteristically cumbersome noun he invented to capture a basic dimension of human existence. Literally, the word might be translated as "how-one-finds-oneself-ness." As Gendlin (1988) has pointed out, Heidegger's word for the structure of affectivity denotes both how one feels and the situation within which one is feeling, a felt sense of oneself in a situation, prior to a Cartesian split between inside and outside. *Befindlichkeit* is disclosive of our always already having been delivered over to the situatedness in which we find ourselves. For Heidegger, *Befindlichkeit* – disclosive affectivity – is a mode of Being-in-the-world, profoundly embedded in constitutive context. Heidegger's concept underscores the exquisite context-dependence and context-sensitivity of human emotional life and thereby helps to ground my claim about the context-embeddedness of emotional trauma.

The existentiality of emotional trauma

I turn now to central features of the phenomenology of trauma, as these were exhibited in a traumatized state that I myself experienced at a conference in 1992, at which I relived the devastating loss that had occurred 18 months earlier:

> There was a dinner at that conference for all the panelists, many of whom were my old and good friends and close colleagues. Yet, as I looked around the ballroom, they all seemed like strange and alien beings to me. Or, more accurately, *I* seemed like a strange and alien being – not of this world. The others seemed so vitalized, engaged with one another in a lively manner. I, in contrast, felt deadened and broken, a shell of the man I had once been. An unbridgeable gulf seemed to open up, separating me forever from my friends and colleagues. They could never even begin to fathom my experience, I thought to myself, because we now lived in altogether different worlds.
>
> (Stolorow 2007: 13–14)

The key that for me eventually unlocked the meaning of the dreadful sense of alienation and estrangement that seemed inherent to the experience of emotional trauma was what I came to call "the absolutisms of everyday life" (Stolorow 2007: 16):

> When a person says to a friend, "I'll see you later" or a parent says to a child at bedtime, "I'll see you in the morning," these are statements . . . whose validity is not open for discussion. Such absolutisms are the basis for a kind of naïve realism and optimism that allow one to function in the world, experienced as stable and predictable. It is in the essence of emotional trauma that it shatters these absolutisms, a catastrophic loss of innocence that permanently alters one's sense of being-in-the-world. Massive deconstruction of the absolutisms of everyday life exposes the inescapable contingency of existence on a universe that is random and unpredictable and in which no safety or continuity of being can be assured. Trauma thereby exposes "the unbearable emdeddedness of being" . . . As a result, the traumatized person cannot help but perceive aspects of existence that lie well outside the absolutized horizons of normal everydayness. It is in this sense that the worlds of traumatized persons are fundamentally incommensurable with those of others, the deep chasm in which an anguished sense of estrangement and solitude takes form.
>
> (Stolorow 2007: 16)

I found an additional and especially illuminating window into the phenomenology of emotional trauma in Heidegger's (1927) existential interpretation of anxiety, which provides extraordinarily rich understanding of states of anxiety at the traumatic extreme of the anxiety spectrum and, in so doing, points the way to a recognition that the possibility of emotional trauma is inherent to the basic constitution of human existence.

Heidegger makes a sharp distinction between fear and anxiety. Whereas, according to Heidegger, that in the face of which one fears is a definite "entity within-the-world" (231), that in the face of which one is anxious is "completely indefinite" (231), "is nothing and nowhere" (231), and turns out to be "Being-in-the-world as such" (230). The indefiniteness of anxiety "tells us that entities within-the-world are not 'relevant' at all" (231):

> The totality of involvements [that constitute the significance of the world] is, as such, of no consequence; it collapses into itself; the world has the character of completely lacking significance.
>
> (Heidegger 1927: 231)

Heidegger makes clear that it is the significance of the average everyday world, the world as constituted by the public interpretedness of the "they,"[3] whose collapse is disclosed in anxiety:

> The "world" can offer nothing more, and neither can the Dasein-with of Others.[4] Anxiety thus takes away from Dasein the possibility of understanding itself . . . in terms of the "world" and the way things have been publicly interpreted.
>
> (Heidegger 1927: 232)

Insofar as the "utter insignificance" (231) of the everyday world is disclosed in anxiety, anxiety includes a feeling of uncanniness, in the sense of "not-being-at-home" (233). In anxiety, the experience of "Being-at-home" (233) in one's tranquilized "everyday familiarity" (233) with the publicly interpreted world collapses, and "Being-in enters into the existential 'mode' of the 'not-at-home' . . . [i.e., of] 'uncanniness'" (233).

Note how closely Heidegger's characterization of anxiety resembles my own earlier description of my traumatized state at the conference dinner. The significance of my everyday professional world had collapsed into meaninglessness. The conference and my friends and colleagues offered me nothing; I was "deadened" to them, estranged from them. I felt uncanny – "like a strange and alien being – not of this world."

Heidegger also presents an ontological *account* of anxiety, in which the central features of its phenomenology – the collapse of everyday significance and the resulting feeling of uncanniness – are claimed to be grounded in authentic (non-evasively owned) "Being toward death" (277). Heidegger claims that "as a basic state-of-mind[5] of Dasein, [anxiety] amounts to the disclosedness of the fact that Dasein exists as thrown[6] Being toward its end [death]" (295).

Why does everyday significance collapse in the wake of authentic Being-toward-death? Significance, for Heidegger, is a system or context of "involvements" (115) – of interconnected "in-order-to's," "toward which's," "for-which's," "in-which's," "with-which's," etc., that govern our practical dealings with entities within-the-world. This system "of assignments or references . . . as significance, is constitutive for worldhood" (121), i.e., for the significance of the world. Any such referential system is anchored in a "for-the-sake-of-which" – i.e., in some possibility of Dasein, some potentiality-for-Being. Within "the horizon of average everydayness" (94), these potentialities-for-Being are prescribed by the "they" – actualizing publicly defined goals and social roles, for example. In authentic Being-toward-death, all such publicly defined potentialities-for-Being are nullified. In order to grasp why this is so, we must examine Heidegger's existential analysis of Being-toward-death.

Existentially, death is not simply an event that has not yet occurred or that happens to others. Rather, according to Heidegger, it is a distinctive possibility, into which we have been "thrown," that is constitutive of our kind of Being ("existence").[7] As such, death always already belongs to our existence as a central constituent of our intelligibility to ourselves in our futurity and finitude. In Being-toward-the-end, "Dasein . . . is already its end" (289): "In Being-toward-death, Dasein comports itself toward itself as a distinctive potentiality-for-Being" (296).

Authentic Being-toward-death has several features, all of which bear upon the collapse of everyday significance in anxiety. First, "we must characterize Being-toward-death as a Being toward a possibility – indeed, toward a distinctive possibility of Dasein itself" (305). In a crucial passage, Heidegger explains:

> The more unveiledly [authentically] this possibility gets understood, the more purely does the understanding penetrate into it as the possibility of the impossibility of any existence at all. Death, as possibility, gives Dasein nothing to be "actualized," nothing which Dasein, as actual, could itself be. It is the possibility of the impossibility of every way of comporting oneself toward anything, of every way of existing.
>
> (Heidegger 1927: 307)

Thus, authentic Being-toward-death as a possibility of Dasein strips everyday significance of the for-the-sake-of-which's that anchor it. In death as possibility, no potentiality-for-Being can be actualized. Everyday significance, which presupposes such actualization, collapses.

Additionally, "Death is Dasein's ownmost possibility" (307):

> Being toward this possibility discloses to Dasein its ownmost potentiality-for-Being, in which its very Being is the issue. Here it

can become manifest to Dasein that in this distinctive possibility of its own self, it has been wrenched away from the "they."

(Heidegger 1927: 307)

Similarly, the "ownmost possibility is non-relational [in that] death lays claim to [Dasein] as an individual Dasein" (308), nullifying all its relations with others:

> This individualizing . . . makes manifest that all Being-alongside [-amid] the things with which we concern ourselves, and all Being-with Others [and thus all everyday public interpretedness], will fail us when our ownmost potentiality-for-Being [death] is the issue.
>
> (Heidegger 1927: 308)

The referential system of everyday significance is for-the-sake-of the "they." Heidegger points out that, in this way of Being, "representability" is constitutive for our being with one another: "Here one Dasein can and must . . . 'be' another Dasein" (284). Insofar as we are actualizing publicly defined roles, any Dasein can substitute for any other. However, in the face of the ownmostness and non-relationality (unsharability) of the possibility of death, the inter-substitutability characteristic of the "they" "breaks down completely" (284):

> No one can take the Other's dying away from him . . . Dying is something that every Dasein itself must take upon itself . . . By its very essence, death is in every case mine . . . [M]ineness . . . [is] ontologically constitutive for death.
>
> (Heidegger 1927: 284)

In authentic Being-toward-death, we are utterly and completely alone. By disclosing our non-substitutability, authentic Being-toward-death tears us out of our absorption in the "they," revealing everyday publicly interpreted worldly possibilities to be irrelevant and useless.

A further feature of authentic Being-toward-death contributes to pulling Dasein out of its absorption in everyday significance. The "ownmost, non-relational possibility is not to be outstripped" (308); "the possibility of nullity . . . is not to be outstripped" (379):

> Anticipation[8] [of death] discloses to existence that its uttermost possibility lies in giving itself up, and thus it shatters all one's tenaciousness to whatever [everyday] existence one has reached.
>
> (Heidegger 1927: 308)

Lastly, death as a possibility is both certain and "indefinite as regards its certainty" (310), i.e., its "when," and it therefore always impends as a constant threat:

> [Death is] a potentiality-for-Being which is certain and which is constantly possible . . . In anticipating the indefinite certainty of death, Dasein opens itself to a constant threat arising out of its "there" [disclosedness]. In this very threat Being-toward-the-end must maintain itself.
>
> (Heidegger 1927: 310)

Here Heidegger makes vividly clear how this constant threat is disclosed in anxiety:

> [T]he state-of-mind which can hold open the utter and constant threat to itself arising from Dasein's ownmost individualized Being, is anxiety. In this state-of-mind, Dasein finds itself face to face with the "nothing" of the possible impossibility of its existence . . . Being-toward-death is essentially anxiety.
>
> (Heidegger 1927: 310)

"The 'nothing' with which anxiety brings us face to face, unveils the nullity by which Dasein, in its very basis, is defined" (356).

Everyday significance is anchored in some publicly defined for-the-sake-of-which, a goal or role whose actualization the referential system of significance is designed to make possible. Such actualizing presupposes some span of going-on-Being in which the actualization can occur. But authentic Being-toward-death is Being toward the constant possibility of the impossibility of existing and, hence, of actualizing anything, a threat that always impends. Authentic Being-toward-death thus annihilates any actualizable potentiality-for-Being that might stably anchor everyday significance. It follows, then, that anxiety, which discloses the constantly impending possibility of the impossibility of existing, should be experienced as a collapse of everyday significance and as a corresponding feeling of uncanniness. But there is a much stronger reason that this should be the case.

Falling into identification with the "they," becoming absorbed in the publicly interpreted everyday world of its practical concerns, is the principal way in which "Dasein covers up its ownmost Being-toward-death, fleeing in the face of it" (295). In the public interpretedness of everydayness, death is understood merely as an event "not yet present-at-hand" (297):

> Death gets passed off as always something "actual"; its character as a possibility gets concealed . . . This evasive concealment in the face of

death dominates everydayness . . . In this manner the "they" provides a
constant tranquillization about death.

(Heidegger 1927: 297–298)

The "they" transforms anxiety in the face of death "into fear in the face of
an upcoming event" (298). In an important passage, Heidegger explains
how absorption in the everyday practical world serves as defensive evasion
of authentic Being-toward-death:

> Everydayness forces its way into the urgency of concern . . . Death is
> deferred to "sometime later" . . . Thus the "they" covers up what is
> peculiar in death's certainty – that it is possible at any moment . . .
> Everyday concern makes definite for itself the indefiniteness of certain
> death by interposing before it those urgencies and possibilities which
> can be taken in at a glance, and which belong to the everyday matters
> that are closest to us.
>
> (Heidegger 1927: 302)

The appearance of anxiety indicates that this fundamental defensive purpose
of absorption in the everyday world of public interpretedness has failed, and
that authentic Being-toward-death has broken through the evasions and
"Illusions of the 'they'" (311) that conceal it. Losing this defensive for-the-
sake-of-which is a principal way in which the everyday world loses its
significance in the anxiety that discloses authentic Being-toward-death.
Dasein feels uncanny – no longer safely at home in an everyday world that
fails to evade the anxiety of authentic Being-toward-death.

I have contended (Stolorow 2007) that emotional trauma produces an
affective state whose features bear a close similarity to the central elements
in Heidegger's existential interpretation of anxiety, and that it accomplishes
this by plunging the traumatized person into a form of authentic Being-
toward-death. Trauma shatters the absolutisms of everyday life, which, like
the illusions of the "they," evade and cover up the finitude, contingency,
and embeddedness of our existence and the indefiniteness of its certain
extinction. Such shattering exposes what had been heretofore concealed,
thereby plunging the traumatized person into a form of authentic Being-
toward-death and into the anxiety – the loss of significance, the uncanniness – through which authentic Being-toward-death is disclosed. Trauma,
like authentic Being-toward-death, individualizes us, but in a manner that
manifests in an excruciating sense of singularity and solitude.

The particular form of authentic Being-toward-death that crystallized in
the wake of my own experience of traumatic loss I would characterize as
a Being-toward-loss. Loss of loved ones constantly impends for me as a
certain, indefinite, and ever-present possibility, in terms of which I now
always understand myself and my world. In loss, as possibility, all

potentialities-for-Being in relation to a loved one are nullified. In that sense, Being-toward-loss is also a Being-toward-the-death of a part of oneself – toward existential death, as it were. It seems likely that the specific features that authentic Being-toward-death assumes will bear the imprint of the nature of the trauma that plunges one into it.

A synthesis: siblings in the same darkness

The two themes that crystallized in the course of my investigations of emotional trauma (its contextuality and its existentiality), along with how they both may find grounding in Heidegger's existential analytic, have now been delineated. On the one hand, emotional experience is inseparable from the contexts of attunement and malattunement in which it is felt, and painful emotional experiences become enduringly traumatic in the absence of an intersubjective context within which they can be held and integrated. On the other hand, emotional trauma is built into the basic constitution of human existence. In virtue of our finitude and the finitude of our important connections with others, the possibility of emotional trauma constantly impends and is ever-present. In Heidegger's vision, we are always already traumatized, to the degree that we exist non-evasively, outside the sheltering illusions of *das Man*.

Here I seek a synthesis of these two central themes – a more encompassing unity in which both the contextuality and existentiality of emotional trauma can be shown to be grounded. I found a pathway to such a synthesis in an unexpected source – certain critiques of Heidegger's philosophy that followed upon the exposure of the depth of his commitment to the Nazi movement (Wolin 1991).

A number of commentators perceive a certain impoverishment characteristic of Heidegger's conception of "Being-with" (*Mitsein*), his term for the existential structure that underpins the capacity for relationality. Authentic Being-with is largely restricted in Heidegger's philosophy to a form of "solicitude" that welcomes and encourages the other's individualized selfhood, by liberating the other for his or her own authentic possibilities. At first glance (I will take a much closer look in the next section), such an account of authentic relationality would not seem to include the treasuring of a particular other, as would be disclosed in the mood of love. Indeed, I cannot recall ever having encountered the word *love* in the text of *Being and Time*, although references to other ontically (empirically) experienced disclosive affect states – such as fear, anxiety, homesickness, boredom, and melancholy – are scattered throughout this book and others written during the same period. Authentic selfhood for Heidegger seems, from this critical vantage point, to be found in the non-relationality of death, not in the love of another. As Lacoue-Labarthe (1990) puts his version of this claim:

"Being-with-one-another," as the very index of finitude, ultimately remains uninvestigated, except in partial relations which do not include the great and indeed overarching division of love and hatred.

(Lacoue-Labarthe 1990: 108)

Within such a limited view of relationality, traumatic loss could only be a loss of the other's selfhood-liberating function, not a loss of a deeply treasured other.

Critchley's (2002) critique is particularly valuable for my purposes here, so I quote from it at some length. Specifically, he pointedly "places in question what Heidegger sees as the non-relational character of the experience of finitude" (Critchley 2002: 169). In a passage deeply resonant with the experience of traumatic loss that lies at the heart of my investigations of trauma, Critchley writes:

> I would want to oppose [Heidegger's claim about the non-relationality of death] with the thought of the fundamentally relational character of finitude, namely that death is first and foremost experienced as a relation to the death or dying of the other and others, in being-with the dying in a caring way, and in grieving after they are dead . . . With all the terrible lucidity of grief, one watches the person one loves – parent, partner or child – die and become a lifeless material thing. That is, there is a thing – a corpse – at the heart of the experience of finitude. This is why I mourn . . . [D]eath and finitude are fundamentally relational . . . constituted in a relation to a lifeless material thing whom I love and this thing casts a long mournful shadow across the self.[9]
>
> (Critchley 2002: 169–170)

Vogel (1994) moves closer yet to the synthesis I have been seeking, by elaborating another dimension of the relationality of finitude. Just as finitude is fundamental to our existential constitution, so too is it constitutive of our existence that we meet each other as "brothers and sisters in the same dark night" (Vogel 1994: 97), deeply connected with one another in virtue of our *common* finitude. Thus, although the possibility of emotional trauma is ever-present, so too is the possibility of forming bonds of deep emotional attunement within which devastating emotional pain can be held, rendered more tolerable, and, it is hoped, eventually integrated. Our existential kinship-in-the-same-darkness is the condition for the possibility both of the profound contextuality of emotional trauma and of the integrative power of human understanding. It is this kinship-in-finitude that thus provides the existential basis of the synthesis for which I have been searching.

In his final formulation of his "psychoanalytic psychology of the self," Kohut (1984) proposes that the longing for experiences of "twinship" is a prewired developmental need that in a proper milieu unfolds maturationally according to a predetermined epigenetic design. In contrast, I regard longings for twinship or emotional kinship as being reactive to emotional trauma, with its accompanying feelings of singularity, estrangement, and solitude. When I have been traumatized, my only hope for being deeply understood is to form a connection with a brother or sister who knows the same darkness. Twinship longings are ubiquitous, not because they are preprogrammed, but because the possibility of emotional trauma is constitutive of our existence and of our Being-with one another in our common finitude.

Implications for Heidegger's conception of *Mitsein*

Having explored the relationality of finitude in the context of my investigation of emotional trauma, I return now to Heidegger's conception of Being-with. Specifically, I will explore the question of whether Heidegger's conception of solicitude can be shown to entail the existential kinship-in-finitude that I have claimed is constitutive of our Being-with one another. (This philosophical question must be distinguished from the psychobiographical question of why Heidegger did not himself flesh out those implications.) I begin this exploration with a discussion of the criticisms of Heidegger's existential analytic offered by two additional commentators – Levinas and Binswanger.

In the early essay "Is ontology fundamental?" (1951), Levinas presents explicit criticism of Heidegger's ontology for reasons that persist throughout Levinas's later writings. Against Heidegger's emphasis on the primordiality of structures of Being (intelligibility), here as in his later works Levinas seeks an ethical relation anterior and irreducible to understanding – a "relation with the other [that] overflows comprehension [understanding]" and that requires "sympathy or love" (Levinas 1951: 5–6):

> The other is not an object of comprehension first and an interlocutor second. The two relations are intertwined . . . To comprehend a person is already to speak with him . . . Speech delineates an original relation [which is] the condition of any conscious grasp . . .
> In comprehending [a human] being I simultaneously tell this comprehension to this being . . . In every attitude in regard to the human there is a greeting . . . A being as such . . . can only be in a relation where we speak to this being. A being is a human being and it is as a neighbor that a human being is accessible – as a face.
> (Levinas 1951: 6–8)

Levinas seems to regard his dialogical philosophy as a "contestation of [Heidegger's claim for] the primacy of ontology" (10):

Reflection offers only the tale of a personal adventure, of a private
soul, which returns incessantly to itself, even when it seems to flee itself.
The human only lends itself to a relation.

(Levinas 1951: 10)

I found Levinas's essay unsatisfying and unconvincing as a critique of
Heidegger. Heidegger's ontology is not a philosophy of the human being as
an isolated adventurer. For Heidegger, Being-in-the-world is always already
"Being-with others" (Heidegger 1927: 155), and solicitude toward others
(*Fursorge*) is an existentiale – a constitutive structure of human existence.
Furthermore, discourse (*Rede*) for Heidegger is a mode of disclosedness
equiprimordial with understanding (*Verstehen*) and affectivity (*Befindlich-
keit*). There is no lack of originary relationality in Heidegger's ontology:
"Being-with is an existential constituent of Being-in-the-world . . . So far as
Dasein is at all, it has Being-with-one-another as its kind of being" (163).
The question I am raising is whether Heidegger's vision of originary
relationality is sufficiently rich and inclusive to encompass or entail the
deep bonds of emotional attunement emphasized in this chapter.

In the context of his efforts to ground psychiatry and psychotherapy in
existential phenomenology, Binswanger mounted a critique of Heidegger's
account of authentic existence. (I rely here on Frie's (1997) rendering of
Binswanger's (1993) critique, as the latter has not been translated into
English.) Binswanger takes exception both to Heidegger's claim that
authentic existence as Being-toward-death is the condition for authentic
Being-with others, and to Heidegger's conception of authentic Being-with
others as emancipatory solicitude or leaping ahead of the other. Such
leaping ahead, according to Binswanger, does not allow for the mutuality
of the reciprocal love relationship. Accordingly, emancipatory solicitude
does not engage the other directly and results in the dissolution of direct
relations between Dasein and the other. There is no path, according to
Binswanger, leading from Heidegger's authentic self to friendship and love
(Frie 1997: 79–84).

In his Zollikon seminar of November 23, 1965, Heidegger responds to
Binswanger's attempt to "supplement" fundamental ontology with a theory
of primordial love:

In *Being and Time* it is said that Da-sein is essentially an issue for itself.
At the same time, this Da-sein is defined as originary Being-with-one-
another. Therefore, Da-sein is also always concerned with others. Thus,
the analytic of Da-sein has nothing whatsoever to do with solipsism or
subjectivism. But Binswanger's misunderstanding consists not so much
of the fact that he wants to supplement "care" with love, but that he
does not see that care has an existential, that is, ontological sense.
Therefore, the analytic of Da-sein asks for Da-sein's basic ontological

(existential) constitution and does not wish to give a mere description of the ontic phenomena of Da-sein.

(Heidegger 2001: 116)

Heidegger is surely right that, whereas his existential analytic is concerned with interpreting ontological structures, including the primordial existentiale, Being-with, Binswanger is largely occupied with describing and theorizing about ontic (psychological) phenomena – such as a primal love presumed to be the source, developmentally, of authentic selfhood. But Heidegger does not, in his rather dismissive response to Binswanger's criticisms, spell out either how authentic Being-toward-death is the condition for the possibility of authentic solicitude, or how authentic solicitude might indeed entail something like friendship or love, in the form of deep bonds of emotional attunement.

Let us first consider the second point, beginning with Heidegger's (1927) distinction between two modes of solicitude – inauthentic and authentic. With regard to solicitude in the inauthentic mode:

> It can, as it were, take away "care" [our existentially constitutive engagement with ourselves and our world] from the Other and put itself in his position in concern; it can leap in for him. This kind of solicitude takes over for the Other that with which he is to concern himself . . . In such [inauthentic] solicitude the Other can become one who is dominated and dependent.
>
> In contrast to this, there is also the possibility of a kind of [authentic] solicitude which does not so much leap in for the Other as leap ahead of him in his existentiell potentiality-for-Being, not in order to take away his "care" but rather to give it back to him authentically as such for the first time. This kind of solicitude pertains essentially to authentic care – that is, to the [authentic] existence of the Other, not to a "what" with which he is concerned; it helps the Other . . . to become free for [his authentic care] . . . [Authentic solicitude] frees the Other in his freedom for himself . . . [It] leaps forth and liberates.
>
> (Heidegger 1927: 158–159)

The mode of discoursing favored in such authentic solicitude Heidegger calls *reticence*, a silent, receptive listening that contrasts sharply with both the intrusiveness of leaping in and the vacuousness of "idle talk" (the mode of discourse of the "they"). In the mode of reticence, we listen in silently to the authentic possibilities of the other. "As a mode of discoursing, reticence gives rise to a potentiality-for-hearing which is genuine, and to a Being-with-one-another which is transparent" (208) – that is, in which we are transparent to ourselves and to one another in our authentic possibilities.

Reticent, authentic solicitude, in Heidegger's account, frees the other for his or her authentic care – that is, to exist authentically, for the sake of his or her ownmost possibilities of Being. But recall that, for Heidegger, being free for one's ownmost possibilities also always means being free for one's uttermost possibility – the possibility of death – and for the existential anxiety that discloses it. So if we are to leap ahead of the other, freeing him or her for his or her ownmost possibilities of Being, we must also free him or her for an authentic Being-toward-death and for a readiness for the anxiety that discloses it. Therefore, according to the claims about the contextuality of emotional life presented throughout this chapter, we must Be-with – that is, attune to – the other's existential anxiety and other painful affect states disclosive of his or her finitude, thereby providing these feelings with a relational home in which they can be held, so that he or she can seize upon his or her ownmost possibilities in the face of them. Is not such attunement to the other's emotional pain a central component of friendship or love? Authentic solicitude can indeed be shown to entail one of the constitutive dimensions of deep human bonding, in which we value the alterity of the other as it is manifested in his or her own distinctive affectivity; it "lets the other be as other" (Raffoul 2002: 217).

Let us now turn to the first point. Heidegger (1927) describes the connection between authenticity and solicitude as follows:

> [Authentic existing,] as authentic Being-one's-Self . . . pushes [the self] into solicitous Being with Others. In light of the "for-the-sake-of-which" of one's self-chosen potentiality-for-Being, [authentic] Dasein frees itself for its world. Dasein's [authenticity] toward itself is what first makes it possible to let the Others who are with it 'be' in their ownmost potentiality-for-Being, and to co-disclose this potentiality in the solicitude which leaps forth and liberates . . . Only by authentically Being-their-selves . . . can people authentically be with one another – not by . . . talkative fraternizing in the "they."
>
> (Heidegger 1927: 344–345)

Authentic Being-one's-self makes authentic solicitude possible. But recall that, for Heidegger, authentic existing always "harbours in itself authentic Being-toward-death" (353); when we seize our ownmost can-be, we always do so "right under the eyes of Death" (434). It is authentic Being-toward-death that singularizes us and lays bare our separateness and self-responsibility, thereby making authentic Being-with one another as separate beings, or authentic solicitude, possible.

Let us look more closely at how authentic Being-toward-death is a condition for the possibility of authentic solicitude. Olafson's (1998) work on the ethical implications of Heidegger's conception of *Mitsein* can help us here. Olafson (1998: 9) aptly characterizes Heidegger's *Mitsein* as a "relation of reciprocal presence" – we are reciprocally present to one another as being in the same world together, disclosing both other beings and ourselves. It is Olafson's central thesis that "implicit in this reciprocity, there is a kind of partnership among human beings and that this partnership carries with it a binding character of a specifically ethical kind" (1998: 11). Olafson's characterization of Heidegger's *Mitsein* in terms of our world-disclosing partnership with one another is quite illuminating:

> [T]he first understanding we have of one another is . . . routed through the world . . . [T]he relation in which we stand to one another [is] rout[ed] through the world as a domain of truth . . . [W]e are all entities that are in the world in the mode of having a world – the same world – and . . . we are, as such, sharers in a common truth . . . [*Mitsein* entails] the reciprocity of presence between beings who are in the world as a domain of truth.
>
> (Olafson 1998: 28–32)

Heidegger's *Mitsein* can thus be understood in terms of "a relation of co-disclosure of the world" (Olafson 1998: 45). Olafson cannot find in Heidegger's unexpanded conception of *Mitsein* a similar "complementarity among human beings in the domain of choice and action" (40), and he seeks to extend Heidegger's account to this domain so that it can encompass ethical obligation to and responsibility for others.

Rather than emphasizing complementarity in choice and action, I wish to flesh out Heidegger's conception of *Mitsein* as a relation of co-disclosure of the world in a somewhat different direction – as it pertains to the theme of kinship-in-finitude that was illuminated in my investigation of emotional trauma. Recall that the world that we co-disclose together as a domain of common truth includes us, ourselves, along with others with whom we share the same human kind of Being (existence). When we disclose the world, we also disclose our own kind of Being, our existence. When we exist authentically, we disclose our Being-toward-death, and we disclose the finitude of our existence in our anxiety. Authentic solicitude requires that we have the ability to comport ourselves authentically toward our finitude and to bear the anxiety of such comportment, because only then are we able understandingly to Be-with – to attune to and be a relational home for – the other's anxiety, as we help free him or her for his or her ownmost and uttermost possibilities of Being. Furthermore, it is the other's authentic solicitude toward us, and the other's attunement to and holding of our existential anxiety, that helps us to exist authentically. Authentic Being-toward-death is a condition for the possibility of authentic solicitude because it makes possible a reciprocal co-disclosure of our common finitude[10] – the existential ground of what I have called our emotional kinship in the same darkness. Such emotional kinship, in turn, must surely, as

Vogel (1994) suggests, have significant ethical implications insofar as it motivates us, or even obligates us, to care about and for our brothers' and sisters' existential vulnerability and emotional pain. And is not such caring the sine qua non of friendship or love, or of a psychoanalytic or psycho-therapeutic attitude?

I close this chapter on a Kantian note. Kant's (1785) "categorical imperative," which he claimed to be the ground of all binding ethical precepts, enjoined, "Act only in accordance with that maxim through which you can at the same time will that it become a universal law" (Kant 1785: 73). Applying Kant's criterion to the ethical maxim to which I alluded in the preceding paragraph, imagine a world in which the obligation to attune to and provide a relational home for others' existential vulnerability and pain – i.e., for the potentially traumatizing emotional impact of our finitude – has become a universal law. In such a world, human beings would be much more capable of owning and living in their existential anxiety, rather than having to revert to the defensive, destructive evasions of it that have been so characteristic of human history. Imagine . . .

Notes

1 I follow the convention adopted by Macquarrie and Robinson, translators of *Being and Time*, of referring to the intelligibility or understandability of beings with the term *Being*, with an upper case *B* (see Heidegger 1927: 22).
2 The claim that our intelligibility to ourselves is always context-embedded renders unnecessary a concept like "the analytic third" (Ogden 1994: 5), which attempts to objectify this embeddedness as if it were some sort of add-on. The emotional experiences of patient and analyst always already contextualize one another, without the presence of any "third subjectivity" being needed.
3 The *"they"* (*das Man*) is Heidegger's term for the impersonal normative system that governs what "one" understands and what "one" does in one's everyday activity as a member of society and occupant of social roles. The "they" is thus a normative authority external to one's own selfhood. "Falling" into identification with the "they" is a flight from or disowning of one's own individual selfhood (Heidegger 1927).
4 The Being-there-with-us of others (Heidegger 1927).
5 "State-of-mind" is a misleading translation of *Befindlichkeit*, Heidegger's term for the existential structure of disclosive affectivity (Heidegger 1927).
6 By the term *throwness* Heidegger designates our already having been delivered over to a situatedness ("facticity") and kind of Being that are not of our choosing or under our control.
7 According to Heidegger, Dasein is distinguished from other entities "by the fact that, in its very Being, that Being is an *issue* for it" (Heidegger 1927: 32). He designates this human kind of Being, which "comports itself understandingly toward that Being" (78), by the term *existence*. In Being as existing, we project ourselves understandingly upon our possibilities, our potentiality-for-Being. In existing, Dasein "is primarily Being-possible . . . [I]t is its possibility" (183). Heidegger's existential analytic seeks the basic structures that make existing possible.

8 *Anticipation* is Heidegger's term for authentic Being-toward-death (Heidegger 1927)

9 Heidegger (1927) seems to point to a similar phenomenon when he notes that the other who has died

> is no-longer-Dasein, in the sense of Being-no-longer-in-the-world . . . In the dying of the Other we can experience that . . . change-over [of Being] from Dasein to Being-just-present-at-hand-and-no-more . . . The "deceased" . . . has been torn away from those who have "remained behind" . . . In tarrying alongside him in their mourning and commemoration, those who have been left behind *are with him*, in a mode of respectful solicitude.
>
> (Heidegger 1927: 281–282)

10 There is also a reciprocal co-disclosure of our *different* finitude, insofar as the possibility of death singularizes us and, existentially, "death is in every case mine" (Heidegger 1927: 284). Insofar as authentic existing discloses both our common finitude and our different finitude, Heidegger points us toward an enigmatic quality of human existence – toward the recognition that it is constitutive of our finite existence to be *both* radically relational *and* radically isolated.

References

Binswanger, L. (1993) *Ausgewahlte Werke Band 2: Grundformen und Erkenntnis Menschlichen Daseins*, edited M. Herzog and H. J. Braun, Heidelberg, Germany: Asanger.

Critchley, S. (2002) 'Enigma variations: an interpretation of Heidegger's *Sein und Zeit*', *Ratio*, 15: 154–175.

Descartes, R. (1641) *Meditations*, Buffalo, NY: Prometheus, 1989.

Freud, S. (1926) 'Inhibitions, symptoms, and anxiety', *Standard Edition*, 20: 77–175, London: Hogarth Press, 1959.

Frie, R. (1997) *Subjectivity and Intersubjectivity in Modern Philosophy and Psychoanalysis*, Lanham, MD: Rowman & Littlefield.

Gendlin, E. T. (1988) '*Befindlichkeit*: Heidegger and the philosophy of psychology', in K. Hoeller (ed.) *Heidegger and Psychology*, Seattle, WA: Review of Existential Psychology and Psychiatry.

Heidegger, M. (1927) *Being and Time*, trans. J. Macquarrie and E. Robinson, New York: Harper & Row, 1962.

—— (2001) *Zollikon Seminars*, edited M. Boss, Evanston, IL: Northwestern University Press.

Kant, I. (1785) 'Groundwork of the metaphysics of morals', in *Practical Philosophy*, trans. M. Gregor, Cambridge: Cambridge University Press, 1996.

Kohut, H. (1984) *How Does Analysis Cure?*, edited A. Goldberg and P. Stepansky, Chicago, IL: University of Chicago Press.

Lacoue-Labarthe, P. (1990) *Heidegger, Art and Politics*, Cambridge, MA: Blackwell.

Levinas, E. (1951) 'Is ontology fundamental?', in A. Peperzak, S. Critchley and R. Bernasconi (eds) *Emmanuel Levinas: Basic Philosophical Writings*, Bloomington, IN: Indiana University Press, 1996.

Ogden, T. (1994) *Subjects of Analysis*, Northvale, NJ: Jason Aronson.

Olafson, F. (1998) *Heidegger and the Ground of Ethics: A Study of Mitsein*, Cambridge: Cambridge University Press.

Raffoul, F. (2002) 'Heidegger and the origins of responsibility', in F. Raffoul and D. Pettigrew (eds) *Heidegger and Practical Philosophy*, Albany, NY: State University of New York Press.

Socarides, D. D. and Stolorow, R. D. (1984/1985) 'Affects and selfobjects', *The Annual of Psychoanalysis*, 12–13: 105–119, Madison, CT: International Universities Press.

Stolorow, R. D. (2007) *Trauma and Human Existence: Autobiographical, Psychoanalytic, and Philosophical Reflections*, New York: Routledge.

Stolorow, R. D. and Atwood, G. E. (1992) *Contexts of Being: The Intersubjective Foundations of Psychological Life*, New York: Analytic Press.

Stolorow, R. D., Atwood, G. E. and Orange, D. M. (2002) *Worlds of Experience: Interweaving Philosophical and Clinical Dimensions in Psychoanalysis*, New York: Basic Books.

Vogel, L. (1994) *The Fragile "We": Ethical Implications of Heidegger's Being and Time*, Evanston, IL: Northwestern University Press.

Wolin, R. (ed.) (1991) *The Heidegger Controversy: A Critical Reader*, Cambridge, MA: MIT Press.

Chapter 7

Reconfiguring psychological agency

Postmodernism, recursivity, and the politics of change

Roger Frie

While psychoanalysts generally agree that psychological change is the objective of their work, there are a diversity of viewpoints on how change actually takes place. In this chapter I will suggest that psychological agency plays a central role in the unfolding intersubjective process of understanding and development that defines post-classical psychoanalysis. The difficulty in discussing agency is that there is so much confusion and debate surrounding its nature. Whereas some define agency using such modernist terms as individual self-mastery and cognitive certitude, postmodernists tend to see agency as an illusory byproduct of the contexts in which we exist. The objective of this chapter is to develop a theoretically coherent and clinically relevant concept of agency that challenges the strict bifurcation between modernism and postmodernism.

I will suggest that psychology agency is generated through our intersubjective engagements and grounded in our reflective capacity. Such a conceptualization is not simply defined by rational free will, nor entirely subverted by discourse and ideology. Indeed, agency is located neither strictly in the individual nor in contexts, but in the interactive, generative space of affect, imagination, and embodiment. Agency is facilitated by openness to difference and, as such, is inherent to the process of therapeutic action. Like therapeutic action, agency is a fluid process characterized by shifts between centering and decentering, certainty and ambiguity. In this sense, I am proposing that the conceptualization of agency is important for moving beyond the paradigms of modernism and postmodernism in which so much psychoanalytic discussion and debate about the nature of human experience is played out.

The status of agency in psychoanalysis is nevertheless complex. The psychoanalytic appreciation of the tension between rationality and irrationality, choice and instinct, conscious will and unconscious desire works against any simple or straightforward definition of agency. With this in mind, I will begin by addressing the conceptualization of agency in the development of a postmodern psychoanalysis, from Freud to Lacan, and from Harry Stack Sullivan to contemporary relational psychoanalysis. I suggest that the evolution of psychoanalysis from a modern to a postmodern position has given way to significant changes in theory and technique, yet the issue of agency has remained a central, unresolved problematic.

In order to develop a reconfigured theory of agency, based on the context-bound reflective capacities of the subject, I turn to the social theory of Anthony Giddens. According to Giddens (1984), agency is to be found, strictly speaking, neither in the subject nor in contexts, but in the inter-dependency of the two. Subject and context are dependent upon one another in such a way that neither can be understood nor defined without the other. There can be no subject without a social context, just as the social context is given meaning through the existence and interaction of subjects. Agency thus is defined not as a mental phenomenon, but as an inherently interactive and emergent process. In contrast to the static, materialistic self that informs the basis of traditional definitions of free will, I view agency as fundamentally embedded in, but not entirely reducible to, social and biological contexts (Martin, Sugarman, and Thompson 2003; Frie 2008). In the final section, I address the way in which this reconfigured concept of agency can open up an ethical space for the politics of choice. Developing a hermeneutic sensibility, I will suggest that a situated theory of agency is necessary to address the sociopolitical realities in which any psychoanalysis inevitably takes place.

The riddle of agency in Freud and Lacan

Freud believed that the power of reason could be used to strengthen the conscious mind, but he also sought to do justice to the unconscious, the so-called underside of reason. Indeed, from the perspective of such Enlightenment ideals as self-mastery and cognitive certitude, the radical nature of Freud's theory of mind cannot be overestimated. By demonstrating the inevitability of distortion in our thinking, Freud presented a conception of the mind essentially combined rationalism with irrationalism.

The tension between these two seemingly oppositional forces – rationalism and irrationalism – is evident in two of Freud's most famous dictums. Freud remarks that that "Where id was, there shall ego become" (1923: 111), yet also states that "The ego is not master in its own house" (1917: 143). The former statement is seen to demonstrate Freud's loyalty to the Enlightenment and forms the corner stone of ego psychology, according to which the objective of psychoanalysis is to help the patient achieve a greater awareness by strengthening his or her ego. The latter statement is often used by proponents of the "decentering" impulse in psychoanalysis, who seek to undermine the Enlightenment view of the ego as the center of all action and motivation.

The work of the French psychoanalyst Jacques Lacan is a primary example of decentration in psychoanalysis. For Lacan, the reality of the unconscious radically undermines the notion of the conscious, rational ego.

Lacan will have no truck with the ideals of American ego psychology, which he believes are based on a misinterpretation of Freud's theory of mind. Lacan rejects outright any notion of the ego as the controlling center of the person and argues instead that the self is split through with unconscious desire. In the place of the ego, he emphasizes the notion of the divided subject.

According to Lacan, Freud's distinction between the unconscious wishes of the id and the conscious strivings of the ego amounts to a split. By presenting the ego as a mere epiphenomenon, an effect of more basic phenomena such as the unconscious and language, Lacan argues that the ego's identity is imaginary. The notion that the ego is a passive effect of forces outside of its control would seem to be borne out by Freud's statement: "Thus in relation to the id [the ego] is like a man on horseback, who has to hold in check the superior strength of the horse" (Freud 1923: 25).

In contrast to his Lacanian interpreters, Freud does not set out to altogether subvert or split the subject. Freud's aim is to show the ways in which human nature is determined both by reason and by the instincts. The very purpose of psychoanalysis, according to Freud, is to strengthen the ego, with the ultimate aim of unifying the ego. Psychoanalytic treatment seeks to heal splits and to restore and enlarge the unity of the ego to the greatest possible extent. As Freud states:

> In actual fact, indeed, the neurotic patient presents us with a torn mind, divided by resistances. As we analyze it and remove the resistances, it grows together; the greater unity which we call his ego fits into itself all the instinctual impulses which before had been split off and held apart from it.
>
> (Freud 1919: 161)

The enlargement of the ego takes place through the facilitation of the ego's communication with, and integration of, the instinctual forces that it previously defended itself against. The expanded ego is achieved not simply through establishing a mastery over the id, but rather, through the integration of the id's impulses within itself. For ego psychology, this amounts to the pursuit of autonomy and emancipation through the growth of self-knowledge, a process that is never fully completed.

From this perspective, the capacity of the ego to turn its gaze on itself and foster a nonpathological, therapeutic split in the psyche is a crucial part of the healing process. It also points to the place of agency in Freud's metapsychology. By turning inward, through the act of reflecting on itself, the ego is able to begin integrating the id's impulses. For Freud, agency is associated with the process of self-reflection and acting on the understanding achieved through reflection. The role of the analyst is to form an alliance between his or her ego and the observing or healthy part of the patient's ego, thereby expanding and strengthening the ego and enabling self-reflection to take place.

In contrast to Freud and his ego psychological adherents, Lacan sees the ego as a source of systematic distortion. As a result, the ego itself cannot be used to overcome that distortion. According to Lacan, the purpose of an analysis is to help the patient accept the splitting and perpetual lack that defines the state of the subject. The fact that the ego is nothing other than an imaginary function is already evident in the "mirror stage," and subsequently reinforced by the subject's entry into language. The formation of the ego through imaginary identifications gives way to the elaboration of the deformations of subjectivity within the "symbolic order." Here the emphasis is on the ways in which human subjectivity is fractured and decentered by the subject's dependence upon language. When the subject acquires language, it is inserted into a predetermined position in the symbolic order. According to Lacan, the symbolic order is irreducible and "cannot be conceived of as constituted by man, but as constituting him" (Lacan 1977: 68). In a manner reminiscent of the later Heidegger, Lacan writes:

> The signifier now becomes a new dimension of the human condition in that it is not only man who speaks, but that in man and through man it speaks, that his nature is woven by effects in which is to be found the structure of language, of which he becomes the material.
>
> (Lacan 1977: 284)

As an effect of the signifier, the subject must endure the semantic instability of language. The endless process of difference, which constitutes the signifying chain, is experienced as a radical dislocation. The subject's "entry" into the preexisting system of language – the symbolic order – exacerbates the process of splitting and the sense of lack first experienced when the subject encounters its specular image. "The subject, too," asserts Lacan, "if he can appear to be the slave of language is all the more so of a discourse in the universal movement in which his place is already inscribed at birth" (Lacan 1977: 148). Seen from this perspective, the subject is born into language, and it is through language that subjectivity is at once constituted and fractured.

According to Lacan, the subject searches for a confirming reflection of his or her self-identity in the other on both the imaginary and symbolic levels. In the imaginary, the subject's identifications result in misrecognitions, and in the symbolic, self-coincidence through the other is rendered unobtainable by the otherness of language. In the face of the imaginary and symbolic, the subject is not only decentered, but radically depersonalized. The fact that language predates and shapes the subject's experience suggests that for Lacan, agency resides not in the subject, but in language itself.

The difficulty of conceptualizing the place of agency in the work of both Freud and Lacan is therefore that it is not always clear who is acting. Freud's structural model of psyche leads to obfuscation of the connection between the subject and agency. Indeed, Freud has less interest in the subject, per se, than he does in showing how the psychic apparatus functions. The deterministic, natural science model employed by Freud results in a language of forces, energies and functions, but not of meanings or intentions per se. In other words, Freud generally attributes agency to the psychic apparatus.

Roy Schafer's (1976) introduction of an "action language" stands out as an attempt to clarify the problem of agency in psychoanalysis. Schafer formulates the problem as follows:

> Psychoanalysts deal essentially with reasons, emphases, choices and the like, [but] as metapsychologists they have traditionally made it their objective to translate these subjective contents and these actions into the language of functions, energies and so forth . . . In keeping with the assumption of thoroughgoing determinism, the word choice has been effectively excluded from the metapsychological vocabulary.
>
> (Schafer 1976: 103)

Schafer seeks to move beyond the structural and deterministic language of classical psychoanalysis. According to Schafer, the patient assumes a sense of agency when she learns to own previously disclaimed emotions and actions in the process of analytic interaction. This, in turn, makes it possible for her to consider new choices and potentially to act in the world in a more constructive fashion.

Schafer's action language is an important step in the evolution of psychoanalytic thinking about agency, but ultimately succumbs to the same dilemmas inherent in Freud's theory of mind. By focusing on the workings of the individual mind, Freud does not account for the intersubjective contexts in which the self-experience necessarily unfolds. A similar argument is formulated by Stolorow and Atwood (1992) in their critique of Schafer. They view his action language as a reification of the Cartesian isolated mind at the expense of intersubjective context, wherein

> the experience of agency is elevated to the ontological core of psychological life. Hence . . . the continual embeddedness of the sense of agency, and of self experience in general, in a nexus of intersubjective relatedness becomes, in Schafer's vision, obscured by the reified image of an omnipotent agent single-handedly creating his own experiences – another variant of the individual isolated mind in action.
>
> (Stolorow and Atwood 1992: 15)

The point is that any theory of agency that links psychological action and change explicitly with the individual subject reiterates the Cartesian split.[1]

By contrast, the same argument cannot be leveled against Lacan, whose thoroughgoing contextualism of the human subject, via the three registers of experience – imaginary, symbolic and Real – complicates the conceptualization of agency. Indeed, as we have seen, for Lacan the person is always subject to the signifier. As a result, the person is conceptualized as a passive recipient or a creation of the symbolic structure in which she always resides. Agency is attributed not to the person, but ultimately to language itself, with the result that language determines, that is to say, "speaks" the person. Thus, whereas Freud's intrapsychic account of agency remains entrenched in Cartesianism, Lacan's theory provides the basis for the postmodern rejection of the subject as agent.

Indeed, we might say that Lacan grants too much importance to structure, and not enough to the agential capacities of the subject. The deterministic assumptions of Lacan's "rewriting" of Freud seem to put into question the reflective and imaginative potential of the subject upon which any theory of agency necessarily depends. My point is that the symbolic is not simply imposed upon the self through language. Nor can imagination be reduced to misrecognition. Rather, the symbolic and imaginary are the enabling mediums through which intersubjectivity is experienced and articulated.

Because the subject has the potential to engage and transform the intersubjective field in which it exists, the notion of agency is implicit in the unfolding nature of this activity. I suggest that we think of agency in terms of our context-bound reflective capacity, thus de-linking it from the individual Cartesian subject. The theory of "situated agency" (Frie 2008) that I wish to elaborate is not the materialistic, static entity of yore, but an emergent process that is grounded in the continuous nature of our intersubjective engagement.

Sullivan and postmodern relational psychoanalysis

The problem is how to account for the role of agency in the clinical setting without attributing the process of change exclusively to either the subject or to the context. It is precisely the strict association of agency with the isolated individual subject that lies at the heart of Harry Stack Sullivan's outright rejection of agency and will. Sullivan's radical stance forms the basis of more recent postmodern approaches in relational psychoanalysis that similarly reject or distance themselves from the notion of agency. As a result, the conceptual status of agency in much interpersonal and relational psychoanalysis is inherently uncertain.[2]

Not wishing to take on the meta-theoretical rhetoric of Freudian psychoanalysis, Sullivan develops a new language with which to describe the analytic process. Sullivan is less interested in creating structure within the person, than in showing how the person relates to and is constituted by his or her environment. Sullivan questions whether the reified, static explanatory concepts like the id, ego, and superego actually contribute to our understanding of human experience, which he sees as dynamic, not static in nature. Sullivan relegates biological drives or instincts to a much more limited role, and emphasizes the importance of interpersonal connectedness. As Sullivan states:

> Everything that can be found in the human mind has been put there by interpersonal relations, excepting only the capabilities to receive and elaborate the relevant experiences. This statement is intended to be the antithesis of any document of human instincts.
>
> (Sullivan 1950b: 302)

Drawing on the sociology of George Herbert Mead, Sullivan argues that the self is always relationally generated and maintained. In an article entitled "The illusion of personal individuality," Sullivan maintains that the content of consciousness is socially derived and gives rise to an illusory sense of self. He argues that: "no such thing as the durable, unique, individual personality is ever clearly justified. For all I know, every human being has as many personalities as he has interpersonal relations" (Sullivan 1950a: 221). Sullivan defines the human being as the total of his or her relations with others and makes possible the development of a theory of "multiple selves." He recommends that clinicians give up their attempt to define a unique individual self and try instead to grasp what is going on at any particular time in the interpersonal field.

For more contemporary representatives of the Sullivanian tradition, such as Edgar Levenson and Philip Bromberg, the formulation of agency is less relevant than understanding "what is going on around here." Talk of agency takes away from the immediate and ever present focus on our relational embeddedness (Levenson 1972) and on the ways in which we exist in multiple self-states (Bromberg 1998) that reflect our ongoing relational interactions and the process of dissociation.

The Sullivanian tradition, as such, has limited interest in a theory of agency. In similar fashion the contemporary theory of multiple self-states makes it difficult to address the question of agency. In Sullivan's (1953a: 191) words, which leave no doubt about his position on agency: "I know of no evidence of a force or power that may be called a *will*, in contradistinction to the vector addition of integrating tendencies." As his comments on the "unique, individual personality" suggest, Sullivan links the notion of agency with the solitary individual. Sullivan's rejection of solipsism leads him to develop a relational grounding for his theory of mind, which anticipates more recent postmodern approaches in psychoanalysis.

The connection between Sullivan and postmodern relational psycho-analysis is particularly evident in the conceptualization of authenticity. As a result of Sullivan's famous dismissal of the notion of the individual self, authenticity, like agency, has long been a tenuous concept in the inter-personal tradition. As Sullivan puts it: "the overweening conviction of authentic individual selfhood . . . amounts to a delusion of unique indi-viduality" (Sullivan 1953b: 16). On the one hand, Sullivan makes an important point because to speak of "authentic existence" can suggest that there is a single way of doing or being that defines us. On the other hand, when authenticity, like agency, is linked to the isolated individual, it is essentially reduced to an artifact of Cartesian thinking, and consequently dismissed.

The belief that "authenticity" refers to a "core" or "true" self is central to the postmodern turn. In relational psychoanalysis, for example, Stephen Mitchell (1993) critiques the notion of authenticity from the perspective of constructivism. Taking the constructivist view of the self as his cue, Mitchell seeks to free authenticity from any explicit connection with a single core of true self: "The sense of authenticity is always a construction, and as a construction, is always relative to other possible self-constructions at any particular time" (Mitchell 1993: 131). Mitchell's aim is to demon-strate the inherently ambiguous nature of authenticity by linking it to the theory of multiple selves. From a postmodern perspective, therefore, the notion of authenticity can seem inherently ambivalent or fleeting because it is always and inevitably a construction.

Postmodernism has shown us that knowledge is always embedded in specific contexts and that understanding can be characterized by difference and uncertainty. Mitchell's discussion of authenticity in psychoanalysis allows for consideration of different types of self-experience.[3] Because of its inherent ambiguity, however, this constructivist perspective bears little resemblance with philosophical and socio-political versions of authenticity that seek to emphasize norms and values in human behavior. From an existential-phenomenological perspective, for example, authenticity implies a better understanding of ourselves in light of the world around us. Self-understanding does not occur in isolation, but through engage-ment with others and the contexts in which we live. As such, authenticity actually permits us to achieve a greater connection to others and the world (Binswanger 1993). This self-understanding is an emergent phenomenon that is at once personal and contextualized. It enables us to make choices and undertake actions that affect our world – hence its ethical and political dimension, about which I will say more later on.

Our capacity to choose one action over another points to a continuity of experience that is usually taken for granted, and only explicitly acknowl-edged when challenged or placed in doubt. Similarly, the notion of multiple constructed self-states relies on a continuity of experience that stands in the way of psychic disintegration and allows for self-perception and understanding over time.

In order to understand the nature of this continuity of experience, it is helpful to draw a distinction between reflective and prereflective domains. The prereflective dimension consists of a basic, nonreflective sense of self, of physical cohesion, and of continuity over time that forms the basis for reflective action and rational processing (which Anthony Giddens (1984) – see below – refers to as "practical consciousness"). From a developmental perspective (see Stern 1985), the process of self-reflection acts upon the prereflective sense of self, thus revealing its ongoing existence, and transforming it into new experiences.

Psychoanalysis is predicated on the possibility of reflection, thus allowing me to comprehend the meaning of actions, behavior, and choices that have not yet been subject to reflection. As such, psychoanalysis is largely concerned with the nature of prereflective experience, or what the later Sartre referred to as "lived experience," which includes the intersubjective realms of embodiment, affectivity and the imagination, and forms the basis for our capacity to understand, reflect, and act. The psychoanalytic process helps us to appreciate the emergent, affective processes on which our reflective capabilities depend.

A crucial factor in the emergent capacity of agency is the human imagination. It is precisely our capacity to imagine new and different ways of being and acting in the world that underlies the rational articulation of change. This is the reverse of the traditional order of things, as Cornelius Castoriadis (1997: 127–128) suggests: "What is most human is not rationality but the uncontrolled and uncontrollable surge of creative radical imagination in and through the flux of representations, affects and desires." From this perspective, reflective cognition presupposes the creative and affective dimension of the imaginary. As Castoriadis states:

> It is because [the human being's] imagination is unbridled that it can reflect; otherwise it would be limited to calculating, to 'reasoning.' Reflectiveness presupposes that it is possible for the imagination to posit as existing that which is not, to see Y in X and specifically, to see double, to oneself double, to see oneself, while seeing oneself as other.
>
> (Castoriadis 1989: 27)

It is the creative potential of the imaginary that makes new and unique patterns of action possible. Agency, on this view, is not an individualized act of rational self-mastery, but a creative process of reflective experience that unfolds in intersubjective contexts.[4]

What makes the imagination so valuable is that it can defy the laws of formal logic. This is particularly the case with the logic of choice: the rational either/or decision that is based on the choice between two or more alternatives. The nature of the imaginary, as Richard Kearney (1988) suggests, is comparable to Freud's account of dreaming. In *The Interpretation of Dreams*, Freud (1900) argues that the alternative "either-or" cannot be expressed in the process of dreaming. Both of the alternatives are usually inserted in the text of the dream as though they were equally valid. On this view, the discourse of the imaginary, like the process of dreaming, consists of both/and rather than either/or. The imaginary, Kearney (1988: 368) observes, "is inclusive, and by extension, tolerant: it allows opposites to stand, irreconcilables to co-exist, refusing to deny the claim of one for the sake of its contrary, to sacrifice the strange on the altar of self-identity." In other words, the imaginary allows us to move beyond the strict logic of either-or scenarios, and imagine new and different ways of being and acting. In contrast to dreaming, which is typically identified with the unconscious, and thus largely inaccessible to the conscious mind, the imaginary can be distinguished from both discursive consciousness and the unconscious. I am suggesting, in other words, that the imaginary is intersubjectively generated, yet highly personal, and that it unfolds at the prereflective level of experience.

In contrast to more radical versions of postmodernism, Mitchell (1993) accounts for the importance of continuity in self-experience. Yet he also embraces a constructivist perspective, and equates agency with a singular, rational self. In order to illustrate his position, Mitchell states:

> It may be that I do everything that I do, but I may do certain things in a very different experiential context than I do other things. The I that does these different things is a quite different I at different times. In fact, as Ogden (1991) has argued, the very sense of being an agent who does things may be missing in more disturbed patients (living in the paranoid-schizoid position); they experience feelings and thoughts as happening to them rather than as generated by them.
>
> (Mitchell 1993: 109)

According to Mitchell, patients may learn to recognize the role of agency in events that were previously experienced more passively. Yet he goes on to suggest, "it seems strained to assume that the self (agent) that is experienced after analysis has facilitated the integration of experiences was there, although disclaimed, all along" (Mitchell 1993: 110).

The problem, as outlined by Mitchell, is based on a familiar dichotomy: the question of whether agency actually facilitates change in the therapeutic setting, or whether agency is itself the consequence of that change. Unfortunately, formulation of change in this manner reduces the question of agency to a basic dualism: we are either determined by our contexts or choose our actions through the expression of our individual will.[5] When applied to the clinical setting, it is impossible (and perhaps quite unnecessary) to tell which came first. By contrast, if we assume that agency is a fluid rather than static concept, one that can be either present or absent in

the same way that experience continuously unfolds between the prereflective and reflective, then we can avoid this dilemma. The assumption of
agency in the clinical setting is akin to the process of centering and decentering; it is not a matter of simple choice, just as therapeutic action is never
a linear process. Agency is an emergent process and never a phenomenon
that we either "own" or "disown."

This tempering of the constructivist impulse seems to be what Irwin
Hoffman has in mind in his discussion of agency. Hoffman's (1991) original
social-constructivist paradigm sought to capture the ambiguity of experience and played an important role in the development of the postmodern
turn in psychoanalysis. In contrast to his earlier approach, Hoffman (1998,
2000) now portrays the world as offering both certainty and uncertainty in
a single dialectical framework, which he refers to as "dialectical constructivism." To this end, he espouses a notion of "free will" that suggests
a major role for conscious choice in construction. Hoffman (2000: vii)
demarcates it as "a space between the source of influence and its impact, a
gap in which I am present as an agent, as a choosing subject".

I previously suggested (Burston and Frie 2006) that Hoffman's discussion
of conscious choice provides an important addition to the constructivist
paradigm. It emphasizes the role of agency in the construction of reality
and potentially includes space for an ethical dimension. As Hoffman (1998)
puts it:

> Only some aspects of reality are socially constructed, in the sense they
> are manufactured by human beings. Among those that are excluded is
> the fact that humans, by their nature, are active agents in the social
> construction of their worlds.
>
> (Hoffman 1998: 77)

With his revised perspective on agency, Hoffman's work allows for recognition of agential experience that cannot simply be reduced to the sociocultural spheres in which we exist. Agency is a historically and socioculturally
situated capacity, yet is never entirely determined by the social, cultural or
biological contexts in which we exist.

At the same time, it seems to me that Hoffman's revision falls prey to the
philosophical conundrums that affect most modernist theories of agency.
On the one hand, Hoffman's introduction of agency into the constructivist
paradigm illustrates the dilemmas inherent in any theory of experience that
focuses primarily on contexts, without also accounting our agential capacity.
On the other hand, a dialectical approach to the subject and context, which
grants agency to the subject at some points, and to context at others, repeats
the dualism characteristic of much modern social theory. By specifying "a
gap" within his theory of construction, Hoffman essentially reifies the
person as an individual agent. In the process, he reintroduces the Cartesian

divide between subject and object into a process that is fundamentally contextualized and emergent.

Beyond agent and structure

It is precisely the need to overcome the perennial divide between the actor (subjectivism) and structure (objectivism) that is at the heart of Anthony Giddens' (1984) approach to the problem of agency. Giddens' perspective on agency is part of his larger theory of structuration, which has been instrumental for the development of a contemporary, post-Cartesian social theory. Although Giddens does not address the issue of agency in psychoanalysis at any length (see Giddens 1991), his approach is directly relevant to our attempt to overcome the dilemmas inherent in psychoanalytic conceptions of agency (see also Moran 1993). It also helps us to see the way in which psychological experience and the reflective capacities of the subject are indelibly linked to social experience.

According to Giddens, the difficulty with an exclusive focus on individual action is that agency can never be separated from the social contexts in which it takes place. Conversely, an exclusive emphasis on structure overlooks the role of individual action and reduces individual participation to a factor of the overall system. Giddens' solution to this fundamental problem is to propose the notion of "recursivity," which suggests that the concepts of subject and society are fundamentally interdependent, not simply interactive. The point is that neither agent nor structure can be understood or conceptualized without the other. Each depends upon the other and exists through an interdependent, or recursive, process. Giddens refers to the coproduction of action and structure as the "recursive nature of social life," in which the structured properties of social activity "are constantly recreated out of the very resources which constitute them" (Giddens 1984: xxiii).

Giddens proceeds by clarifying the interdependent roles of action and structure. Giddens suggests that the actions of individuals within society are social properties of a social system. He states that actions do not "create social systems, but reproduce and transform them, remaking what is already made in the continuity of praxis." Indeed, for Giddens (1984: 171), "human societies, or social systems, would plainly not exist without human agency. But it is not the case that actors create social systems." In other words, our actions do not simply produce results of our own choosing because we act in and through a structure. Persons act by means of structure, thereby remaking structure, which in turn remakes us as actors, in an ongoing process. Agency, on this view, is neither a capacity of the individual nor a function of the social context. In the same way, structure is both the medium and outcome of agential practices.

Giddens' theory of structuration is relevant from a number of different perspectives. While the major problem with theories centered exclusively on structures is that they view the agent only as a bearer of structures, Giddens emphasizes the importance of the reflexive capacity of the subject. But he does so in a way that avoids the snares of Cartesianism. Indeed, Giddens moves beyond the strict association of agency with rational reflection. Instead, he suggests that knowledge is expressed principally as "practical consciousness," which refers to the ability to conduct action without the necessity for conscious reflection. As Giddens (1984) states:

> Human agents or actors – I use these terms interchangeably – have, as an inherent aspect of what they do, the capacity to understand what they do while they do it. The reflexive capacities of the human actor are characteristically involved in a continuous manner with the flow of day-to-day conduct in the contexts of social activity. But reflexivity operates only partly on a discursive level. What agents know about what they do, and why they do it – their knowledgeability as agents – is largely carried in practical consciousness. Practical consciousness consists of all the things which actors know tacitly about how to "go on" in the contexts of social life without being able to give them direct discursive expression.
>
> (Giddens 1984: xvii–xxiii)

The knowledge involved in practical consciousness thus has a tacit character that comes about through our direct involvement with the world around us. Subjects act, understand and act anew by means of the capacity to understand what they do while they do it. This is undertaken without the need to discursively account for what they do. Giddens thereby also takes issue with the postmodern emphasis of the structuring capacity of language by arguing that subjects act both linguistically and nonlinguistically.

The point, for Giddens, is that the actions of the agent take place with the knowledge of consciousness of the agent, though this is usually only at the level of practical consciousness. Even those moments when an agent reflects upon an activity and thematizes the action within discursive consciousness, what is considered a specific event is in reality part of the ongoing process of action and reflection. As such, the notions of individual choice and will are inevitably a reification of the process of recursivity. As a result, agency is conceptualized as a process, a continuous flow of events, rather than a series of discrete "mental" events.

Not surprisingly, the view of agency developed by Giddens in his theory of structuration has many similarities with the early philosophy of Heidegger (see Giddens 1984: xxii). In *Being and Time*, Heidegger (1996) rejects the Cartesian view of the subject, arguing that existence manifests itself not through the process of rational reflection, but as "being-in-the-world." Accordingly, the person is not simply *of* a particular sociocultural context, and this context does not *only* form the background for activity. The embeddedness of the person in sociocultural contexts is so profound as to render any absolute distinction of action from context nonsensical.

According to Heidegger, persons are "always and already in the world" in such a way that there is no possibility of separating the self and world. From this perspective, we can never exist outside of our world of experience. We come to know ourselves through our engagement with others and the world. Yet we find ourselves "thrown" into a world we neither create nor control. As a result, Heidegger suggests that it is up to each of us to take up the possibilities of self-understanding into which we are thrown and shape them "authentically" into lives that are our own.[6] In other words, the capacity for agency and authenticity is possible only as a result of our being-in-the-world, which can be experienced as both enabling and constraining.

With Heidegger, then, such notions as individual subjectivity and interior processes lose their primacy because understanding comes to be seen as constituting the fundamental structure of human Dasein. For the hermeneutic tradition that follows from Heidegger, there is no psychological experience that is not constituted by the sociocultural and interpretive contexts in which we find ourselves. Indeed, according to Gadamer (1994: x–xi) this understanding is not simply a "method" to be juxtaposed with conceptualization or explanation. Rather, with understanding "a dimension is opened up that is not just one among other fields of inquiry but rather constitutes the praxis of life . . . Hermeneutics encourages not objectification, but listening to one another."

As self-interpreting beings, persons are always contributors to the sociocultural contexts in which they exist and participate. In other words, experience is always contingent on the context and our communal relations that constitute our personhood by way of interpretations and practices. In his elaboration of the hermeneutic position, Charles Taylor describes the human agent not as a solitary, rational actor, but as one who exists in a space of questions. "These are the questions to which our framework-definitions are answers, providing the horizon within which we know where we stand, and what meanings things have for us" (Taylor 1989: 30). This perspective throws up a strong challenge to the image of an agent free from all frameworks (or contexts). According to Taylor, such a person would be

in the grip of an appalling identity crisis. Such a person wouldn't know where he [or she] stood on issues of fundamental importance, would have no orientation in these issues whatsoever . . . a person without a framework altogether would be outside our space of interlocution.

(Taylor 1989: 31)

The hermeneutic conceptualization of agency thus seeks to move beyond the objectivist view of a reality. In contrast to the disengaged, individual subject, Gadamer (1994: x) states that "there is now an Other, who is not an object for the subject, but someone to whom we are bound in the reciprocations of language and life." In other words, understanding and self-interpretation are communally forged. Situated agents can reason and act only as a result of the social, cultural, and biological contexts in which they are embedded.

Agency and the politics of choice

Given this alternative reading of agency in the work of theorists as diverse as Giddens, Heidegger, Gadamer or Taylor, it is possible to ask whether the postmodern critique unnecessarily conflates agency with the isolated, rational Cartesian subject. Indeed, in this final section I will suggest that agency remains a vitally important concept for psychoanalysis and the politics of change. The difficulty is that when agency is misread as a Cartesian artifact, the process of action is no longer given the serious consideration it deserves.

The postmodern critique of the subject runs into difficulty when social contexts (be they disrupting social discourses or subtle ideologies) are seen as the only appropriate level of analysis. If contexts are used not only to describe but also to explain the nature of human action, we run the risk of reducing meaning to a one-sided causal pattern between the context (cause) and the action (effect). Because persons are more than living enactments of their contexts, the analysis of contexts must also account for the construction of personal meaning. This meaning-making process occurs despite the continual fragmentation and dislocation of human experience. Any conceptualization of agency must thus account for the way in which human experience shifts between centering and decentering, integration and disintegration. Indeed, the postmodern concepts of multiplicity, fragmentation and difference need to be linked with an appreciation of the role of agency, meaning-making, and personal responsibility. Without such an appreciation, the focus on multiplicity of selves and the fragmentation of identity has the potential to overlook the psychological and social harm these experiences can carry. Fragmented, dissociated selves have limited political meaning or value; what meaning they have lies in the language and metaphors of tragedy (Glass 1993). Multiplicity, which entered relational treatment as an innovative theory of dissociative psychopathology, has the potential to render the subject helpless.

Without a coherent notion of agency, which points to our emergent capacity to make choices and see things in ways that are different, new, or fresh, our ability to confront real political challenges is undermined. Theory and actual practice appear to be in conflict here. The problem is that although postmodernism theory is thoroughly intriguing as a radical form of critique, postmodernism actually undermines its own political relevance when it dismantles agency and skirts relativism. Without a substantive conception of political agency, it is hard to see how progressive political forces can realistically make a difference. Similarly, the challenge for postmodern influence in psychoanalysis is to demonstrate that it can transform as well as subvert. Within the clinical setting, the uncovering of difference, multiplicity and perpetual lack, while important, does not go far enough. The person's potential for reflective action, continuity and meaning-making is equally important.

This problem is perhaps most evident in the poststructuralist analysis of the self. According to Foucault, for example, theories of self derive from the social and cultural practices specific to an historic epoch and currents of power whose interest it is to define the self in ideological terms. This Foucauldian perspective demonstrates issues of power and repression involved in all human experience. Although a resourceful subversion of the dominant value system, it is nevertheless problematic when it comes to the question of political action.

Although postmodernism is generally associated with the politics of the left (especially in North America), one of the strongest arguments against the postmodern reductionism actually derives from a contemporary neo-Marxist perspective. In contrast to the view that all human experience can be reduced to social discourses and ideologies the literary critic, Terry Eagleton (1991, 1996), sees agency as undeniably central to any theory of human behavior, whether political or psychological. Indeed, one might well ask whether politics and psychology ever can or should be separated from one another, as they frequently are by psychoanalysis (see Marcuse 1955).

From his standpoint, Eagleton charges that radical versions of postmodernism contain

> no adequate theory of such agency, since the subject would now seem no more than the decentered effect of the semiotic process; and its valuable attention to the split, precarious, pluralistic nature of all identity slides at its worst into an irresponsible hymning of the virtues of schizophrenia.
>
> (Eagleton 1991: 198)[7]

In other words, to assume that persons have no voices other than the prevailing discourses in which they exist not only dismantles agency but also potentially undermines the possibility of psychological, social and political change. As Eagleton concludes: "the left, now more than ever, has need of strong ethical and even anthropological foundations." Without "any adequate theory of political agency", "postmodernism is in the end part of the problem rather than the solution" (Eagleton 1996: 134–135).

The point is that the uncovering of ideology, discourse or power still confronts the dilemma of accounting for how to create change. Within the clinical setting, the analyst must guard against stopping the work of analysis where the self has been shown to be infused with otherness. That is, if persons arrive at beliefs within an ideology, whether personal, political or psychological, do they not also have the capacity to modify that ideology? For Eagleton, this points to a sense of personal and psychological continuity, however minimal, on which the potential for agency is based: "a certain provisional stability of identity is essential not only for psychological well-being but for revolutionary political agency" (Eagleton 1991: 198).

Clearly, the objective must be to keep sight of the situational and context-bound reflective capabilities of the psychological agent, despite the subordination of the subject to organizing structures and discourses that are either outside of our awareness or beyond our control. Agency, like the subject, can never exist outside of the social discourses and ideologies that inevitably impact on our actions; yet we still retain the possibility to affect our contexts – as the recursive process of structuration suggests. In contrast to the static, disengaged subject on which the notion of free will is based, I suggest that we think of agency as a fluid, dynamic process that is fundamentally embedded, but never fully determined or exhausted by the biological and sociocultural contexts in which we exist (Martin et al. 2003; Frie 2008).

Concluding remarks

Postmodernism has surely made us aware of the dangers implicit in grand narratives and universals. As a result of the postmodern critique, we can appreciate the way in which all concepts are inevitably filtered through the lens of culture and ideology. Postmodernism has shed light on the ethnocentrism, naive realism, and rampant individualism that once characterized much psychoanalytic theory and practice. We now recognize that our insights, generalizations and understandings all arise within specific contexts and are necessarily limited. Such themes as difference, plurality, and irregularity are rather refreshing changes from past adherence to sameness and strict rationality.

But there is an important caveat. The fascination with postmodernism, whether in its moderate or radical versions, has led to a general devaluing of agency. I have argued that the very possibility for change and transformation arises because of our capacity to imagine, reflect, understand and act in ways that are potentially new and different. In other words, social and cultural discourses not only position us, but also provide us with the resources to respond to the situations in which we find ourselves. What is needed, in effect, is the recovery of our reflective capacities. Such a recovery cannot return to the traditional notion of an unchanging, fixed subject, but instead requires a notion of a changing, dynamic person, situated in multiple contexts, and grounded in lived experience. Like the person, agency is neither concrete nor static, and certainly bears no relation to the romantic Western notion of the self-creating individual. Psychological agency, on this view, is an intersubjective, embodied, and affective emergent process, which is central to any account of human experience.

Notes

1 Schafer's later (1983, 1992) "narrative" approach introduces a hermeneutic sensibility to the embedded nature of experience and thus overcomes some of the difficulties inherent in his "action language."

2 When referring to the role of agency in interpersonal psychoanalysis, I will focus specifically on the Sullivanian tradition. I have examined the lesser known, and largely overlooked, existential-phenomenological approach to agency at length elsewhere (Frie 2003). Within the interpersonal school, this approach includes such existentially oriented analysts as Erich Fromm, Rollo May, Leslie Farber, and Benjamin Wolstein (for a more recent addition to this tradition, see the work of John Fiscalini 2004). The fact that these analysts are generally neglected by the contemporary tradition of relational theorists is, I believe, a result of the strict association of such notions of agency and will with isolated individualism. Indeed, many relational psychoanalysts (see Mitchell 2002) associate agency with Sartre's concept of freedom and responsibility, thus overlooking a majority of existential-pheneomenological philosophers who were critical of Sartre's philosophy. A closer reading of existential-phenomenological approach in psychoanalysis demonstrates that the error of this postmodern critique. The work of this group of analysts was radically influenced by such anti-Cartesian philosophers as Martin Heidegger and Martin Buber. On the whole, they sought to move beyond the notion of an isolated individual, though an argument can be made for the fact that they did not sufficiently account for the contexts of experience, including the situated nature of agency. Within the contemporary relational tradition, the concept of agency figures perhaps most prominently in the work of Jessica Benjamin (1988), whose Hegelian and Habermasian approach, however, bears little similarity to multiple self-state theorists (Bromberg 1998). Given her perspective on the self and subjectivity, I would not refer to Benjamin as "postmodern."

3 Mitchell later questions more radical versions of postmodernism in psychoanalysis over the issue of authenticity, whilst still retaining an ambiguous notion of the "I." For a fuller discussion of Mitchell's position, see Burston and Frie (2006: 276–277).

4 Habermas (1987: 333–334) makes an important (and appreciative) critique of Castoriadis, which is worth noting here. Castoriadis distinguishes between two realms of imaginary experience: the "social imaginary" and the "individual unconscious," which constitutes the monadic core of subjectivity in early childhood. To the extent that the individual unconscious constitutes a "unique private world that runs up against the socially institutionalized world in the course of childhood development and gets integrated in and subordinated to the latter after the resolution of the oedipal conflict," Castoriadis' approach would seem to remain firmly entrenched in the developmental (and monadic) metapsychology of classical psychoanalysis. In contrast, I view the imaginary less in terms of a

developmental stage, then as a central and continuous dimension of human experience that is both intersubjective and personal in nature.

5 It is worth noting the way in which Mitchell approaches the problem of agency over the course of his writings. In *Relational Concepts in Psychoanalysis*, Mitchell (1988) devotes an entire chapter to the problem of "will," drawing in particular on the work of Farber and the early Sartre. A short time later, during in his full-fledged embrace of postmodernism, Mitchell (1993) has little truck with agency, equating it (and phenomenology in general) with Cartesianism. In his last, posthumously published book, *Can Love Last?*, Mitchell (2002) contrasts personal agency with social and psychological forces that are outside of our awareness. Mitchell (2002: 184–185) suggests that while psychotherapists and psychoanalysts "struggle daily with the problem of reconciling these two perspectives . . . No theorist has managed to systematically elaborate their confluence, but clinicians work this out in rough and ready fashion all the time." Given this statement, Mitchell presumably was referring to psychoanalytic theory and the work of Giddens, Bauman and other social theorists who seek in different ways to overcome this basic dualism.

6 For a more detailed and critical discussion of authenticity, being-with, and problem of choice in the early Heidegger, see Frie (1997) and Robert Stolorow (Chapter 6 in this book.)

7 Eagleton here is making a direct reference to the work of Deleuze and Guattari (2004).

References

Benjamin, J. (1988) *The Bonds of Love: Psychoanalysis, Feminism, and the Problem of Domination*, New York: Pantheon.

Binswanger, L. (1993) *Grundformen und Erkenntnis Menschlichen Daseins*, Heidelberg: Asanger.

Bromberg, P. (1998) *Standing in the Spaces: Essays on Clinical Process, Trauma, and Dissociation*, Hillsdale, NJ: Analytic Press.

Burston, D. and Frie, R. (2006) *Psychotherapy as a Human Science*, Pittsburgh, PA: Duquesne University Press.

Castoriadis, C. (1989) 'The state of the subject today', *Thesis Eleven*, 24: 5–43.

—— (1997) *World in Fragments: Writings on Politics, Society, Psychoanalysis, and the Imagination*, Stanford, CA: Stanford University Press.

Deleuze, G. and Guattari, F. (2004) *Anti-Oedipus: Capitalism and Schizophrenia*, New York: Continuum.

Eagleton, T. (1991) *Ideology: An Introduction*, London: Verso.

—— (1996) *The Illusions of Postmodernism*, Oxford: Blackwell.

Fiscalini, J. (2004) *Coparticipant Psychoanalysis: Toward a New Theory of Clinical Inquiry*, New York: Columbia University Press.

Freud, S. (1900) *The Interpretation of Dreams*, in *The Standard Edition of the Complete Psychological Works of Sigmund Freud*, 4–5, London: Vintage, 2001.

—— (1917) 'A difficulty in the path of psychoanalysis', in *Standard Edition*, 17: 137–144, London: Vintage, 2001.

—— (1919) 'Lines of advance in psycho-analytic therapy', in *Standard Edition*, 17: 159–168, London: Vintage, 2001.

—— (1923) 'The ego and the id', in *Standard Edition*, 19, London: Vintage, 2001.

Frie, R. (1997) *Subjectivity and Intersubjectivity in Modern Philosophy and Psychoanalysis*, Lanham, MD: Rowman & Littlefield.
—— (2003) 'Between Modernism and Postmodernism', in R. Frie (ed.) *Understanding Experience: Psychotherapy and Postmodernism*, London: Routledge.
—— (2008) 'The situated nature of psychological agency', in R. Frie (ed.) *Psychological Agency: Theory, Practice and Culture*, Cambridge, MA: MIT Press.
Gadamer, H.-G. (1994) 'Foreword', in J. Grodin, *Introduction to Philosophical Hermeneutics*, New Haven, CT: Yale University Press.
Giddens, A. (1984) *The Constitution of Society*, Berkeley, CA: University of California Press.
—— (1991) *Modernity and Self-Identity*, Stanford, CA: Stanford University Press.
Glass, J. (1993) *Shattered Selves: Multiple Personality in a Postmodern World*, Ithaca, NY: Cornell University Press.
Habermas, J. (1987) *The Philosophical Discourse of Modernity: Twelve Lectures*, trans. F. Lawrence, Cambridge, MA: MIT Press.
Heidegger, M. (1996) *Being and Time*, Albany, NY: State University of New York Press.
Hoffman, I. Z. (1991) 'Discussion: toward a social-constructivist view of the psychoanalytic situation', *Psychoanalytic Dialogues*, 2: 287–304.
—— (1998) *Ritual and Spontaneity in the Psychoanalytic Process: A Dialectical-Constructivist View*, Hillsdale, NJ: Analytic Press.
—— (2000) 'At death's door: therapists and patients as agents', *Psychoanalytic Dialogues*, 10: 823–846.
Kearney, R. (1988) *The Wake of Imagination*, London: Routledge.
Lacan, J. (1977) *Ecrits*, New York: Norton.
Levenson, E. (1972) *The Fallacy of Understanding: An Inquiry into the Changing Structure of Psychoanalysis*, New York: Basic Books.
Marcuse, E. (1955) *Eros and Civilization: A Philosophical Inquiry into Freud*, New York: Beacon.
Martin, J., Sugarman, J. and Thompson, J. (2003) *Psychology and the Question of Agency*, Albany, NY: State University of New York Press.
Mitchell, S. A. (1988) *Relational Concepts in Psychoanalysis*, Cambridge, MA: Harvard University Press.
—— (1993) *Hope and Dread in Psychoanalysis*, New York: Basic Books.
—— (2002) *Can Love Last? The Fate of Romance Over Time*, New York: Norton.
Moran, F. (1993) *Subject and Agency in Psychoanalysis: Who is to be Master?* New York: New York University Press.
Schafer, R. (1976) *A New Language for Psychoanalysis*, New Haven, CT: Yale University Press.
—— (1983) *The Analytic Attitude*, New York: Basic Books.
—— (1992) *Retelling a Life*, New York: Basic Books.
Stern, D. (1985) *The Interpersonal World of the Infant: A View from Psychoanalysis and Developmental Psychology*, New York: Basic Books.
Stolorow, R. and Atwood, G. (1992) *Contexts of Being: The Intersubjective Foundations of Psychological Life*, Hillsdale, NJ: Analytic Press.
Sullivan, H. S. (1950a) 'The illusion of personal individuality', in *The Fusion of Psychiatry and Social Science*, New York: Norton, 1964.

—— (1950b) *Tensions Interpersonal and International*, in H. Cantril (ed.) *Tensions that Cause War*, Urbana, IL: University of Illinois Press.

—— (1953a) *Interpersonal Theory of Psychiatry*, New York: Norton.

—— (1953b) *Conceptions of Modern Psychiatry*, New York: Norton.

Taylor, C. (1989) *Sources of the Self: The Making of the Modern Identity*, Cambridge, MA: Harvard University Press.

Chapter 8

Attitudes in psychoanalytic complexity

An alternative to postmodernism in psychoanalysis

William J. Coburn

> [I]t is the attitude of the analyst toward the patient and toward the process that is most potent in whatever that change process may be.
>
> (Estelle Shane)

The modernist search for the grand narrative may not be all that it was once cracked up to be, but neither necessarily is its more subversive, post-modernist alternative – notwithstanding its ground-breaking and crucial challenge to the presumed legitimation and legislation of knowledge: "[W]ho decides what knowledge is, and who knows what needs to be decided?" (Lyotard 1984). These questions are as essential and vitally applicable to the arena of psychotherapy and psychoanalysis as they were, and are, to the more global political and scientific culture at large. Postmodernist implications for psychotherapy and psychoanalysis, how-ever, have certainly infiltrated key psychoanalytic concepts and clinical approaches, and not necessarily for the better (Frie 2003).

Psychoanalytic complexity, as a unique, multidisciplinary paradigm in its own right, offers a compelling alternative to either the Scylla of adopting the reified, "objective" truths and realities of Cartesianism or the Charybdis of the dissolution of the self, personal agency, emotional responsibility, individuality, and historicity. Frie (2003) and Orange (1995, 2001) have posited persuasive alternatives to this dichotomous perspective in their elaboration and application of the existential-phenomenological tradition and *perspectival realism*, respectively.

This chapter explores an additional alternative to the either/or limitations of modernist assumptions and radical postmodernist thought – an alternative that revolutionizes ideas about development, transference, countertransference, defense, trauma, clinical epistemology, and especially therapeutic action. In particular, it underscores past and present self-organizing activity (as opposed to moment-by-moment interpretive construction) and highlights the role of emergent *attitudes* that naturally flow from a psychoanalytic complexity sensibility. These attitudes bear upon the trajectory of the therapeutic relationship in important ways. It eschews the more radical relativism and deconstructionism found in postmodernism in favor of the more moderate "post-structuralism" of which Cilliers (1998) writes in his descriptions of complexity. Whereas the approaches of Derrida and Lyotard, for instance, "acknowledge that it is not possible to tell a single and exclusive story about something that is really complex . . . the acknowledgement of complexity, however, certainly does not lead to the conclusion that anything goes" (Cilliers 1998: viii) or that everything is left up to social construction (Hacking 1999). Whereas emotional experience and meaning are not pictured as rule-driven, static, or hard-wired, they also are *not* envisioned as solely the result of interpretive activity and moment-by-moment construction by the analytic dyad. Instead they are more profitably understood as emergent and patterned (or "soft-assembled") through the cooperation of all the constituents of a relational system, past, present, and imagined future. The therapeutic advantage of such a sensibility lies not in any technical prescriptions or developmental expectations, but through the therapist's essential attitudes and presuppositions about the patient, the therapeutic relationship, how systems work, what it means to be human, how we are unremittingly situated contextually, and how we arrive at truths. Especially salient in this chapter is the exploration of the role of the convergence of thinking and working clinically on three essential levels of discourse – the phenomenological, the interpretive, and the metaphysical – as well as the role of personal situatedness, emotional responsibility, and potential freedom. These themes are taken up at length below. First, let us turn to the ideas of complexity and complex systems.

Complexity and complex systems

Drawing from the work of complexity theorists from a variety of disciplines,[1] I previously described and elaborated the nature of complexity and complex systems (Coburn 2007). This interdisciplinary and multidisciplinary paradigm, invented by no one in particular, provides psychoanalysis with a rich, explanatory framework with which to investigate and understand experiential worlds and their corresponding meanings. It conveys a strong respect for the complexity of human experiencing and its high degree of context-dependency, context-sensitivity, and historicity. It is interested in the self-organization of the constituents of any relational system and presumes that what emerges from such systems is not pre-designed or rule-driven but is fluid, unpredictable, irreducible, and dynamic. Psychoanalytic complexity rejects the notion that emotional experience is reducible to individual "intrapsychic" life, to biological drives, to internalized self and object representations, or even to the here-and-now interpretive activity of the analytic participants alone. It offers us the means of expanding our awareness and understanding of the larger relational contexts responsible for the truths at which we eventually arrive.

At the base of complexity theory lies a substantial alteration in our more familiar world-views, one that invariably challenges many of our customary presumptions about truth, reality, the therapeutic relationship, and, more broadly, the origins of emotional experience and emotional meaning. Henri Atlan once commented that "[r]andomeness is a kind of order, if it can be made meaningful; the task of making meaning out of randomness is what self-organization is all about" (Atlan 1984: 110). And I would add: the task of making meaning out of apparent randomness *or* out of too much order is much of what psychoanalysis is all about. A complexity sensibility is concerned with the emergence and patterning of emotional experience from the self-organization and cooperation of many parts and with the conditions necessary to produce adaptive change.

Briefly, let's look at the nature of a complex adaptive system with which the characteristic complexity is often associated. The essential characteristics of such a system include the presence of a large number of elements that interact in a dynamic fashion, which interaction does not have to be physical but does require the ongoing transference of information from one constituent to another. System interactions need to be rich, which means that any element of the system influences and is influenced by many others. Interactions are also nonlinear, which insures that small changes can have large results, and vice versa. Moreover, complex systems share the quality of recurrency, that is, the "effect of any activity can feed back onto itself, sometimes directly, sometimes after a number of intervening stages" (Cilliers 1998: 4).

Complex systems are also understood to be open, in the sense described by Thelen and Smith (1994); this enables them to interact with their environment. As Cilliers states, "Instead of being a characteristic of the [complex] system itself, the scope of the system is usually determined by the purpose of the description of the system, and is thus often influenced by the position of the observer" (Cilliers 1998: 4). The process of framing, then, is a way of defining specific systems as either a system, subsystem, or suprasystem; any element can be considered a system in its own right, as can any system be understood as an element, depending upon the observer's perspective. Complex systems operate under conditions far from equilibrium; in the context of human life, "equilibrium is another word for death" (Cilliers 1998: 4). And importantly, a complex system has a history: Cilliers states, "Not only do they evolve through time, but their past is co-responsible for their present behavior" (Cilliers 1998: 4). This speaks to the limitations of naive constructivist perspectives in which psychological phenomena arising between two people, along with their corresponding interpretations, are believed to have been "constructed" in the moment, quite apart and somehow insulated from both individuals' relational histories.

Finally, the nature of a complex system is such that

> Each element in the system is ignorant of the behavior of the system as a whole, it responds only to information that is available to it locally . . .
> If each element "knew" what was happening to the system as a whole, all of the complexity would have to be present in that element.
>
> (Cilliers 1998: 4–5)

For Cilliers, the notion of each element "knowing" the status of the system as a whole constitutes either a "physical impossibility" or a leap to metaphysical descriptions.

A complexity sensibility compellingly dissuades us from thinking of our world, including our experiential worlds, as containing disparate, unrelated parts (that is, if we are speaking explanatorily). At the same time, it underscores that our experiential worlds often do not necessarily reflect, in a one-to-one, palpably felt correspondence fashion, the originary and contemporary sources of those worlds and the meanings we attribute to them. Whereas it posits a world-view fundamentally incompatible with presumptions we may have had about separateness of self and other, personal agency, free will, the individuality of personal minds, the solid, static nature of truth, emotional development as epigenetic and teleological, or the rule-based and design-based nature of the universe, nevertheless complexity does not preclude the possibility of *experiencing* our selves and the world in a myriad of ways (that is, if we are speaking *phenomenologically*), including feeling radically separate, disengaged, estranged, or even nonexistent (Atwood et al. 2003). It is our attitude about and the tension engendered by the ubiquitous discrepancy between these three levels of discourse – the phenomenological, the interpretive (discussed below), and the explanatory – that is heavily implicated in how we work clinically and in what, ultimately, proves to be mutative for our patients. This attitude offers a useful alternative to the decontextualizing impact of constructivist approaches whose clinical narratives may remain too fluid and ultimately indeterminate.

Attitudes and therapeutic action

Much has been written in psychoanalysis about explicit attitudes with which one should approach the clinical setting. Schafer's (1983) work is but one example of the attention paid to explicit recommendations about essential attitudes in the psychoanalytic endeavor. Of course Freud (1912, 1913) before him had elaborated similar objectivist/observer attitudes that were to guide the analyst, which included neutrality, anonymity, abstinence, and discipline. More contemporarily, Lichtenberg et al. (1996) outlined ten guidelines describing how the analyst should approach the clinical setting, reflecting a notable instance of the conscious use and advantage of adopting certain attitudes. Aron (1996), in cautioning us about the attitude with which the analyst's self-disclosure is conveyed – an authoritative final word on the truth of something about the analyst, or the offer of a provisional, "to the best of my knowledge" opinion – demonstrated awareness of an essential ingredient that runs throughout all human relating: the inevitability of any word, action, even an "implicit relational knowing" (D. N. Stern et al. 1998: 905), being accompanied by an *attitude*. Also, recall that Ferenczi (1928), in discussing empathy, actually identified two related processes: *Einfühlung* and *Abschätzung*, meaning empathy and assessment. *Empathy* here refers to the registering in one individual of the feelings of another. *Assessment* refers to the formulation and appraisal of that feeling state, which appraisal is ultimately conveyed to the other in the form of an implicit attitude. Any theoretical perspective, however well intentioned and aimed at objectivity, neutrality, fairness, or benevolent curiosity it may have been, has always arrived with implicit (and not necessarily intended) attitudes that, in and of themselves, determine much of what happens relationally, much of our arrived-at truths. For instance, Freud's contention that each clinician should arrive at the consultation room prepared as a skilled, objective, dispassionate surgeon (Freud 1912, 1913), ready to discern and reveal the unconscious of the other, was accompanied by an underlying *attitude* that it *was indeed possible* to situate oneself in that manner, to *be* that *objective* and *neutral*. We can well imagine the potential ramifications of an attitude that abjures, however cautiously, the likelihood of our subjectivities having a substantial impact on our patients, in contrast to one that assumes it outright. It is the latter, more implicit form of attitude – that is, one that *accompanies* a theoretical perspective and is not explicitly recommended in the spirit of technical prescription – with which this chapter is concerned and in which we find instances of the impact of one's subjectivity as it is intertwined with one's theories.

Examining and appreciating the impact of an individual's subjectivity on the relational surround is not new. Intersubjective systems theory (Atwood and Stolorow 1979), for instance, originally emerged, in part, from an appreciation for the role of the highly individualized, context-specific, and context-dependent nature of a theorist's subjectivity in the formation of his or her approach to the clinical surround. And it is not surprising that elements of continental philosophy – Gadamer (1975) for instance – informed aspects of intersubjective systems theory and other contextualism-based sensibilities (Orange 1995). As Orange points out, not only does Gadamer's concept of *prejudice* beautifully illustrate the inevitability of human beings being situated in a perspective, or an *attitude*, but it also underscores that this prejudice actually provides pathways to – as opposed to obfuscating – the understandings at which we arrive over time. Thus we witness one among many perspectives that not only acknowledges the quintessentially subjective nature of human perceiving and experiencing but that underscores the way in which it provides the very conduit for deepening our understanding of our selves and others.

It is evident and by now well documented that a psychoanalytic complexity sensibility offers a detailed and powerful explanatory framework for hypothesizing about the emergence of emotional experience and the meaning-making process, but we are, of course, interested in how ideas about complexity influence how we relate and interact with our patients and in what way therapeutic action might derive from such a sensibility. Given that specific, personal attitudes accompany any theoretical persuasion, therapists naturally want to understand and account for – not *control* for – the impact these attitudes have on the patient and on the clinical surround in general. In what follows, I briefly delineate some of the essential attitudes or organizing themes that coalesce in a complexity-informed treatment and that inform aspects of the trajectory of the analytic relationship. I then focus on two of these attitudes in particular that are especially interrelated and substantially implicated in therapeutic action. Appreciating the influence of these attitudes highlights the contrast between them and the more radical constructivist sensibilities that "maintain that there are no truths about the (patient's) mind to be discovered and no self-knowledge to be gained" (Eagle 2003). Instead they help expand an individual's sense of his or her life truths and realities by *contextualizing* and *situating* their experiences across broader historical and present-day contexts.

A psychoanalytic complexity sensibility presumes individual, inescapable, context-embedded *prejudices* and the impossibility of even temporary disembeddedness (Coburn 1999) from such personal situatedness. There are no "time-outs" from embodying our necessarily delimited experiential horizons. Also, it is assumed that the multiple sources of our experiential world and the meanings we attribute to it are always active. We are continually informed by our history, our current state of mind, and our current environment, just as we are perpetually shaped by our past, our present, and our imagined future (Loewald 1972; D. N. Stern 2004). And at no time can the lines be clearly delineated among these essential sources of our experiential worlds.

An additional attitude – that of valuing the concept of *autocatalysm* (the process of a system's generating its own agent of change) – includes assuming the advantage of courting surprise and of accepting the inevitability of being startled in the midst of an analytic relationship. This attitude acknowledges that novelty can emerge at any moment, and it is left to us to determine the usefulness and meaning of what does emerge. And further, what might emerge at any moment is understood as a product and property of the highly contextualized, dialogic exchange in analysis – what Winnicott (1971) so beautifully underscored in his conceptualization of play between people. What does emerge is always a property and product of the larger system of which each of us is a part.

Furthermore, attitudinally we value complexity itself, in the *phenomen-ological* sense of the term. That is, we value attending to how the system feels, whether it feels too ordered, predictable, familiar, or repetitive, or whether it feels too random, unpredictable, or unstable. We value learning to detect when the system is poised more toward the center of the orderliness/randomness spectrum, and we appreciate reflecting on the contexts that allow for this to happen.

Another attitude that emanates from a complexity perspective is *fallibil-ism*, which concept Orange (1995) has taken up in great detail. We embody a sense of emotional conviction about our arrived at truths but simul-taneously attempt to hold such truths lightly, leaving room for a change in or expansion of those truths in the next moment, the next day, or the next year. This attitude articulates with that of *incompressibility* – another means of defining *complexity*. Human experiencing and meaning-making are irreducible or *incompressible* and can be witnessed only as a function of time as one's experiential world unfolds, *over time.* Analytic exploration and meaning-making are not a process of unpacking an individual's intrapsychic or "internal" world with the aim at arriving at static truth. They are also not a process of negating the presence of individual minds and falling prey to the analyst's interpretive activity alone. What is emerging is changing, and the change process then informs what emerges next. As complexity theorists are wont to say, *the rules of the game change as a result of the play.*

An additional and essential attitude pertains to an unremitting respect for the complexity of human experience and the meanings we may attribute to it. This includes a sense of compassion (Orange 2006) toward the peculiarities and idiosyncrasies of each of our emotional worlds and an appreciation for how an individual is uniquely situated in the world at a given moment. This is a valuable expansion of our continuing attempts to leave behind the more traditional veridicality/distortion dichotomy (Gill 1984) as we listen to an individual's narrative. This also highlights and cautions us about our natural propensity to slide into truth and reality assessments at the expense of relentlessly attending to emotional meaning – the sine qua non of the analytic endeavor.

As we can extrapolate from the descriptions of complexity in the previous section, a striking characteristic of complex systems, especially when applied to the domain of human experiencing, is the ubiquitous discrepancy between how systems *work* and how systems *feel.* That is, individual emotional life is pictured here as an emergent property of larger, inter-penetrating relational systems, of which each of us is a constituent, and not as the product of one specific component or person. Thus, whereas I may *experience* my emotional world as *mine*, it is understood explanatorily as derivative of a larger relational network. A dramatic implication of this metaphysical assumption is that, despite however much we may feel a sense of ownership and/or authorship of our own emotional lives, it is the systemic context that gives rise to and defines such life. On the one hand, then, we consequently, and ultimately, cannot claim ownership or authorship of our emotional lives, but instead we are often left with a sense of having been propelled into a specific emotional situation. This reflects an instance in which the *phenomenological* directly reflects an *explanatory* assumption. Heidegger referred to such situatedness as *Befindlichkeit* or "how-one-finds-oneself-ness" (Heidegger 1927; see also Stolorow 2007: 2). And yet, on the other hand, despite the unremitting contextuality of one's personal situatedness, one must take what one has been given and claim it to be one's own, or most certainly suffer the consequences of an attenuated existence or outright disavowal, phenomenologically speaking. Indeed what brings many of our patients to the consultation room is the anguish of finding oneself in an emotional situatedness that is felt to be either too painful to bear (e.g., traumatic states) and/or felt to be not of one's authorship or ownership (e.g., relational compliance and accommodation, see Brandchaft 2007). This reflects one of the more ironic conundrums of human emotional life – that, phenomenologically and interpretively, we must seize responsibility (i.e., this is *my* emotional life, this is how I *find* myself) for that which, explanatorily, was not of our making. This points us to the two interrelated attitudes that are coextensive with a psycho-analytic complexity sensibility and are especially implicated in our understanding of therapeutic action and therapeutic change. I refer to these attitudes as, first, *valuing the distinction among three levels of discourse: phenomenological description, interpretive understanding, and metaphysical/ explanatory assumptions*[2] and second, *valuing the conundrum of personal situatedness, emotional responsibility, and potential freedom.* These two attitudes articulate with one another in key ways – the first providing the underpinnings and foundation for the second.

In regards to the first attitude, previously I (Coburn 2002, 2007) articulated the importance of distinguishing, in contexts of theoretical discussions, two levels of discourse: the *phenomenological* and the *explanatory*. The necessity and utility of this distinction emerged in light of the fact that many essential concepts in psychoanalysis were muddled by not distinguishing clearly enough on what level of discourse one might be speaking at a given moment. Elsewhere I write that

> Psychoanalytic complexity . . . fosters an insistence on distinguishing between those [psychoanalytic terms] that refer to lived, subjective experience, on the one hand, and those that refer to theoretical explanation, on the other hand. This distinction obviates the invariable confusion that arises when the language of experience (phenomenology) and the language of theory (explanation) are conflated. The use of the term "self" provides a glaring example: viewed through a

. psychoanalytic complexity theory lens, it denotes a dimension of experience and not a theoretical explanation for such an experience.

(Coburn 2007: 6)

A closer examination of this distinction yields the necessity of refining it, which refinement includes the addition of the realm of *interpretive understanding*. Beginning with the first level of discourse, *phenomenological description* refers to a realm of discourse grounded in felt experience that can variously range across a wide spectrum of relative states of formulation. Whereas this range of states can extend to relatively vague, unformulated though nevertheless potentially accessible states of mind and mood (D. B. Stern 1997), it primarily includes those emotional experiences that are conscious and articulable, and thus, those that can be reflected upon. In this realm of discourse, speaking of "the self" would refer to one's *experience* of oneself – anxious, sad, calm, perplexed, disoriented, centered, and so forth. And it can refer to the *experience* of having *parts*,[3] or aspects of oneself from one moment or context to the next, which is generally required for the experience of conflict to obtain. In this language, referring to "this part of me" or "that part of me" references aspects of our felt experiential world and *not* the presumption of the presence of any objectified psychic parts that are sometimes presumed to be dormant and sometimes not (i.e., something akin to the Freudian dynamic unconscious).

The second level of discourse, *interpretive understanding*, pertains to organizing principles that variously and context-dependently shape an individual's experience world, including the coalescence of emotional meaning that gets associated with aspects of that experiential world. Like *phenomenological description*, this realm is both process and content organized, in that emotional themes are highly specific and, over time, identifiable, just as they are dynamic and context-driven. These themes organize and impart emotional meaning to what otherwise would be unformulated, insignificant, or inconsequential emotional impressions. *Unlike* phenomenological description, they generally are not considered as aspects of one's experiential world until arrived at and reflected upon through a dialogic relationship centered on a spirit of inquiry and interpretation. Thus when we speak of one's emotional themes, the patterning of one's historical and contemporary relationships, or of the dynamic and often implicit processes of affect regulation, we are speaking in the domain of *interpretive understanding*.

The third level of discourse, *metaphysical/explanatory assumptions*, is less content organized and more concept and process oriented. It refers to one's foundational (sometimes unconscious) assumptions about *how things work*, to one's convictions about the underpinnings and origination of emotional experience and meaning. An example would be the assumption that all human experiencing and meaning-making is inextricably embedded in a larger world context or complex system of which each of us is but a part. Another related example, following a complexity sensibility, is the assumption that such experiencing and meaning-making can never be attributed solely to one's past, to one's present, or to one's imagined future and that the proportion of these influences remains forever indeterminate. This happily subverts the more traditional obsession with determining whether a specific facet of experience is *transference* or *real*, or *history-based* or *here-and-now formulated*. Speaking on the level of metaphysical assumptions, as the term is employed here, does not address the nature of individual experience, nor the themes that organize it, but rather references the broad universal presuppositions – our convictions about the way things work – that organize the contents and processes of the previous two realms of discourse. The "philosophical unconscious" (Stolorow and Orange 2003: 518) is another term that well describes this third level of discourse.

Valuing distinguishing between these three levels of discourse not only is crucial in subverting conflation and muddle in conversations about psychoanalytic theory, but also is an essential attitudinal ingredient implicated in the emergence of therapeutic action in psychoanalysis and psychotherapy. Much of human emotional pain and strife, or alternatively, emotional and relational numbness and complacency resulting in the narrowing of one's affective horizons, is attributable to the ubiquitous, felt discrepancies between these three levels of discourse, as the clinical instance below reflects. This first attitude also provides the foundation and preconditions for the inevitability of the phenomenology of the second attitude – that of *valuing the conundrum of personal situatedness, emotional responsibility, and potential freedom*, to which I now turn.

As Heidegger (1927) extensively explored, we are *thrown* into life circumstances over which we have no control and yet in which we may find a life possibility, a potential freedom that our emotional situatedness might offer us. Heidegger referred to this as "finite freedom" (Heidegger 1927: 436). Phenomenologically speaking, I believe one's ability to grasp a life possibility that ultimately can be *one's own* (Sartre 1943) emerges partly out of an awareness of the systemic contexts that have been responsible for *determining* our situatedness to begin with. In other words, this attitude suggests that, in the absence of a situational awareness, included in which is a deepened understanding of the contextual forces (past, present, and imagined future) that conspire to situate us affectively in the very place we *find* ourselves, there cannot obtain an appreciation for the extent to which we can exercise what we think of as free will, autonomy, agency, and individuality. Experientially speaking, there can be no doubt of the veracity of such states as autonomy or agency. At the same time, the constitution of these states is entirely systemically and contextually derived. Assuming these aspects of experience outright, without a previously garnered sense of our fatedness and contextuality, leaves us blind to the forces that have conspired in determining potentially unwanted aspects of our experiential worlds (e.g., emotional convictions about loathsome defects in oneself, or painful and repetitive attributions of traumatic life circumstances to flaws in one's individual mind or psyche). Therapeutically, a broadened aware-ness of the very contexts – our history, our current state of mind, and our environment – that are implicated in determining where and how we find ourselves offers us life possibilities from which we might choose. Herein lies a resolution to, or perhaps dissolution of, dichotomies such as determinism versus autonomy/individuality, or self versus no-self.

Thus, given a complexity sensibility, and given that these two inter-twined attitudes emanate from such a sensibility and doubtless permeate a complexity-informed, analytic relationship, let us turn to a clinical instance to grasp more clearly not only the relationship between these two attitudes but also the manner in which they are implicated in therapeutic action and therapeutic change.

Clinical example

When Cindy arrived at my office on a cold and blistery January day (in Los Angeles), she slowly and tentatively unbuttoned her wool coat in a manner suggesting the unwrapping of a package whose contents were sure to be unwelcome if not toxic. An extraordinarily attractive woman of 36 years, she proceeded to speak of a five-year romantic relationship, still ongoing, the essential problems of which centered, she felt, on her excruciating inability to determine the source of her intense ambivalence and equivocation about being close to this man. Specifically, her primary preoccupation appeared to be her inability to assess whether the relationship difficulties were, essentially, *her* fault, due to her presumed personality defects, or if they were attributable to the glaring flaws that resided in the partner whom she had chosen. I commented that either perspective seemed to render her completely responsible for her relationship predicament, given that, in the event it rested with *his* being the owner of the intransigent flaws, her having chosen this man to begin with was serving as yet another, alternative confirmation of her *own* defects and perceptual disabilities. Either way, the source of her general lifelong dysfunction (i.e., anxiety, depression, substance abuse, etc.) and now her relationship woes and uncertainties resided in her mind – she was the root cause. Could I fix her or somehow cure her of her defects? Immediately I sensed an impending disjunction and the likelihood of an impasse when I suggested that perhaps there were additional factors in her history, in her environment, and in her life in general that might be contributing to her distress. At that moment, I felt one of my own attitudes or emotional convictions – that of the contextuality of all emotional experience, meanings, and corresponding organizing principles

– slamming abruptly into hers. At my suggestion, she gazed at me with incredulity and promptly corrected me about the source of her despair. It was all in *her* head. She was the owner and author of her distress and of the trail of dismembered relationships she had left in her wake. This was a foundational theme – one that we articulated and reflected upon over the course of several years – whose philosophical underpinnings rest in the realm of questions about the origination, ongoing authorship, and presumed ownership of one's experiential world.

Despite my own personal and clinical propensity toward a complexity sensibility and its attendant contextualist attitudes, my essential, conscious aim in my work with Cindy, as best as I can determine, was to investigate collaboratively the details of her *experience* of her defectiveness and her *experience* of the corresponding world that continually disappointed her and that was, more or less, presumably of her own making. And despite the overall spirit of inquiry that I believed we both imbued in our relationship and our work together, my more implicit attitudes – particularly the two under discussion here – doubtless crept into our exploratory dialogue. She of course knew that I felt differently about the authorship and ownership of her personal experience, her beliefs and emotional convictions. Space in this chapter does not allow for a thorough discussion of her own reasons – past, present, and imagined future – for adhering so tenaciously to a perspective organized around the need to take complete responsibility for her emotional life and her relationship behavior. However, themes of accommodation and compliance (Brandchaft 2007) became evident over time, themes, we discovered, in which she had been held responsible not solely for her own painful affect but for that of others as well. Over time, Cindy began to feel that perhaps she was not as utterly responsible for her sense of her self and the ways she interacted with others as she had been led to believe and that, furthermore, there were indeed forces in her life, past and present, that conspired to shape her emotional life (the phenomenological) and the organizing themes (the interpretive) underlying it. In other words, her phenomenology expanded to include the contextuality of her emotional experience. And given my attitudes about the sources of and responsibility for one's emotional life, I cannot exclude the possibility that her shift in perspective to what I think of as a more contextualist frame of mind was yet another act of accommodation on her part – this time to *me*, as opposed to the traumatogenic others in her past. This concern remains for the two of us to ponder and articulate, and indeed the freedom to do so might in and of itself stand as a distinguishing feature between a pathological accommodation (Brandchaft 2007) and a conscious, useful one. That said, Cindy and I did arrive at a reflective, conscious sense of our colliding attitudes about the origins of emotional experience and the degree to which we may or may not be responsible for it. And this was done through the lens of the two attitudes under consideration. Let's examine for a moment the interface between Cindy's initial attitudes and those derived from a psychoanalytic complexity perspective.

Initially, Cindy understood her experience of herself and her relational world as emanating *from* herself, from her defects and flaws in particular (about which she felt excruciating shame). She understandably took her felt experiences (phenomenological description) at face value, relegating them to the level of metaphysical/explanatory assumption. I *feel* responsible for my state, therefore I *am* responsible for it. Previously she had not taken into consideration the organizing themes that shaped her experience (interpretative understanding), nor had she considered the metaphysical assumptions of a complexity perspective that holds that all emotional experience, including our underlying organizing themes, is inextricably embedded in a larger context of which each of us is but a part and that such experience is always informed by one's history, one's current state of mind, and one's environment – the lines of demarcation among which are dynamic and can never be clearly drawn. I believe grasping the distinctions among these three levels of discourse – phenomenological description, interpretive understanding, and metaphysical/explanatory assumptions – and their relationship to one another proved mutative for Cindy. I also believe that her considering this perspective, over time, did not obtain via my educating or persuading her but rather through her sensing my implicit attitudes about these ideas in the context of my fundamentally attempting to explore, collaboratively, her emotional world and her emotional convictions. I think she felt that I was more interested in exploration and in establishing an emotional connection with her than I was in her adopting my complexity-informed attitudes, but of course I can never be certain about that.

The second attitude, buttressed by the first, played an essential role for Cindy as well. Initially Cindy felt that she was the author and owner of her emotional experience and of her life context in general. When things went wrong, it was her fault. She was not quagmired in the familiar "what did I do to deserve this?" or the "why do bad things always happen to me?" perspective. Reflecting a variation on the Heideggerian theme of thrownness. Cindy's sense of herself and her life was that *she* had thrown, and continued to throw, herself into a emotional situatedness in which, though felt to be entirely of her own making, she remained hopelessly and powerlessly embedded. Paradoxically, she had little sense of control or authorship over that which she felt she alone had already authored. Cindy's conundrum of accommodatively having had to assume personal responsibility for her emotional life and behavior, on the one hand, and her relentless conviction that she would forever remain powerlessly confined in that sense of responsibility, on the other hand, remained a substantial source of anguish and perplexity for her. Seemingly paradoxical, it wasn't until she began to consider that a variety of other sources (the first attitude), in addition to herself, had conspired to place her in her current emotional situatedness that she was able to begin considering what freedom, if any at all, might be garnered from the *possibilities* (Heidegger 1927; Sartre 1943) that had been given her (the second attitude). In this instance, Cindy's increased *situational awareness* of her context-embeddedness – that she is but a constituent of a larger relational system – helped facilitate an increased tendency toward thinking about possibilities that could become *her* possibilities. For Cindy, that meant in part that she could begin understanding her life (and relationship) circumstances as being not entirely of her making and thus reconsider her sense of guilt and shame for all that she previously felt she had authored on her own. Over time, we discovered that her decreased sense of guilt and shame liberated her to be more proactive in reversing many of her relationship decisions (i.e., she didn't feel as much of that sense of "well, you've made your bed, and now you have to lie in it!"). In this instance, at least for Cindy, grasping a life possibility of her own (Heidegger 1927; Sartre 1943) actually meant relinquishing a complete, overarching, and archaic sense of emotional responsibility.

Concluding remarks

In this clinical instance, like many that we clinicians encounter, a spirit of inquiry into Cindy's emotional life and its corresponding meanings inevitably led to a deepening of our understanding of the contexts – past, present, and imagined future – that were and are responsible for such life to begin with. Often this deepening entails an appreciation for the relationship between felt experience and the greater interpenetrating relational systems that give rise to it, as well as for a corresponding sense that, to a significant degree, we consequently are not the authors and owners of our personal affectivity and situatedness. In the metaphysical/explanatory sense, there is no free will, individuality, or personal agency. In the phenomenological sense, the degree to which we may *experience* free will and personal agency nevertheless always remains context-dependent. However, the idea that we are not the authors and owners of our personal affectivity and situatedness need not slide into constructivist assumptions that there are no essential truths and realities to be discovered. Instead of eliminating the concept of individual minds, for instance, from our psychoanalytic armamentarium, a psychoanalytic complexity perspective helps us contextualize those minds in broadening our understanding of the sources and origins of our emotional experience. This proves to be a useful corrective to the wide swing of the modernist/postmodernist pendulum found in deconstructionism. An acknowledgment of and appreciation for the relationship between the three different levels of discourse help subvert the endless obsession with dichotomizing modernist and postmodernist views of the self and self-narrative. Additionally, coming to appreciate our embeddedness in a larger world context for which we cannot be held responsible – but for which we ultimately must take responsibility – is an essential constituent in the potential for garnering a personal sense of freedom, of agency, and of what is true and real.

In addition to a spirit of curiosity and inquiry, complexity-informed attitudes – two in particular that have been elaborated here – are clinically instrumental in helping expand one's sense of one's unbidden personal situatedness, on the one hand, and of one's potential for developing alternate organizing principles and courageously engaging one's *finite freedom*, on the other hand.

Acknowledgements

I am deeply indebted to Robert Stolorow, Estelle Shane, Donna Orange, Roger Frie, and Nancy VanDerHeide for their invaluable input and editorial help in the preparation of this chapter.

Notes

1 Some of these theorists include Poincaré et al. (1900), Waddington (1966), Thom (1974), Lorenz (1993), Prigogine and Holte (1993), Kauffman (1995), Bak (1996), Cilliers (1998), and Taylor (2001). For an elaboration of the nature of complexity and complex systems, see Coburn (2002, 2007). For their insightful treatment of complexity in psychoanalysis, I am deeply indebted to Galatzer-Levy (1978), Sashin and Callahan (1990), Moran (1991), Varela et al. (1991), Lichtenberg et al. (1992), Spruiell (1993), Thelen and Smith (1994), Shane et al. (1997), Stolorow (1997), Miller (1999), Palombo (1999), Scharff (2000), Beebe and Lachmann (2001), Charles (2002), Ghent (2002), Magid (2002), Sander (2002), Shane and Coburn (2002), Sucharov (2002), Trop et al. (2002), Bacal and Herzog (2003), Dubois (2005), Harris (2005), Piers (2005), Seligman (2005), Thelen (2005), Bonn (2006), Orange (2006), Pickles (2006), Steinberg (2006), and Weisel-Barth (2006).
2 These particular designations were arrived at in a dialogue with Robert Stolorow; we began discussing the distinction between the levels of discourse of phenomenology and of explanation. After some discussion, it became evident that a refinement and elaboration of these distinctions were necessary; these three terms were intersubjectively derived and remain of ambiguous origin.
3 See Coburn (2007) for an elaboration of the advantage of distinguishing between levels of discourse in comparing and contrasting intersubjective systems theory and relational theory.

References

Aron, L. (1996) *A Meeting of Minds: Mutuality in Psychoanalysis*, Hillsdale, NJ: Analytic Press.
Atlan, H. (1984) 'Disorder, complexity, and meaning', in P. Livingston (ed.) *Disorder and Order*, Saratoga, CA: Anma Libri.
Atwood, G. E. and Stolorow, R. D. (1993) *Faces in a Cloud: Intersubjectivity in Personality Theory*, Northvale, NJ: Jason Aronson.

Atwood, G. E., Orange, D., and Stolorow, R. D. (2003) 'Shattered worlds/psychotic states: a post-cartesian view of the experience of personal annihilation', *Psychoanalytic Psychology*, 19: 281–306.

Bacal, H. and Herzog, B. (2003) 'Specificity theory and optimal responsiveness: an outline', *Psychoanalytic Psychology*, 20: 635–648.

Bak, P. (1996) *How Nature Works: The Science of Self-Organized Criticality*, New York: Copernicus.

Beebe, B. and Lachmann, F. M. (2001) *Infant Research and Adult Treatment: A Dyadic Systems Approach*, Hillsdale, NJ: Analytic Press.

Bonn, E. (2005) 'Turbulent contextualism: bearing complexity toward change', prepublished paper.

Brandchaft, B. (2007) 'Systems of pathological accommodation and change in analysis', *Psychoanalytic Psychology*, 24(4): 667–687.

Charles, M. (2002) *Patterns: Building Blocks of Experience*, Hillsdale, NJ: Analytic Press.

Cilliers, P. (1998) *Complexity and Postmodernism: Understanding Complex Systems*, London: Routledge.

Coburn, W. J. (1999) 'Attitudes of embeddedness and transcendence in psychoanalysis: subjectivity, self-experience and countertransference', *Journal of The American Academy of Psychoanalysis*, 27: 101–119.

—— (2002) 'A world of systems: the role of systemic patterns of experience in the therapeutic process', *Psychoanalytic Inquiry*, 22(5): 655–677.

—— (2007) 'Psychoanalytic complexity: pouring new wine directly into one's mouth', in P. Buirske and A. Kottler (eds) *New Developments in Self Psychology Practice*, Northvale, NJ: Jason Aronson.

Dubois, P. (2005) 'Perturbing a dynamic order: dynamic systems theory and clinical application', prepublished paper.

Eagle, M. (2003) 'The postmodern turn in psychoanalysis: a critique', *Psychoanalytic Psychology*, 20: 411–424.

Ferenczi, S. (1928) 'The elasticity of psycho-analytic technique', in S. Ferenczi and M. Balint (eds) *Final Contributions to the Problems and Methods of Psycho-Analysis*, New York: Brunner/Mazel.

Freud, S. (1912) 'Recommendations to physicians practising psychoanalysis', *Standard Edition*, 12: 109–120, London: Hogarth Press.

—— (1913) 'On beginning the treatment: further recommendations on the technique of psychoanalysis', *Standard Edition*, 12: 121–144, London: Hogarth Press.

Frie, R. (2003) 'Introduction: between modernism and postmodernism: rethinking psychological agency', in R. Fried (ed.) *Understanding Experience: Psychotherapy and Postmodernism*, New York: Routledge.

Gadamer, H.-G. (1975; 2nd edn 1991) *Truth and Method*, trans. J. Weinsheimer and D. Marshall, New York: Crossroads.

Galatzer-Levy, R. (1978) 'Qualitative change from quantitative change: mathematical catastrophe theory in relation to psychoanalysis', *Journal of the American Psychoanalytic Association*, 26: 921–935.

Ghent, E. (2002) 'Wish, need, drive', *Psychoanalytic Dialogues*, 12: 763–808.

Gill, M. (1984) 'Transference: a change in conception of only in emphasis?', *Psychoanalytic Inquiry*, 4: 489–523.

Hacking, I. (1999) *The Social Construction of What?*, Cambridge, MA: Harvard University Press.

Harris, A. (2005) *Gender as Soft Assembly*, Hillsdale, NJ: Analytic Press.

Heidegger, M. (1927; English trans. 1962) *Being and Time*, trans. J. Macquarrie and E. Robinson, New York: Harper & Row.

Kauffman, S. A. (1995) *At Home in the Universe: The Search for Laws of Self-organization and Complexity*, New York: Oxford University Press.

Lichtenberg, J., Lachmann, F. and Fosshage, J. (1992) *Self and Motivational Systems: Toward a Theory of Psychoanalytic Technique*, Hillsdale, NJ: Analytic Press.

—— (1996) *The Clinical Exchange: Techniques Derived from Self and Motivational Systems*, Hillsdale, NJ: Analytic Press.

Loewald, H. W. (1972) 'The experience of time', *Psychoanalytic Study of the Child*, 27: 401–410.

Lorenz, E. N. (1993) *The Essence of Chaos*, Seattle, WA: University of Washington Press.

Lyotard, J. F. (1984) *The Postmodern Condition: A Report on Knowledge*, Minneapolis, MN: University of Minnesota Press.

Magid, B. (2002) *Ordinary Mind: Exploring the Common Ground of Zen and Psychotherapy*, Boston, MA: Wisdom.

Miller, M. L. (1999) 'Chaos, complexity and psychoanalysis', *Psychoanalytic Psychology*, 16: 355–379.

Moran, M. G. (1991) 'Chaos theory and psychoanalysis: the fluidic nature of the mind', *International Review of Psycho-Analysis*, 18: 211–221.

Orange, D. M. (1995) *Emotional Understanding: Studies in Psychoanalysis*, Hillsdale, NJ: Analytic Press.

—— (2001) 'From Cartesian minds to experiential worlds in psychoanalysis', *Psychoanalytic Psychology*, 18: 287–302.

—— (2006) 'For whom the bell tolls: context, complexity, and compassion in psychoanalysis', *International Journal of Psychoanalytic Self Psychology*, 1(1): 5–22.

Palombo, S. R. (1999) *The Emergent Ego: Complexity and Coevolution in the Psychoanalytic Process*, Madison, CT: International Universities Press.

Pickles, J. (2006) 'A systems sensibility: commentary on Judith Teicholz's "Qualities of Engagement and the Analyst's Theory"', *International Journal of Psychoanalytic Self Psychology*, 1(3): 301–316.

Piers, C. (2005) 'The mind's multiplicity and continuity', *Psychoanalytic Dialogues*, 15(2): 229–254.

Poincaré, L., Guillaume, C. E. et al. (1900) *Rapports présentés au Congrès international de physique réuni à Paris en 1900 sous les auspices de la Société française de physique*, Paris: Gauthier-Villars.

Prigogine, I. and Holte, J. (1993) *Chaos: The New Science: Nobel Conference XXVI*, St Peter, MN: Gustavus Adolphus College.

Sander, L. W. (2002) 'Thinking differently', *Psychoanalytic Dialogues*, 12: 11–42.

Sartre, J.-P. (1943; English trans. 1948) *Being and Nothingness*, trans. H. Barnes, New York: Philosophical Library.

Sashin, J. I. and Callahan, J. (1990) 'A model of affect using dynamical systems', *Annual of Psychoanalysis*, 18: 213–231.

Schafer, R. (1983) *The Analytic Attitude*, New York: Basic Books.

Scharff, D. E. (2000) 'Fairbairn and the self as an organized system', *Canadian Journal of Psychoanalysis*, 8: 181–195.

Seligman, S. (2005) 'Dynamic systems theories as a metaframework for psychoanalysis', *Psychoanalytic Dialogues*, 15(2): 285–319.

Shane, E. and Coburn, W. J. (2002) 'Prologue', *Psychoanalytic Inquiry*, 22: 653–654.

Shane, M., Shane, E. and Gales, M. (1997) *Intimate Attachments: Toward a New Self Psychology*, New York: Guilford.

Spruiell, V. (1993) 'Deterministic chaos and the sciences of complexity: psychoanalysis in the midst of a general scientific revolution', *Journal of the American Psychoanalytic Association*, 41: 3–44.

Steinberg, M. C. (2006) 'Language, the medium of change: the implicit in the talking cure', prepublished paper.

Stern, Daniel N. (2004) *The Present Moment in Psychotherapy and Everyday Life*, New York: Norton.

Stern, Daniel N., Sander, L., Nahum, J., Harrison, A., Lyons-Ruth, K., Morgan, A., Bruschweilerstern, N. and Tronick, E. (1998) 'Non-interpretive mechanisms in psychoanalytic therapy: the "something more" than interpretation', *International Journal of Psychoanalysis*, 79: 903–921.

Stern, Donnel B. (1997) *Unformulated Experience: From Dissociation to Imagination in Psychoanalysis*, Hillsdale, NJ: Analytic Press.

Stolorow, R. D. (1997) 'Dynamic, dyadic, intersubjective systems: an evolving paradigm for psychoanalysis', *Psychoanalytic Psychology*, 14(3): 337–364.

—— (2007) *Trauma and Human Existence: Autobiographical, Psychoanalytic and Philosophical Reflections*, New York: Analytic Press.

Stolorow, R. D. and Orange, D. M. (2003) 'Book review of *Mistaken Identity* by L. Brothers', *Psychoanalytic Quarterly*, 72: 515–518.

Sucharov, M. (2002) 'Representation and the intrapsychic: Cartesian barriers to empathic contact', *Psychoanalytic Inquiry*, 22(5): 686–707.

Taylor, M. C. (2001) *The Moment of Complexity: Emerging Network Culture*, Chicago, IL: University of Chicago Press.

Thelen, E. (2005) 'Dynamic systems theory and the complexity of change', *Psychoanalytic Dialogues*, 15(2): 255–283.

Thelen, E. and Smith, L. B. (1994) *A Dynamic Systems Approach to the Development of Cognition and Action*, Cambridge, MA: MIT Press.

Thom, R. (1974) *Modèles mathématiques de la morphogenèse: recueil de textes sur la théorie des catastrophes et ses applications*, Paris: Union général d'éditions.

Trop, G. S., Burke, M. L. and Trop, J. L. (2002) 'Thinking dynamically in psychoanalytic theory and practice', in A. Goldberg (ed.) *Progress in Self Psychology*, Hillsdale, NJ: Analytic Press.

Varela, F. J., Thompson, E. and Rosch, E. (1991) *The Embodied Mind: Cognitive Science and Human Experience*, Cambridge, MA: MIT Press.

Waddington, C. H. (1966) *Principles of Development and Differentiation*, New York: Macmillan.

Weisel-Barth, J. (2006) 'Thinking and writing about complexity theory in the clinical setting', *International Journal of Psychoanalytic Self Psychology*, 1(4): 365–388.

Winnicott, D. W. (1971) *Playing and Reality*, London: Penguin.

Chapter 9

Identity, identification, imagination
Psychoanalysis and modern European thought after the postmodern turn

Anthony Elliott

In recent years several psychoanalytic authors working within the European tradition of contemporary critical thought have addressed anew the problem of the constitution of the human subject (see, among others, Green 1985; Castoriadis 1987, 1997; Laplanche 1987; Anzieu 1989; Kristeva 1989, 1993; in addition, for a comprehensive synthesis of these trends, see Elliott 2004). Essential to all such recastings of subjectivity is a shift away from an Oedipal-centred to a pre-Oedipal perspective, from a Lacanian-inspired theory of the linguistifaction of the subject to a post-Lacanian theory of pre-verbal, imaginary significations. Moreover, these far-reaching investigations have raised afresh the question of human creation, the question of representation and fantasy, and the question of the imaginary constitution of the socio-symbolic world. In doing so they offer alternative perspectives on the very nature of representation and repression in the structuration of social action and thus potentially contribute to a reconsideration of social theory more generally.

The essential value of such a reappraisal of the constitution of the subject for critical social theory lies in its stress on the unconscious aspects of social reproduction – that is, on the ways in which a society's structures are reproduced through a redoublement of a primary, if inaccessible, field of the subject's imaginary productions. This stress on the irreducibly creative, imaginary fabrications of the subject is particularly suggestive for social theorists seeking to grasp the potential reach of contemporary recursive theories of the structured features of human action – without which there could be no reflexivity in personal life and thus no recursivity in society (see, for example, Bourdieu 1977; Giddens 1984, 1990). In today's recursive theories, structured features of action are conceptualized as unregulated but regular with reference to more preconscious than conscious dispositions. In conceptualizing the mysteries of such recursive dispositions, however, most theorists make recourse only to limited notions of the unconscious (as, say, a reservoir of memory traces) or to pre-psychoanalytic understandings of tacit assumptions or shared dispositions. By contrast, what post-Lacanian perspectives indicate must be grasped is not how dispositions or memory traces are pressed into structured action with reference to preconscious or even unconscious figurations, but rather how structured action is structured at each and every moment with reference to primitive identificatory processes, pre-verbal sensory experience of others and objects, as well as the ongoing impact of a primary protorepresentation or instituting fantasy. For a critical social theory that addressed recursive dispositions in this way would provide a framework within which other concerns, such as the imaginary constitution of bodily and sensory experience, could be recast.

This chapter seeks to address and critique some of the claims of post-Lacanian conceptualizations of the human subject. I shall do so by focusing in particular on the recent psychoanalytic departures of Julia Kristeva and Jean Laplanche on the status of primary repression as a condition for the constitution of the subject. The chapter goes on to suggest ways in which the analyses set out by Kristeva and Laplanche can be further refined and developed, partly through a reconsideration of the intertwining of unconscious representation and repression as developed in the writings of Cornelius Castoriadis, Thomas Ogden and others. The final sections of the chapter are reconstructive and innovative in character. For existing psychoanalytical accounts I suggest we should substitute the concept of *rolling identification*, the psychical basis of the shift from self-referential representational activity to an elementary form of intersubjectivity. Rolling identifications are defined as a representational flux that permits human subjects to create a relation to the self-as-object and pre-object relations. Such primal identification, it is suggested, operates through a *representational wrapping of self and others*. The chapter concludes with a consideration of the significance of primary repression, and the politicization of identification.

Freud on the unconscious, representation and repression

In classical Freudian theory, the creation of the human subject occurs in and through repression. Primary repression, Freud wrote, "consists in the psychical (ideational) representative of the drive being denied entrance into the conscious" (1915: 148). The outcome of primary repression, which arises from the non-satisfaction of infantile needs, is the bonding or fixing of drives to representations. But Freud stops short of spelling out the precise implications of primary repression for the structuration of subjectivity. Instead, his own theoretical and clinical accounts of the development of subjectivity centre upon the concept of secondary repression, or "repression proper", as formulated in the Oedipus and castration complexes. In Freud's scheme, it is the paternal breakup of the imaginary child–mother dyad which initiates "repression proper", and constitutes the development of identity and culture.

However, Freud's construction of Oedipal repression as constitutive of identity obscures as much as it illuminates. The view that the small infant (re)presents or discovers *itself* through Oedipal identifications implies that subjectivity is a given, and not a phenomenon to be explicated. The inconsistency here is that the infant surely cannot identify with Oedipal presentations unless it already has a more rudimentary sense of subjectivity. Moreover, it seems that this problem is only compounded if we reverse the logic in operation here, as Lacan does, and trace the imaginary ego as modelling and misrecognizing itself in specular images. For, as various commentators have noted (Castoriadis 1987; Elliott 1999), the specular relation is constituted as a *relation* only to the extent that it is shaped by psychic space itself. And in Lacan's account, this (mis)copying is linked to further alienation through the constitution of the subject via a phallocentrically organized structure of language and culture.

By contrast, the psychoanalytic direction of contemporary theory involves a renewed emphasis upon primary repression and identification. Kristeva (1987, 1989) and Laplanche (1987) provide detailed treatments of the topic. Here it is suggested that the dynamics of primary repression and identification involve an elementary gap between self and other, a gap which is the very condition for the arising of the subject. Primary repression is thus not merely a preparatory step for the constitution of Oedipal identity. Rather, primary repression is considered as elementary to the establishment of subjectivity itself. In what follows, I shall critically examine some of the central theoretical issues on primary repression as discussed by Kristeva and Laplanche. Following this, I shall attempt to sketch an alternative account of primary repression as linked to the dynamics of subjectivity and intersubjectivity.

Primary repression and the loss of the thing: Kristeva's exploration of the imaginary father

For several decades, Kristeva has focused on recasting the relations between subjectivity and society in a series of works situated at the intersection of psychoanalysis, feminism and modern European thought, including *Tales of Love* (1987), *In the Beginning was Love* (1988), *Strangers to Ourselves* (1991), and *New Maladies of the Soul* (1993). Her work blends linguistic and psychoanalytical theory to advance a novel account of how pre-verbal experience – maternal, infantile, poetic – enters into, shapes, distorts and disrupts language through processes of art, literature and psychoanalysis. The result has been a radical opening of the intersections between psychoanalysis and critical social theory, which in turn has provided a transformative political and feminist dimension to Freudian thought and an enhanced psychoanalytical dimension to critical social theory.

Kristeva's various discussions of the constitution of repressed desire demonstrate a persistent concern with human imagination and the creativity of action. In order to adequately grasp Kristeva's contribution to the development of a theory of the human subject, it is necessary now to situate her work in the context of Lacan's "return to Freud". Having undertaken her psychoanalytic training with Lacan, it is perhaps not surprising that Kristeva's early writings should emphasize the ordering power of the Symbolic, of language as such. In Lacan's rewriting of Freud, the human subject comes to language, and adopts a position of speaker, from a devastating primordial loss. The pain of this loss leads to a repression that at once buries memories of fulfilment experienced through contact with the phallic mother on the one hand, and catapults the subject-to-be into a Symbolic order of individuation, differentiation and cultural signification on the other. In her early work Kristeva accepts these basic tenets of Lacanian theory, but she contrasts Lacan's account of the Symbolic order with a revaluation of the persistence and force of repressed libidinal desires, somatic dispositions and affects – a kind of unconscious rhythm that Kristeva terms "the semiotic". Prose and poetry are symbolic forms that Kristeva has psychoanalytically deconstructed to try to capture something of "the semiotic" or "maternal body" that remains truly inexpressible. She finds in acts of artistic expression that press language to its limits – that is, in the ruins of the symbolic – a zone, by definition incommunicable, in which desire bursts forth. Is this zone a set of organized subjective meanings, a language, or is it prelinguistic, and hence indescribable? Not so much prelinguisitic according to Kristeva, as an expression of the prolinguistic: affects, bodily dispositions, silences, rhythms.

In her recent work, Kristeva has become especially interested in Kleinian psychoanalysis, or more specifically Klein's elaboration of Freud's theory of representation or the proto-fantasy. A close reading of Klein, argues Kristeva, demonstrates that the child, from the very beginning of life, is consumed with anxiety:

> No matter how far back Klein reaches into childhood, she always discovers a fantasizing ego. A sundry entity made up of verbal and non-verbal representations, sensations, affects, emotions, movements, actions and even concretizations, the Kleinian phantasy is a wholly impure theoretical construct that defies the purists as much as it fascinates clinicians, particularly those who specialize in children, psychosis, or the psychosomatic disorders.
>
> (Kristeva (2001: 137)

Moreover, the fantasy-like omnipotent construction of the primary object – the breast – is first and foremost a construction from within, that is, of unstable representational distinctions between *inside* and *outside*, between *inner* and *outer*. "From the outset", writes Kristeva (2001: 63), "the primal object of the paranoid-schizoid position emerges, in Klein's view, if and only if it is an *internal object* constructed through a fantasy of omnipotence". As Kristeva notes, rightly in my view, Klein's notion of the internal object is entirely distinct from Lacan's order of the imaginary, for Lacan primarily stressed the visual side of fantasy. Lacan's account of spectral distortion – that narcissism is constituted through the intermediary of the object as a function of the subject's absorption in a reflecting surface – underscores the role of the scopic function in the structuration of the ego and the object. Yet what of transverbal representations, affects, emotions, sensations? Here – and make no mistake about it – Kristeva, a "post-Lacanian", speaks up for Klein's understanding of the internal object, primarily since the Kleinian approach offers a fruitful conceptual map for grasping heterogeneous psychic representations that are altogether missing in Lacan's "return to Freud".

As with her previous work, especially *Tales of Love*, *Black Sun*, and *New Maladies*, Kristeva repositions Klein's clinical and conceptual approach to ask: what is psychic representation? Here Kristeva applauds Klein for uncovering *diverse domains of representation* – not only verbal or symbolic representations, but also affects, sensations, gestures, and even "concretizations" to which fantasies are sometimes reduced in psychotic suffering. In Klein's theory, says Kristeva, the centrality of wish and fantasy to human subjectivity is borne of sensation and affect. The movement of the Kleinian investigation, rooted in clinical experience with children and which contributes significantly to our understanding of both psychosis and autism, is fundamental for grasping the richness and multilayered creativity of the psyche. In exploring the transverbal archaic realm, a realm that belies visual representation, Klein went beyond the "secondary imagination" which runs throughout the whole tradition of Western thought to the primary fantasy or constitutive imagination. Kristeva makes an interesting case for the contemporary relevance of Klein's hypothesis of a proto-fantasy, or the instituting fantasy. The correctness of Klein's psychoanalytic theory is confirmed, she argues, by more recent studies that portray the psyche, lodged between anxiety and language, in the form of "pre-narrative envelopes" (Daniel Stern), "nameless dreads" (Wilfred Bion) and "life narcissisms" (André Green). Such a focus on the psychic representative prior to representation also connects strongly with Kristeva's own theoretical account of semiotic articulations, defined as a heterogeneous play of unconscious forces – of drives and desires – which exert a pulsional pressure within language itself, and which may be discerned in the rhythm, tone and disruption of speech.

This brings us to an important aspect of Kristeva's interpretation of Freud, an aspect I want to concentrate on in some detail. In her recent writing, Kristeva connects the constitution of subjectivity to the imaginary tribulations of the pre-Oedipal phase rather than to the Oedipal symbolic process alone. According to Kristeva, the primary identifications of narcissism already represent an advancement over the affective, representational flux of auto-eroticism. She describes primary identification as the "zero degree" that shapes psychic space itself, and links this arising of the subject to Freud's notion of a "father in individual prehistory". In this "prehistory", the child forges an initial identification, prior to sexual division, with a maternal-paternal container. As Kristeva explains this *pre-Oedipal* identification:

> Freud has described the One with whom I fulfil the identification (this "most primitive aspect of affective binding to an object") as a Father. Although he did not elaborate what he meant by "primary identification", he made it clear that this father is a "father in individual prehistory" . . . Identification with that "father in prehistory", that Imaginary Father, is called "immediate", "direct", and Freud emphasizes again, "previous to any concentration on any object whatsoever . . . The whole symbolic matrix sheltering emptiness is thus set in place in an elaboration that precedes the Oedipus complex".
> (Kristeva 1987: 267)

And again, on the sexual indistinction of primary identification:

> The archaeology of such an identifying possibility with an other is provided by the huge place taken up within narcissistic structure by the vortex of primary identification with what Freud called a "father of personal prehistory". Endowed with the sexual attributes of both parents, and by that very token a totalizing, phallic figure, it provides satisfactions that are already psychic and not simply immediate, existential requests; that archaic vortex of idealization is immediately an other who gives rise to a powerful, already psychic transference of the previous semiotic body in the process of becoming a narcissistic Ego.
> (Kristeva 1987: 33)

Note here that the reference to an *other* ties the emergence of identity to the intersubjective field. Note too that this identification with the imaginary father (which is less a partial object than a pre-object) *constitutes* primary repression; it "bends the drive toward the symbolic of the other" (Kristeva 1987: 31).

Kristeva argues that primary identification arises, not from the child's desire for the pre-Oedipal mother, but from an affective tie with the *mother's desire for the phallus*. Echoing Lacan, she contends that the child comes to realize that the mother herself is lacking, incomplete. In this connection, the child encounters the desire of the other: that the mother's desire is invested elsewhere, in the imaginary phallus. For Kristeva, identification with the imaginary father functions as support for the loss of the maternal object, and provides an imaginary lining to subjectivity which guards against depression and melancholia. Yet, because the investment in this imaginary father comes from the inside, the emergence of identity is itself a precarious, fragile process.

Enigmatic messages: Laplanche

Like Kristeva, Laplanche is also concerned with reconceptualizing the conditions of primal identification and repression, with the purpose of mapping the inaccessible, unconscious significations between the individual subject and the intersubjective realm. Laplanche suggests that an elementary form of subjectivity is constituted when the small infant enters into an identification with certain "enigmatic signifiers" in the pre-Oedipal phase, a phase which initiates the binding of unconscious drives through primal repression. Though highly technical in formulation, what Laplanche means by the notion of enigmatic signifier, roughly speaking, is the uncanny decentring influence of the Other upon our psychical life. This process of decentring, says Laplanche, occurs at the crossroads of language, body and desire – wherever another's "message" (Laplanche's term) implants itself as a perplexing question or foreign body in the human subject's psyche. Subjectively speaking, the role of enigmatic signifiers is one always at work in the emotional life of the subject, and yet the sort of specific enigmas or perplexing messages that tend to dominate a person's experience of self derive, by and large, from childhood. According to Laplanche, enigmatic messages conveyed by parents (at first by the mother) are especially consequential for the development of subjectivity since such implantations arise prior to the establishment proper of the signifying character of the symbolic order.

If the enigmatic message is integral to the psychic origins of the unconscious, it is equally central to human subjectivity itself, so that Laplanche is able to develop a neo-Lacanian critique of the trajectory of both psychosexuality and identity. He outlines the foundational force of an opaque, impossibly paradoxical Otherness – the result of intrusive and exciting adult enigmas – so that the human subject can never get to the heart of family secrets or sexual researches but must live nevertheless with these enigmas through the continual emotional work of translation, reconstruction and binding. In any case, this is so since adult messages always-already outstrip the small infant's capacity for emotional processing and affective response. Laplanche calls this the "fundamental anthropological situation" of humans, the fact that the infant wouldn't survive without the care and nurturance provided by the adult, a situation that locates the infant as struggling to comprehend the adult's expressions of feeling, gestures of care and conveyances of relatedness. For try as the infant might to comprehend elements of the adult's communication – attempting a kind of "proto-understanding" through the primitive translation and binding of adult enigmas – there is always a left-over or residue, which for Laplanche constitutes the unconscious and primal repressions.

More than merely perplexing, however, enigmatic messages are completely mysterious. For the enigmatic message is itself, in an uncanny sort of way, always scrambled, overloaded with signification, impenetrable. Laplanche's account of all this might perhaps be likened to the sense of strangeness an adult might feel when, having entered a room, he or she discovered people talking a highly specialized language, like the jargon of nuclear physics, nanotechnology or deconstruction. For Laplanche, messages are enigmatic because they are compromised by the repressed unconscious lodged inside us: a contradictory condensation of unconscious desires invades the enigmatic signifiers, such that the adult does not know what it wants of the infant in any case. This is a version of the classic psychoanalytic doctrine that the small infant's unconscious is formed with reference to the parental unconscious.

Laplanche's favourite stage of infant development appears to lie with the earliest transactions between mother and child, the pre-Oedipal realm where floating needs and appetites meet with scrambled and mysterious adult messages, which he uses to illustrate the paradox of primal seduction. Returning the Freud's discussion of maternal care and devotion as central to the origins of the infant's psychic life, Laplanche argues that the breast is a carrier of maternal fantasy which transmits opaque sexual significations within the mother–child relation. The child, says Laplanche, receives a sexually distorted, overloaded message from mother, a message which the child is emotionally unable to process or translate.

Primary repression rethought: rolling identifications and representational wrappings of self and other

There is, I believe, much that is of interest in Kristeva and Laplanche on the constitution of the unconscious through primary repression. Both Kristeva and Laplanche, in differing theoretical ways, underline the importance of primary repression as the support for the arising of an elementary form of subjectivity, which is subsequently secured through the Oedipus and castration complexes. However, there are also serious theoretical difficulties arising from their work. Kristeva has been much criticized, in both psychoanalytic and feminist circles, for linking the moment of identification with the imaginary father. For feminists such as Cornell (1991: 68–71), this has the effect of reinscribing gender stereotypes within the pre-Oedipal phase, resulting in a denial of woman's imaginary. Cornell's critique of Kristeva interestingly stresses that it is from a reading of the desire of desire, the desire of the Other, that primary identification arises and grants the subject's assent to identity in the symbolic order. From a feminist angle, Cornell is especially attuned to the abjection of the mother that this moment of identification involves, though she is also to some degree aware of the positioning of desire as an external, impersonal force (the desire of desire) rather than as emanating from the child's desire *for* the mother. From a related but distinct perspective, Laplanche's work has also been criticized for its neglect of the more creative dimensions of sexual subjectivity. As Jacqueline Rose has pointed out, Laplanche's reinterpretation of primary repression means that the "child receives everything from the outside", desire being inscribed within the repressed unconscious via the deformations of parental sexuality itself (Fletcher and Stanton 1992: 61). In my view, these criticisms are indeed valid. The standpoints of Kristeva and Laplanche are flawed in respect of the power accorded to the other (imaginary father/seduction) over psychic interiority, or the outside as constitutive of desire itself. By contrast, I suggest that we must develop a psychoanalytic account of subjectivity and intersubjectivity which breaks with this inside/outside boundary.

For these accounts I suggest we should substitute the delineation of an elementary dimension of subjectivity formed in and through primary intersubjectivity – a mode dependent upon the fixation of primal repression and identification. In the constitution of primary intersubjectivity, the small infant actively enters into the push-and-pull of object – or, more accurately, pre-object – relations. This is less a phenomenon of the other "breaking in" from the outside than one of ordering psychic interiority within intersubjective boundaries of shared, unconscious experience. The organizing of shared, unconscious experience occurs through a process that I call *rolling identification*. Derived from the representational flux of the unconscious, rolling identifications provide for the insertion of subjectivity into a complex interplay between self-as-object and pre-object relations. Rolling identifications literally spill out across libidinal space, with representational flux passing into objects, and objects into psychical life, in a ceaseless exchange. Here the rudimentary beginnings of pre-self experience arises from factors such as sensory impressions of autistic shapes and objects (Tustin 1980, 1984; Ogden 1989), which form feelings of warmth, hardness, coldness, texture and the like; a primitive relation to bounded surfaces (Ogden 1989), such as the child's own body, the body of the mother as well as non-human substances; and from maternal rhythmicity (Kristeva 1984), including tone, breath and silences.

There is a proto-symbolic as well as a sensory poetics at work here. Persons and things may not yet be objects, but the small infant constantly invests and assimilates what is outside itself – though, once again, it must be stressed that the monadic core of the subject as it functions during this elemental form of intersubjective experience is, in fact, diametrically opposed to all that we understand by the terms "inside" and "outside". As Castoriadis (1987) says,

> Here there is no way of separating representation and "perception" or "sensation". The maternal breast or what takes its place, is a part without being a distinct part, of what will later become the "own body" and which is, obviously, not yet a "body".
>
> (Castoriadis 1987: 294)

There is thus something of an infinite regress operating here, such that a primitive psychological organisation of experience is constituted by identificatory incorporations of the (m)other that structure relations to self, others and the object-world in an ongoing way. Does the other, in some way, transport the infant to the heart of reality, a mix of proto-subject and proto-world? How can the libidinal articulations of the babbling child become somehow "organized" within the uncontrollability that otherness necessarily brings?

Now as regards the psychoanalytic notion of primary repression, it can be said that all individuals develop a framework for reworkings of psychical organisation, based on sensory modes of organising experience which remain undivided at the level of psychic reality. The analysis of the sensory core of the primal subject worked out by Thomas Ogden, rather than that of Castoriadis himself, is very useful here. Reaching back to the earliest days of the pre-Oedipal, Ogden theorizes what he terms an "autistic-contiguous position", described by him as "a sensory-dominated mode in which the most inchoate sense of self is built upon the rhythm of sensation, particularly the sensations of the skin surface" (Ogden 1989: 31). Such autistic-contiguous experience is not a biological or prepsychological phase of development, but is rather psychodynamically operative from birth and functions in the life of the subject in large part from connections and relations of a sensory kind. Like Castoriadis, Ogden stresses that the infant's earliest relations with objects comes from contact with the care-taking other in a presymbolic, sensory-dominated mode. Theorizing the autistic or undivided nature of such experience in neo-Kleinian terms, Ogden notes that the infant's relationship to the object is quite different to the depressive position (where there is a relationship between subjects) and also to the paranoid-schizoid position (where both self and other are treated as objects). Rather, the nascent subject's undivided or autistic "experience" or "state" is that of nonreflective sensory Being, the first imaginative elaboration of bodily needs.

In one sense, Ogden aestheticizes imagination, so that – thanks to the autistic-contiguous valorization of bodily experience – subject and object, sensation and representation pass fluently into each other so as to ensure the possibility of a presymbolic break-up of the psychical monad. The neo-Kleinian Ogden thus adds particular insight and intriguing depth to Castoriadis's paradoxical claim that the "autism is undivided", in the sense that he details the small infant's or proto-subject's relationship to the object in the autistic-contiguous position. As Ogden (1989) writes,

> It is a relationship of shape to the feeling of enclosure, of beat to the feeling of rhythm, of hardness to the feeling of edgedness. Sequences, symmetries, periodicity, skin-to-skin "moulding" are all examples of contiguities that are the ingredients out of which the beginnings of rudimentary self-experience arise.
>
> (Ogden 1989: 32)

Ogden, together with Castoriadis, stands out among psychoanalysts who have preserved certain universal elements of Freud's original account of the psychic origins of the human subject, while at the same time expanding and refining it in a systematic manner to account for the primary force of representation and repression in the constitution of the unconscious. In what follows, I shall draw – although selectively and critically – upon their ideas. On the basis of both his clinical work and the reconstruction of diverse traditions in contemporary psychoanalysis, Ogden has identified the forms of object-relation – or, more accurately, relations to the pre-object – that derive from autistic-contiguous modes of experience. The nursing experience, the experience of being held, of being rocked to sleep, sung to as well as caressed by the mother: Ogden's discussion of rhythmicity and experiences of sensory contiguity that make up a person's earliest relations with objects is highly persuasive. But I do not think that he unearths sufficiently the essential nature of such primary, autistic or what I term rolling identifications as a constructive process, one in which the internalized attributes of pre-objects and part-objects are employed in the service of a transformation or working through of the psyche.

Ogden sees us all as permanently producing and reproducing primitive representations of pre-objects or proto-objects in our dealings with things and other people, drawing upon elementary identifications from the autistic-contiguous mode to bolster the shape and content of our more mature, multiple identifications with self and others in daily life. Yet what does this radically imaginary positing of elementary identifications consist of? Ogden posits the existence of basic mechanisms whereby external experiences are taken in, of primitive identificatory processes by which contiguity of surfaces may be introjected. But he does not provide a satisfactory account of the imaginary constitution of sensory surfaces, the elements of creation in the subject's constitution of a sensory world, nor the initial unmediated identity of the infant, sensation, affect and representational flux. Ogden says that autistic identifications provide a kind of "sensory floor" to psychic experience. And yet if we reflect on the pre-Oedipal tie of infant (proto-subject) and breast (proto-object), it can be said that the making of fluid identifications from experiences of rhythmic rocking or sucking involves more than the constitution of the breast as an object, as separate or different from the subject. From the angle of the monadic core of the psyche, what is important about rhythm, texture, boundedness, warmth, coldness and the like is the undifferentiated, unmediated quality of identification as a process. Before experiences of hardness or softness are located as representations of what the proto-subject finds in interpersonal contact, the proto-subject just *is* hardness or softness. But, *pace* Ogden, I argue that there must be some minimal representational colouring involved here – which I seek to delineate with reference to Freud's concept of primary repression and also the representative prior to representation, of which more shortly.

Rolling identifications veer away in erratic directions, and their elaboration is plural, multiple, discontinuous. The elementary form of identification, the pre-identification presupposed by internalization, saturates libidinal space. The mode of identification flows, continually *rolls* out anew. Before the differentiation proper of self and other, this modality of psychic organization is basic to the wealth of images, fantasies and feelings that circulate within intersubjective communication. To capture the nature of rolling identification, we must connect the auto-erotic indistinction between the self and the nonself of which Castoriadis speaks with the concept of primary identification and repression. Now primary identification "does not wait upon an object-relationship proper" (Laplanche and Pontalis 1985: 336). It is constituted, rather, through a process of incorporating a pre-object; or, as Kristeva says, primary identification "bends the drive toward the symbolic of the other" (Kristeva 1987: 31). But how, exactly, is the drive "bent" in the direction of the other? How does the subject make this shift from self-referential representational fulfilment to primary intersubjectivity? How, in any case, does the presentation of otherness enter into the construction of the psyche? Several factors suggest themselves on the basis of the foregoing observations. To begin with, the infant's subjectivity – marked by representational flux – can be thought of as becoming *internally split* once the emergent relation to the pre-object is established. Primary identification, and the general narcissism which it ushers in, is therefore closely bound up with loss. Loss here is understood as a result of the preliminary dissolution of basic representational self-sufficiency. As Castoriadis expresses this:

> Once the psyche has suffered the break up of its monadic "state" imposed upon it by the "object", the other and its own body, it is forever thrown off-centre in relation to itself, orientated in terms of that which it is no longer and can no longer be. *The psyche is its own lost object.*
>
> (Castoriadis 1987: 296–297, original italics)

The subject, simply, suffers the loss of self-referential representational fulfilment, and it substitutes a relation to pre-objects and self-as-object as the basis for creating "a place where one lives" (Winnicott 1971).

To be sure, the possible adaptive reactions must register basic relational connections. Indeed, this is the outlook described by Kristeva and Laplanche – the subject is referred beyond itself via an imaginary anchor in parental significations. This standpoint, while more sophisticated than most, is still inadequate however, since its conception of the subject and the unconscious is too simple. In my view, the relation between the rudimentary beginnings of subjectivity and primary intersubjectivity – the psychical registration of self-as-object and pre-object relations – cannot be understood outside of the representational dynamics of desire itself. Now in Freud's account of the nascent subject's fall from pre-Oedipal Eden, basic relational connections are established in the psyche through the arising of the affect of unpleasure associated with hunger. The nascent subject creates a hallucinatory representation of the breast in an attempt to avoid the terrors of reality, which in Freud's theorization involves a primordial wound incurred by the absence of the mother. Through hallucinatory wish fulfilment, the nascent subject imagines the mother present in fantasy, even though she is in fact missing in actuality. Originary fantasmatic representation for Freud is thus the prototype of all further representations, fantasy and dream formation in the psyche. The "original representation" is what cannot be included within any self-grasping or self-reflexivity of the subject's imaginary productions, but whose very absence marks the stratified and intercommunicating elaborations of our imaginary worlds, as a kind of vortex around which desire circulates.

As far as a foundational myth of the psychic constitution of the subject goes, Freud's narrative is, one might claim, at once too subject-centred and not focused enough on the imaginary domain. His treatment of how unpleasurable affect, drawing on traces of reality, triggers the creation of the hallucinated breast contains rich insight, with its subtle examination of the origins of imaginary creation. Certainly when Freud speaks of the pre-Oedipal infant as having "created an object out of the mother" (1926: 170) he captures with original insight the breathtakingly innovative and creative dimensions of the imaginary domain. For the most part, however, Freud's speculations here fail to do justice to the lucidity of his concepts. For what allows the nascent subject's originary representation to become the prototype of all further representations is conceptualized by Freud only at the level of the hallucinated breast as "object". Yet, as Castoriadis notes, this supposedly "original" hallucination is, in fact, a secondary formation – based on the elaboration of quite complex connections between subjectivity, part-objects and objects. As Castoriadis sees it, it is not hallucinatory wish fulfilment (a secondary figuration) which shapes the paradox of representation. For Castoriadis, the roots of our unconscious lives develop out of the creation of an *Ur-Vorstellung*, an instituting fantasy or proto-representation which must be absent from the unconscious if, para-doxically, we are to function as "subjects of the unconscious".

Just as Castoriadis would have us concentrate on the monadic core of the psyche (the nascent subject as "unitary subjective circuit") and accordingly refashions the psychoanalytic doctrine of *anaclisis* ("leaning-on") to eluci-date how the psyche "lends itself to socialization", Ogden would have us concentrate on the presymbolic, sensory mode in which surface contiguity cements a person's earliest relations with objects. As Ogden (1989: 33) puts this: "These sensory experiences with 'objects' (which only an outside observer would be aware of as objects) are the media through which the earliest forms of organized and organising experience are created". But even if we recognize that radically imaginary processes and experiences of sensory contiguity contribute to the earliest "structure" of psychological organisation, we are still confronted with the dilemma of how the nascent subject encounters shared experience. There is also the further problem of determining exactly what facilitating factors are necessary for primary or rolling identification to unfold.

Now contemporary research concerning human subjectivity suggests that the psyche's capacity to produce unconscious representations from the earliest days of life is not separated off from the time/space environments of other persons in the manner that classical Freudian theory supposes, and for which Castoriadis (and in some senses Ogden too) provides a challeng-ing justification. In recent research, work has focused on the earliest and most primitive phases of psychic functioning, emphasising the role of the mother in a very different manner from Freud and Castoriadis. The rela-tion between the nascent subject (infant) and other (mother) is revalued as essentially creative, and the constitution of psychic structure is held to depend upon various affective exchanges and communicative dialogues. Feminist psychoanalysts (for example, Luce Irigaray), in particular, have stressed that the maternal body plays a constitutive role in emotional life and the structuring of the psyche. From this perspective, the use of the symbolic father or phallus to conceptualize the emergence of individuation in the Freudian and Lacanian standpoints is shown to rest on a masculinist inability to envision the mother as both a containing and a sexual subject within the child's psychic world. As Irigaray has argued, the failure to represent the umbilicus – in psychoanalytic theory as well as in cultural life more generally – as a symbol of connection with, and separation from, the mother has led to the continuing dominance of the phallus in contemporary theory.

This revaluing of the intersubjective sphere as it concerns the develop-ment of the psyche also incorporates a recognition that the creative play of subjectivities structures a potential space within which a web of psychic and sociosymbolic identifications can unfold. Various theorists emphasize how

psychic space and the location of otherness are interwoven in the constitution of subjectivity and the frame of intersubjectivity. In the work of
Irigaray, this investigation emerges as part of an attempt to rework the
psychoanalytic conceptualization of the child–mother dyad, giving special
attention to bodily flows and to experiences of fluidity as itself other.
Anzieu (1989) discusses the archaeology of a "skin ego", a preverbal
writing made up of traces upon the skin. Hélène Cixous similarly seeks to
explore the repudiation of the body in the nascent subject's imaginary
relationship to the phallic mother. There is also research in psychology
suggesting that interaction between the psyche and its environment starts in
the womb, and that from the moment of birth the infant is engaged in
creative and active communications with the world (see Stern 1985;
Chamberlain 1987).

    The general characteristics I outlined in the foregoing discussion regard-
ing primary or rolling identification, if they are valid, are also relevant for
describing how the psyche opens up to externality (otherness, difference) in
a predominantly imaginary mode. Now Odgen's account of the earliest
experiences of sensory contiguity, I have suggested, comes close to filling
out in detail Castoriadis's philosophical construction of the radically
imaginary as genuine psychic creation. Yet if we return to Odgen and his
discussion of how the earliest sensory experiences with "objects" are the
media through which psychical production is created, we see that, although
his discussion is subtle and intricate, he does not in fact specify the
facilitating conditions necessary for the structuration of such primitive
psychic organisation. Indeed, there is a passage in Ogden where he appears
to rule out the necessity of considerations of representation in the autistic-
contiguous mode altogether. "The rudiments of the sensory experience itself
in an autistic-contiguous mode", writes Ogden (1989: 35), "have nothing to
do with the representation of one's affective states, either idiographically or
symbolically".

    However, and here I return to threads of my argument concerning
primary or rolling identification, Ogden's assertion cannot stand without
some explanation of the status of the *representative prior to representation*.
According to the view I am proposing, there is a *representational wrapping
of self and other* achieved through primary repression and identification. By
this I mean that the subject establishes a preliminary ordering, to use a kind
of shorthand, of pre-self experience, otherness and difference as the basis
for the elaboration of psychic space itself. Such representational wrapping
does not just "register" other persons and the object world, but is the
central mechanism which makes their humanization possible. *Representational wrapping spirals in and out of intersubjective life, ordering and
reordering both psychical imagination and the social process of which it is
part.* What I am suggesting is that the status of the representative prior to
representation, though never explicit theorised by Freud as such, is turned

from the outset towards otherness and sociality. I say "turned towards" in the sense not of a representational incorporation of difference (as the psyche functions here in a presymbolic mode), but rather as the minimal capacity for the registration of pre-self and pre-object experience in the productive imagination.

The significance of primary repression, and the politicization of identification

How far do the concepts of primary repression, rolling identification and representational wrapping lead us to rethink the constitution and/or positioning of the subject in terms of socio-symbolic signification? The insights of Freud, and of contemporary psychoanalysis more generally, should of course lead us to caution in this respect. Whatever the radicalizing possibilities of this more differentiated rendering of repression and identification that I have presented, identity requires meaning, and therefore symbolic law, which constitutes subjectivity in its sociocultural dimensions. The transition from a fantasy world of representation to socio-symbolic signification refers the individual subject beyond itself. The break-up of the psychical monad, and crucially the socialization of the psyche, are the medium through which a relation to the Other is established, and therefore to broader cultural, historical and political chains of signification.

However, none of this means that human subjects can be reduced to mere "supports" of symbolic law. Contrary to Lacanian and related deterministic theories, "history" is not fixed once and for all, and offers no guarantees with regard to the organization of power. Thus the connection between law and desire, ideology and the affective, is not a fixed reality instituted by the symbolic. Freud's account of Oedipus, as Kristeva comments, "was not, as he has been too easily accused of, to respect the paternal law of taboos that sketch our social interplay . . . [but rather] to sort out the types of representations of which a subject is capable" (Kristeva 1987: 9–10). In this respect, representational forms, I have suggested, are shaped to their core in and through pre-Oedipal processes of repression and identification. As an elementary elaboration of pre-self experience and pre-object relations, primal repression permits the *representational splitting of the subject*, which is bound up with pleasures and traumas of the intersubjective network itself. This elementary organization of psychical space will be repressed with entry to the socio-symbolic order, thus cementing the reproduction of "social imaginary significations". However, these elementary, representational wrappings of self and other are never entirely repressed. Pre-Oedipal representations, at the outer limit of our symbolism and discourse, cannot be shut off from identity and culture, and continually burst forth anew within any of our symbolic systems.

The argument I am developing here is closely linked to that of Kristeva, who sees us all as permanently swept along by semiotic forces, bearing at the very core of our identity something intrinsically resistant to symbolic articulation yet always-already derailing or overriding our interpersonal dialogue. Kristeva, who is very much taken with Freud's notion of a "father in prehistory", is divided in her more recent work as to the possibilities for transforming the symbolic order through the semiotic on the one hand, and the necessity of identification with the imaginary father for the production of individual identity on the other. Some critics, like Cornell (1991, 1993), interpret this as a turn from the semiotic to an idealized relation to the paternal function. Even if this is so, however, it is surely possible to step back from Kristeva's inflation of the paternal function and instead stress, as I try to do, more creative possibilities arising from the fluid, rolling and multiple identifications stemming from the imaginary constitution of sensory experience. From this angle, then, what is the sociocultural significance of primary repression and rolling identification? What is at issue here is the interlacing of representational wrapping of pre-self and pre-object connections on the one hand and socially instituted representations on the other hand. If we understand that social significations are taken up and invested by subjects within the matrix of former pre-Oedipal modes of generating experience, we can see that there are a wealth of fantasies, identifications, contiguities and rhythmicities available to the subject as she or he creatively engages with cultural forms. Such early, pre-Oedipal modes of generating experience provide not only a support for identity, but also the identificatory basis from which to re-imagine our world. Representational wrappings of self and other – constituted in and through primal repression – infuse the power of the radical imagination and help to contest, question and destabilize our relation to the symbolic order.

Applied to the field of social difference and sexual identity, recognition of the imaginary valorization of sensory experience becomes a vision of alternative meanings and desires positioned against closure in the name of socio-symbolic reproduction. Developing upon the work of Castoriadis, Kristeva, Laplanche and Ogden, I argue that the autistic-sensory forms the imaginary basis for the constitution of the subject. In the pursuit of radical imagination, there are meanings and values embedded in this domain of the pre-Oedipal which are of vital importance. Representational wrappings of pre-self and pre-object connections, as an ongoing unconscious process of identification, are resilient enough to always threaten or destabilize the hierarchical closure imposed on meaning and language in the socio-symbolic order. The dream of radical imagination is thus, in part, the dream of retracing the shared representational and affective modes of generating experience which link us ineluctably together.

The politics of difference require creativity, innovation, reflectiveness, in order to enact the different itself. In pursuit of the new, the different, beyond the constraint and domination of the current social order, there are values and affects embedded in the subject's relation to primal identification which are of vital importance. Primal identification, and the repression which consolidates it, opens a preliminary distance between the self and others, and is thus a foundation for personal and collective autonomy. For this link to the other, prior to mirror asymmetry and the imprint of social significations, can offer a prefigurative image of a cultural condition in which relatedness, fulfilment and creativity are more fully realized. The role of unconscious representation in dreaming the new lies precisely in this connection to the other, primary intersubjectivity, a condition from which we might imagine self, society, politics and ethics anew.

References

Anzieu, D. (1989) *The Skin Ego*, New Haven, CT: Yale University Press.

Bourdieu, P. (1977) *Outline of a Theory of Practice*, Cambridge: Cambridge University Press.

Castoriadis, C. (1987) *The Imaginary Institution of Society*, Cambridge: Polity.

—— (1997) *World in Fragments*, Stanford, CA: Stanford University Press.

Chamberlain, D. (1987) 'The cognitive newborn: a scientific update', *British Journal of Psychotherapy*, 4: 30–71.

Cornell, D. (1991) *Beyond Accommodation*, New York: Routledge.

—— (1993) *Transformations*, New York: Routledge.

Elliott, A. (1999) *Social Theory and Psychoanalysis in Transition: Self and Society from Freud to Kristeva*, London: Free Association Books.

—— (2004) *Subject to Ourselves: Social Theory, Psychoanalysis and Postmodernity*, Boulder, CO: Paradigm.

Fletcher, J. and Stanton, M. (eds) (1992) *Jean Laplanche: Seduction, Translation and the Drives*, London: ICA Publications.

Freud, S. (1915) 'Repression', *Standard Edition*, 14: 141–158, London: Hogarth Press.

—— (1926) *Inhibitions, Symptoms and Anxiety. Standard Edition*, 20: 75–174, London: Hogarth Press.

Giddens, A. (1984) *The Constitution of Society*, Cambridge: Polity.

—— (1990) *The Consequences of Modernity*, Cambridge: Polity.

Green, A. (1985) Réflexions libres sur la représentation de l'affect. In *Propédeutique: La métapsychologie revistée*, Paris: Champvallon, 1995.

Kristeva, J. (1984) *Revolution in Poetic Language*, New York: Columbia University Press.

—— (1987) *Tales of Love*, New York: Columbia University Press.

—— (1988) *In the Beginning was Love*, New York: Columbia University Press.

—— (1989) *Black Sun: Depression and Melancholia*, New York: Columbia University Press.

—— (1991) *Strangers to Ourselves*, London: Harvester.

—— (1993) *New Maladies of the Soul*, New York: Columbia University Press.

—— (2000) *The Sense and Non-Sense of Revolt: The Powers and Limits of Psychoanalysis*, New York: Columbia University Press.

—— (2001) *Melanie Klein*, New York: Columbia University Press.

Laplanche, J. (1987) *New Foundations for Psychoanalysis*, Oxford: Blackwell.

Laplanche, J. and Pontalis, J. B. (1985) *The Language of Psychoanalysis*, London: Hogarth.

Ogden, T. (1989) *The Primitive Edge of Experience*, Northvale, NJ: Jason Aronson.

Stern, D. (1985) *The Interpersonal World of the Infant*, New York: Basic Books.

Tustin, E. (1980) 'Autistic objects', *International Review of Psycho-Analysis*, 7: 27–40.

—— (1984) 'Autistic shapes', *International Review of Psycho-Analysis*, 11: 279–290.

Winnicott, D. (1971) *Playing and Reality*, New York: Basic Books.

Chapter 10

Naturalizing relational psychoanalytic theory

Arnold H. Modell

The "hard problem" for relational theory is: how is meaning constructed between two different subjectivities, between two private and separate minds? How is shared knowledge, shared beliefs and shared imagination established within a relationship? Each one of us constructs our own inner world of private meaning in accordance with everything that we have experienced, everything that we know, and everything that we value. How is meaning constructed between two semi-autonomous consciousnesses?

With regard to this question, the Russian linguist Mikhail Bakhtin noted that creating meaning between two autonomous consciousness is not a question of a redoubling, or mirroring of the other's experience but it is a matter of *translating* the (combined) experience into an altogether different perspective, into new categories of valuation (Todorov 1984). Something analogous occurs when things go well in a psychoanalytic treatment. When successful, the combined experience of the two participants creates new meanings.

This problem of meaning creation within a dyad was investigated in the nineteenth century by Charles Sanders Peirce, who described *A Third* that would mediate the relationship within the semiotic dyad (Muller 2000). The term *The Third* was introduced into psychoanalysis by Brickman (1993) and Ogden (1994). Although Winnicott did not use this term, he suggested a solution to the problem of shared meaning and anticipated The Third when he described the shared illusion of the child's transitional object. Winnicott said:

> of the transitional object it can be said that it is a matter of agreement between us and the baby that we will never ask the question "did you conceive of this or was it presented to you from without?" The important point is that no decision on this point is expected. The question is not to be formulated.

(Winnicott 1951: 239)

In the squiggle game Winnicott (1989) showed how a shared imagination proceeds in a stepwise fashion. He makes a drawing, the child completes the drawing, he then completes the child's drawing and so forth. He and the child build upon each other's construction of meaning.

Postmodern thinkers believe that reality is socially constructed. When this assumption was applied to the psychoanalytic relationship this has led to a more egalitarian view that transference is the product of two subjectivities, that the analyst is not a neutral, "blank screen" that receives only the patient's projections. The person of analyst, his or her conscious and unconscious communications of feelings contribute to the formation of the transference. If transference is co-created, the analyst is not the sole judge of what is true, and further, the analyst is not the only one who knows. I believe that this egalitarian attitude has had a beneficial effect upon psychoanalytic treatment, but there remains a deep and fundamental problem with the concept of social constructivism. Social construction is really a misnomer as it omits reference to the body, meaning construction is deeply embodied for the meaning of experience is a selective process ultimately based on feelings.

As the philosopher Robert Nozick (2001) observed, everything cannot be a social construction, what we think and what we believe cannot simply be a matter of a relativistic judgment for this will lead to an infinite regression. Nozick cites William James who tells the story of a person approaching him after a lecture and saying: "The world rests on a large turtle" (Nozick 2001: 21). "And what does the turtle rest upon?" James asked. "Another turtle," said the person. "And what does that turtle rest upon?" "More turtles, Professor James, there are turtles all the way down." Our knowledge and beliefs cannot be simply socially constructed, they must be grounded upon something: that something is our embodied selves. It is for this reason it is necessary to naturalize relational theory.

The asymmetric perception of the other's feelings and intentions

Philosophers once questioned whether an individual's consciousness and the privacy of the self makes it logically impossible to know other minds. The existence of other minds was seen as a problem for philosophy to solve. For example, in a dialogue between the philosophers J. Wisdom and J. Austin, a symposium on other minds, Wisdom asks: "How does one know of another creature that he is angry?" (Wisdom and Austin 1962: 775) He answers that logically one cannot know the mind of another unless one believes in mental telepathy. Austin, in response, suggests another possibility: that emotions entail public display and that we can work out rules for accepting the testimony (of our senses). Today, such philosophical discussions are moot for we know that when another person expresses anger that anger is communicated and perceived, invariably unconsciously, and variably consciously, because that is the way our minds and brains are constructed. Such knowledge is involuntary and may or may not be conscious, we do not need logical rules, as Austin proposed, recognizing the feeling in the other is an expression of inclusive fitness. As social animals we are required to perceive the feelings of the other. Empathy is now understood as part of our evolutionary heritage. I will suggest that recognizing the intention of others is an archaic function of the brain while awareness of our own intentions represents a higher order cognitive function – in certain respects we can know the intention of the other better than we can know our own intentions. As the philosopher Thomas Nagel (1995) observed, people are often unaware of their own motives, and we often understand others better than they understand themselves. Our capacity to do so rests upon an archaic function, the involuntary communication of feelings and its unconscious/conscious perception by the other.

Darwin fully recognized the adaptive advantage in perceiving and interpreting the communication of feelings both within one's own and other species. An animal's capacity to correctly interpret the feelings of another individual within its own or in other species obviously adds to their inclusive fitness. In his book *The Expression of the Emotions in Man and Animals*, Darwin said:

> With social animals, the power of intercommunication between the members of the same community, and with other species, between the opposite sexes, as well as between the young and the old, is of the highest importance to them. This is generally effected by means of the voice, but it is certain that gestures and expressions are to a certain extent mutually intelligible.
>
> (Darwin 1872: 60)

Feelings are communicated involuntarily through different modalities such as the voice, facial expression and bodily gestures. In psychoanalysis, when faces are not seen, feelings are communicated by means of the tone of voice, its pitch, cadence and rhythm. In that case, both participants become intensely aware of the meanings conveyed by the sound of the voice. It is by means of feeling that we give meaning to words. We all know that words conveyed without feeling have no meaning, they are just empty talk. Infant research (Beebe and Lachmann 2002) has focused on the gazing dialogue that occurs between mother and child, the mother's face is the primary source for the intersubjective communication of feelings. Facial expressions have been standardized as a research tool. It has been shown that facial expressions are universal markers of specific feelings, universal in the sense that they transcend cultural differences (Eckman and Sorenson 1969). This allows neurobiologists who investigate feelings in human subjects to employ the so-called Eckman faces, as a standardized method for the investigation of intentionality.

In the discussion that follows I make the Freudian assumption, that *mental processes are in themselves unconscious*, that an unconscious process precedes conscious awareness. I believe *that unconscious processes occupy an intermediate area between neurophysiological events and consciousness*. In addition to unconscious memory, the perceptual unconscious is a continuously flowing stream operating in the here and now. That is to say, thoughts and feelings are processed unconsciously before entering consciousness. The subject communicates feelings involuntarily while the recipient, the other, also initially receives that communication unconsciously. If an unconscious process precedes conscious awareness, this would also mean that interpretation of the other's feelings occurs involuntarily and unconsciously. When it comes to conscious awareness of feelings, as I have noted, there is an asymmetry in that we are better able to characterize the feeling of the other as compared to the feelings that occur within ourselves. The recipient of the feeling, rather than the one who communicates the feeling, is better positioned to correctly interpret its meaning.

From an evolutionary perspective, that of inclusive fitness, there is an obvious benefit in being able to accurately and correctly interpret the intentions of the other. As Darwin indicated, this is an archaic function that is shared by most social animals. Self awareness is a late acquisition both developmentally and phylogenetically. While chimps, bonobos, gorillas, dolphins and elephants can recognize themselves in the mirror, self recognition is not the same as self awareness. We may be the only animal that has the capacity for self reflection and self awareness, but as Darwin noted, the capacity to detect feelings in the other is widespread among social animals. For example, dogs are known to able to correctly interpret the mood of their owner; they can observe whether their owner is angry, depressed or joyous. But self awareness is not a cognitive capacity that we attribute to dogs. It is debatable whether a dog has a sense of self but no one believes that dogs have the capacity for self reflection. Dogs do not interpret what they are feeling, they simply feel. Dogs do not say to themselves: "I am feeling angry or I'm frightened."

We believe that young babies do have a sense of self , what Daniel Stern refers to as a "core self," but self awareness or self reflection is a later development (Stern, 1985). The unconscious communication of feeling that occurs within a dyad is now widely acknowledged to occur shortly after birth. Mother and infant reciprocally respond to each other's feelings. We are far from knowing the details of the neurophysiology of this mutual attunement, but it has been proposed that mirror neurons are activated (Gallese 2001) so that an intersubjective, empathic process may be present at the beginning of life. Edward Tronick (2003) views this process as occurring within a shared dyadic consciousness in which the mother invests the baby's feelings with meaning. The mother by virtue of her more complex consciousness interprets the baby's feelings and thus facilitates the baby's self awareness. This does not preclude the fact that the baby creates meaning for itself by means of what Winnicott described as the "spontaneous gesture." While babies provide their own meaningful motoric gestures it is the mother who endows the baby's *feelings* with meaning. The parent teaches the baby to recognize themselves as a subject. Kohut (1977) has also described this process as the function of the self-object. The baby's acquisition of the meaning of feelings, based on the mother's empathic response, occurs before the acquisition of language but it is of course greatly enhanced by language.

All of this is to suggest that a dyad, such as the analytic dyad, contains an implicit, built-in asymmetry regarding the perception and interpretation of feeling. Being the recipient of the communication of feeling rather than the one who's expressing the feeling allows the recipient a greater degree of freedom of interpretation. I suggest that this is a background condition of the analytic dyad. This asymmetry works in two directions. We know of course that the analysand can often accurately interpret the meaning of their analyst's feelings, feelings that may be outside of the analyst's awareness. Such perceptions of the analyst's feelings may trigger a specific transference response in the patient. In this sense transference can be understood as a co-creation, a mixture of a past construction and a present awareness.

In addition to recognizing specific emotions in the other, we perceive whether or not the other person is attending to us, we have an overall sense of the other's attention or indifference. We have an innate capacity to sense whether we are "cathected" by the other. Or to express it differently, we are always aware of whether or not we enter into the other's subjectivity. This state of indifference towards the analyst, expressed as non-communication of feeling, appears in certain disorders of the self which I have viewed as a sign of an illusion of omnipotent self-sufficiency (Modell 1980). The absence of feeling is an (apparent) absence of desire as feelings are object seeking. This state of unrelatedness, being alone the presence of the other, may have been considered by Heidegger as an ontological category, a mode of being with the other in the world. Heidegger speaks of objects being available or unavailable with regard to their use (Dreyfus 1997). I will comment on this further in a later section. If someone is in a state of unrelatedness in psychoanalysis, the analyst is not available for use.

Selection and simulation

As an underlying principle let us assume that one of the functions of the self is to select what is perceived in accordance with its value and significance to the individual. Here our entire life history comes into play. This selectionist process informs intentionality by endowing perceptions with value, what Freud might have described as cathexis. Intentionality can be usefully defined as the directing of action towards a *future* goal that is chosen and defined by the individual. The key words here are *chosen and defined*. Intentionality encompasses not only actions into the world but also imaginary wishes and desires. I have discussed these principles in greater detail in *Imagination and the Meaningful Brain* (Modell 2003). One of the functions of the self is to internally simulate the effect of one's intentions prior to action. *The self creates a remembered future.* I believe that Freud recognized this process when he described signal anxiety, that one unconsciously simulates the possible danger that can result from a forbidden wish. Signal anxiety represents the anticipation of danger that has not yet occurred, signal anxiety is future oriented. As a background to the discussion that follows let us keep in mind these self-functions of selection and simulation.

With these principles in mind let us now consider how the unconscious perception of feelings might be interpreted. We believe that there are degrees of freedom in interpreting feelings, ranging from an involuntary unconscious interpretation to a fully conscious, complex association to the feeling. When feelings are aroused in association to the memory of trauma, whether conscious or unconscious, the interpretation of these feelings will depend on the degree to which the traumatic memory has been recontextualized by means of subsequent experience (Modell 1990). When a traumatic memory is unmodified, imagination is constricted and feelings are interpreted involuntarily. Consider this example: a psychiatrist became intensely frightened if he noted any indication of irrationality or what he feared to be craziness in his wife. This state of affairs was in contrast to the ease and comfort he had in dealing with irrationality in his patients, he did quite well with very sick patients, especially schizophrenics. The meaning of his intense anxiety in response to his wife's presumed irrationality could be traced to the fact that the age of two or three, he inferred that he was a witness to his mother having a spontaneous miscarriage. He was unable to remember the event but he did reconstruct that in all probability his mother became "hysterical" and was emotionally distraught for an undetermined period of time. He felt as if his mother had simply and inexplicably gone crazy. When this man then became panicked as a response to his wife's presumed irrationality, we could infer the presence of an unconscious metaphoric process that melded or blended this childhood memory with his current perceptions and found a correspondence. In *Imagination and the Meaningful Brain* (Modell 2003) I have suggested that this unconscious imaginative process utilizes the memory of emotional categories, these categories are in turn are based on patterns of metaphoric correspondences between the past and present. His wife's presumed irrationality served as a metonymic trigger creating anxiety which in turn was interpreted unconsciously as an indication that his wife was going crazy. An unconscious selective process simulated an image of an untenable future relationship. I believe that an unconscious process constantly scans our conscious perception for similarities or differences with a significant affective memories.

Unconscious ties to the body of the other

Shortly after birth newborn human infants can imitate an adult's gestures such as protrusion of the tongue (Meltzoff and Moore 1977). These observations further suggest that the infant has an inborn body schema that responds to and mirrors the body of the other. It seems probable that the gestures of the experimenter activate mirror neurons in the infant (Gallese 2001). This can also be thought of as a kind of unconscious kinesthetic empathy. In later development this kinesthetic empathy may be experienced as feeling oneself into the body of the other. For example, as adults when watching a dance performance we obtain pleasure through a vicarious identification with the dancer's movements. This unconscious mirroring or simulation of the other can provide a stage for constructing imaginary scenarios of future interactions.

The discovery of mirror neurons shows that empathy is an embodied neurophysiological process (Thompson 2001). It is not been generally recognized however that empathy can be placed in the service of simulating and anticipating the future response of the other. Metonymic associations evoked through empathy can be understood as contributing to the transference and countertransference responses within the psychoanalytic dyad. Transference and countertransference reactions implicitly contain an internal simulation of the anticipated response of the other. Transference and countertransference responses are implicitly directed towards the future.

Who is a subject?

Empathy is of course a fundamental dimension of intersubjectivity. Some researchers such as Colwyn Trevarthen (2001) claim that intersubjectivity is present at birth. The truth of this assertion would then depend upon one's definition of a "subject." Within the dyad how does one define a "subject?" (There is an extensive psychoanalytic and philosophic literature on this topic which I will not attempt to summarize) I would suggest that we recognize the other as a subject, or correspondingly feel ourselves to be a subject, when there is a sense of being understood. This process depends upon the communication and interpretation of feelings. An analysand, who, for whatever reason, stops communicating is no longer a subject for the analyst. I would claim that being a subject rests on a mutual understanding of the feelings that are communicated, whether that communication relies on acts of speech, or gestures. A subject is defined by the existence of a communicative bond of feeling.

Let me illustrate this assertion by referring to an account of a primat-ologist who gradually became a subject to a troop of baboons (Smuts 2001). Barbara Smuts describes how she accommodated herself to the baboons' style of communication.

> In the process of gaining their trust I changed almost everything about me including the way I walked and sat and the way I held my body, and the way I used my eyes and voice. I was learning a whole new way of being in the world – the way of the baboon. I was not literally moving like a baboon – my very different morphology prevents that – but rather I was responding to the cues that the baboons used to indicate their emotions, motivations and intentions to one another, and I was gradu-ally learning to send such signals back to them. As a result, instead of avoiding me when I got too close, they started giving me very deliberate dirty looks, which made me move away. This may sound like a small shift, but in fact it signaled the profound change from being treated as an *object* that elicited a unilateral response processes (avoidance), to being recognized as a *subject* with whom they could communicate. Over time they treated me more and more as a social being like themselves, subject to the demands and rewards of relationship.
>
> (Smuts 2001: 295)

Perceiving the other as a subject is a precondition for collaboration. Colla-borating with the other is a capacity that is acquired in early childhood. Trevarthen (2001) notes that children do not simply observe others; they interact with others and develop the capacity for a shared joint attention. This starts at around 9 to 14 months:

> the child alternates between monitoring the gaze of the other and what the other's gazing at, checking to verify that they are continuing to look at the same thing. Infants between nine and 18 months look to the eyes of the other person to help interpret the meaning of an ambiguous event.
>
> (Gallagher 2007: 228)

Different modes of being with the other in the world

Heidegger's concept of *dasein* as a description of modes of everyday human existence does have relevance for relational theory. His philosophy allows us to recognize that aspects of the therapeutic relationship are features of ordinary life (Heidegger 1962; Dreyfus 1997). This is indeed a very broad subject which, as I am not a philosopher, I'm not prepared to discuss. But I shall instead focus on three aspects of *dasein*: the self and other within a frame; the other utilized to ensure one's safety in the world; and finally, states of non-relatedness.

We know that some relationships are demarcated and set apart from ordinary life in that they occur within a frame or a boundary. This is not simply a matter of a role assignment for the boundary consists of rules regarding the expression of feelings. Three examples of such relationships would be: teacher–student; physician–patient; analyst–analysand. These are asymmetric relationships, that are constrained by mutually understood rules. The doctor, teacher, or analyst, should not retaliate when provoked, should not have tantrums, and should not attempt to sexually seduce the other. The boundary or frame of the analytic relationship is somewhat different from the others in that it is designed to maximize the freedom of the imagination. It has been rightly described as a play space. Play is fundamentally paradoxical: the essence of play is freedom and spontaneity. This freedom must occur within certain constraints; all play is a voluntary activity, yet play is circumscribed and restrained by the "rules of the game." Play illustrates a profound truth that freedom exists by means of restraints (Modell 1990).

Gregory Bateson (1972) recognized that within a play space affects have an as-if quality. He observed animals in a zoo engaged in mock fighting and reasoned that some sort of communication or set of signals must exist that would tell the participants: "this is only play," "this is not ordinary life." This "as if" quality of the frame that contains the play space of a psychoanalysis may permit some patients to experience feelings within the frame that they could not allow themselves to experience in ordinary life. This is not to imply that these feelings are not real, but it does make a difference that the object of one's feelings is not someone who is present in ordinary life, but is someone who is inside the frame that separates the game from life as it is ordinarily lived.

I will now consider the use of the other as a guarantor of one's safety in the world. Due to the human infant's prolonged dependency, and the fact that we, unlike other animals, do not possess an inborn set of defensive reflexes, the mother becomes a protective environment that is interposed between the self and the dangers of the world. In *Object Love and Reality* (Modell 1968) I described how for certain patients the person of the analyst and the analytic relationship itself becomes invested with qualities of a transitional object, analogous to the child's belief in the teddy bear which assures the child safety of the world as long as the object is not lost. I described a type of transference in which the analyst was endowed with nearly magical properties that would protect the individual from coming to harm in the world. This is a mode of object relatedness that has obvious roots in an archaic maternal relationship. But this does not mean that the other is perceived as a subject but instead is seen as a tool, as an object to be used, in the older psychoanalytic literature one would call the other a "part object." I now believe this form of relatedness to be universal, as it is an unconscious aspect that is present in most intimate relationships.

I will now consider being with the other in a state of non-relatedness. You will recall that one becomes a subject when one's communications are understood. This is not possible if feelings are not communicated. Some years ago I described a group of patients who defend themselves from becoming a subject to the other by means of their non-communication of feelings (Modell 1975, 1980). They feel as if they are not in the world or imagine themselves to be encased in a plastic bubble or within a cocoon. They do not become a subject to the other because they wish to maintain an illusion of omnipotent self sufficiency. Feelings are object seeking and an expression of desire. One avoids becoming a subject by impeding the other's knowledge of one's self. Hubert Dreyfus, in his interpretation of Heidegger's *Being and Time* (Dreyfus 1997), comments that no one is understandable without the other. He describes this process as producing a *shared clearing*. Defending against this " shared clearing" by non-relating is also a way of being in the world that is not necessarily an expression of psychopathology, as it occurs at times in everyone's life. States of non-relatedness should also be recognized as a part of relational theory. We periodically need to re-establish our separateness from the other. We need to re-establish the privacy of the self. I have described this in greater detail elsewhere (Modell 1990). My emphasis on the centrality of feelings again underlines that relational theory cannot be detached from bodies.

References

Bateson, G. (1972) 'A theory of play and fantasy', in *Steps to an Ecology of Mind*, New York: Ballantine.

Beebe, B. and Lachmann, F. (2002) *Infant Research and Adult Treatment*, Hillsdale, NJ: Analytic Press.

Brickman, H. (1993) 'Between the devil and the deep blue sea: the dyad and the triad in psychoanalytic thought', *International Journal of Psychoanalysis*, 74: 905–915.

Darwin, C. (1872) *The Expression of the Emotions in Man and Animals*, Chicago, IL: University of Chicago Press.

Dreyfus, H. (1997) *Being – in – the – World*, Cambridge, MA: MIT Press.

Eckman, P. and Sorenson, E. (1969) 'Pan-cultural elements in facial display of emotion', *Science*, 164: 86–88.

Gallagher, S. (2007) 'Moral agency, self consciousness, and practical wisdom', *Journal of Consciousness Studies*, 14(5–6): 199–223.

Gallese, V. (2001) 'The shared manifold hypothesis', *Journal of Consciousness Studies*, 8(5–7): 33–50.

Heidegger, M. (1962) *Being and Time*, San Francisco, CA: Harper.

Kohut, H. (1977) *The Restoration of the Self*, New York: International Universities Press.

Meltzoff, A. and Moore, M. (1977) 'Imitation of facial and manual gestures by human neonates', *Science*, 78(5): 997–1015.

Modell, A. H. (1968) *Object Love and Reality*, New York: International Universities Press.

—— (1975) 'A narcissistic defense against affects and the illusion of self-sufficiency', *International Journal of Psychoanalysis*, 56: 275–282.

—— (1980) 'Affect and their non-communication', *International Journal of Psychoanalysis* 61: 259–267.

—— (1990) *Other Times, Other Realities*, Cambridge, MA: Harvard University Press.

—— (1993) *The Private Self*, Cambridge, MA: Harvard University Press.

—— (2003) *Imagination and the Meaningful Brain*, Cambridge, MA: MIT Press.

Muller, J. (2000) 'Hierarchical models in semiotics and psychoanalysis', in J. Muller and J. Brent (eds) *Peirce, Semiotics and Psychoanalysis*, Baltimore, MD: Johns Hopkins University Press.

Nagel, T. (1995) 'Freud's permanent revolution', in *Other Minds*, New York: Oxford University Press.

Nozick, R. (2001) *Invariances*, Cambridge, MA: Harvard University Press.

Ogden, T. (1994) 'The analytic third: working with intersubjective clinical facts', *International Journal of Psychoanalysis*, 75: 3–19.

Smuts, B. (2001) 'Encounters with animal minds', *Journal of Consciousness Studies*, 8(5–7): 291–309.

Stern, D. (1985) *The Interpersonal World of the Infant*, New York: Basic Books.

Thompson, E. (2001) 'Empathy and consciousness', *Journal of Consciousness Studies*, 8(5–7): 1–32.

Todorov, T. (1984) *Mikhail Bakhtin: The Dialogical Principle*, Minneapolis, MN: University of Minnesota Press.

Trevarthen, C. (2001) 'Intrinsic motives for companionship in understanding: their origin, development, and significance for infant mental health', *Infant Mental Health Journal*, 22(1–2): 95–131.

Tronick, E. Z. (2003) 'Of course all relationships are unique', *Psychoanalytic Inquiry*, 23(3): 473–491.

Winnicott, D. W. (1951) *Transitional Objects and Transitional Phenomena: D. W. Winnicott Collected Papers*, New York: Basic Books.

—— (1989) *Psychoanalytic Explorations*, Cambridge, MA: Harvard University Press.

Wisdom, J. and Austin, J. (1962) 'Symposium: other minds', in W. Barret and H. Aiken (eds) *Philosophy in the Twentieth Century*, New York: Random House.

Postscript

From postmodern skepticism to the search for psychoanalytic understanding

Donna Orange

Postmodernism, as our contributors have noted in various ways, stands in the philosophical tradition of skepticism. From ancient Greece (Pyrrho, Carneades, Sextus Empiricus) through Montaigne and Hume to twentieth-century poststructuralism/postmodernism, skeptics have protested against exaggerated claims to knowledge, unmasked dogmatism, and relativized totalizing worldviews. The resulting skepticism has ranged from an extreme refusal to make any truth claims (pyrrhonism) to an epistemically modest and pragmatic injunction to hold theory lightly and suspend judgment. The recent emphases on difference, rupture, ambiguity, social constructivism, and dissolution or multiplication of the subject have followed the more extreme tradition, while hermeneutics and pragmatism have remained closer to Aristotle's injunction to seek in every domain the kind of knowledge and degree of certainty appropriate to it.

This book has included, in addition to efforts to show what postmodernism can contribute to psychoanalysis, attempts to move beyond radical postmodernism from several points of view. Each moderates the extremes of skepticism by claiming that there are elements or forms of human life we must take seriously: complexity, agency, self-experience, mutual understanding, suffering and trauma. The authors show us how we can understand these human basics psychoanalytically without reverting to modernist rationalism and empiricism, both forms of what French philosophers tend to call "intellectualism". A particularly problematic effect of this intellectualism is reductionism.

All the authors abhor the reductionistic (it-all-comes-down-to) assumptions of Enlightenment claims to objective knowledge, present in both past and present forms of psychoanalysis. It seems ironic, however, that the deconstructive tools developed to combat Freudian and Kleinian essentialisms could themselves result in new reductionisms. Not only have some psychoanalysts rushed to embrace neuroscience, now "neuropsychoanalysis", but also many seem to have become impatient with the irreducible complexity of lived human experience: the intractability of human suffering and folly. Reductionism is surely a temptation for clinicians of all

theoretical persuasions. The problem is that some of the strongest advocates of psychoanalytic postmodernism have tended to subtract out lived
experience in their focus on constructed categories, on narrative and fiction,
on enactment, on dissociation, and even on multiple selves. Indeed, any of
our psychoanalytic categories may become reductionistic if we believe we
know better than our patients about their lives and sufferings.

At the same time, some readers might wonder, given the philosophers
whom many of us study – Buber, Heidegger, Gadamer, Merleau-Ponty,
Levinas – whether we are not turning the clock back rather than moving
beyond postmodernism. In response, it is important to consider the history
of twentieth-century French philosophy. From the 1930s through the 1950s,
phenomenology and existentialism were all pervasive. Levinas had brought
Husserl and Heidegger to Sartre, while himself revisiting, if not receding
into the social background, first into the concentration camps and afterwards into Jewish studies. A generation later, Foucault, Derrida, and
Lyotard dominated the scene, teaching that nothing was stable, and everything was potentially reversible. When "l'affaire Heidegger" erupted in
the 1980s, and the extent of Heidegger's Nazi involvement became clear,
along with the anti-Semitism of a leading American postmodernist, Paul de
Man, the shine fell off postmodernism, and there began a strong return
to ethics. Levinas' claim was that ethics is first philosophy, that it precedes
both ontology (versus Heidegger) and epistemology (versus deconstructive
postmodernism).

Radical postmodernism thus became radically passé just at the moment
that American relational psychoanalysis became enamored of its constructivism and deconstructionism. The apparent return to so-called modernist
(or pre-postmodern) thinkers in our book echoes the philosophical movement in European philosophy to retrieve ethical sources – from Socrates to
Buber and Levinas – and to understand psychoanalysis as relational in a
positive sense.

Hermeneutics, for example, originally the study of rules for interpreting
texts, became, in the hands of Hans-Georg Gadamer, a philosophy of dialogic understanding. Understanding and interpretation, no longer methods
for doing something to texts or persons, became, we might say, radically
intersubjectivized. Understanding became what emerges in conversation with
another person, from, and with whom, one learns and is surprised. Philosophical hermeneutics thus shares the postmodernist suspicion of subject-
object thinking, Enlightenment intellectualism, essentialism, authoritarianism, and exaggerated claims to possess the truth. Instead, truth emerges in a
self-correcting (a concept from pragmatism) and mutual dialogic process:

> The basic model of reaching an understanding together is dialogue or
> conversation . . . a conversation is not possible if one of the partners
> believes himself or herself to be in a clearly superior position in

comparison with the other person and assumes that he or she possesses a prior knowledge of the erroneous prejudgments in which the other is entangled. If one does this, one actually locks oneself into the circle of one's own prejudices. Reaching an understanding dialogically is impossible if in principle one of the partners in a dialogue does not allow himself or herself to enter into a real conversation.

(Gadamer 2007: 70)

Here we see how it is possible to reject the extreme skepticism of some postmodernists, to avoid a return to dogmatism, and to embrace a search for understanding, for making sense together.

Psychoanalysis, as my co-editor noted in the Introduction, was from its inception both thoroughly grounded in the Enlightenment tradition and radically subversive of its modernist rationalism. In post-Freudian and post-Kleinian psychoanalysis, the rationalistic claims to know what is true of the patient's psyche have radically come loose. We no longer see ourselves as the knowing authorities in the psychoanalytic situation, but rather as full participants in the intersubjective situation and partners in the search for understanding, never fully achieved. Some contemporary psychoanalysts, concerned to unmask the oppressive categories of gender, sexual orientation, race, and cultural difference, have embraced postmodern deconstructionism in its more radical forms. In a recent discussion of the effects of continuous trauma in the South African struggle against apartheid, for example, a postmodernist analyst was able only to address the presumption of reality of the events described, and completely unable to understand the terror being described or to connect with the traumatized person sitting next to her. What do you mean by saying these people were really in danger? What kind of narrative construction is this? This kind of attitude creates a kind of disengagement from emotional experience that can resemble the distance of the authoritarian Freudian analyst, and tends to encourage a confrontational clinical approach. In this radical postmodernism, the ironic result can be a kind of performative contradiction – affirming the analyst's participation while remaining the detached player of a game of chess. As a result, it can appear as though some postmodern analysts are more interested in the objectives of their reductionistic deconstruction than in the actual living other person. Certainly this is not true of all who regard themselves as postmodernist, but radical postmodernism seems to subtract out the connection to the other person in all its complexity.

Most of the contributors to this book, on the contrary, wish to find a way of thinking and working that avoids such distancing. While moderately skeptical in outlook, they develop such concepts and values as attention to experiential complexity; awareness of the existential effects of emotional devastation; concepts of agentic and embodied personhood; non-reductionistic understandings of development; and of the possibility of emergent meaning within intersubjective fields. Many of the contributors would describe themselves as phenomenologists and have sought to describe various ways of thinking about a dialogical psychoanalysis that can keep us close to the lifeworlds of our patients.

So we need a middle ground or path. One avenue of thinking and practice, which many contributors to our book are bringing to psycho-analysis, moves beyond radical postmodernism by drawing on the under-valued traditions of dialogical and ethical phenomenology. What might such a dialogical and phenomenological alternative to radically skeptical postmodernism look like? I think it would mean at least three important things: first, a moderate postmodernism whose focus on lived experience leaves aside, "brackets", or suspends our interest in categories, dualisms, and in the "facts" studied by the natural sciences; second, viewing related-ness as our primary human situation, and specifically I-You, or dialogic, relatedness as the condition for the possibility of agentic subjectivity; third, embracing the indispensable asymmetry of our work that leads many psychoanalysts and therapists to live out the quiet discipline of placing ourselves in the background.

The primacy of lived experience means that, as psychoanalysts, we concern ourselves with what our patients are suffering. We attempt to understand their suffering – including their ways of coping with it until now – through our own situated and limited lived experience. We try to notice when our patient feels that we make him or her an It – reducing, observing, diagnosing, judging, knowing better, controlling, distancing – and when we seem to connect as a We, the I and You of genuine dialogue, of com-munion. Instead of "treating" depression or psychosis, we undergo the situation with the other. Carrying our preconceptions – personal, cultural, and theoretical – as lightly as possible, we attempt together to make sense of, to understand the patient's suffering within the always-already living relation in which we find ourselves and which we continue to develop together. It is written that we should rejoice with those who rejoice and weep with those who weep. Unfortunately, in our work with devastated human beings, we weep more often.

Working as dialogical analysts also means seeing relatedness as our primary human situation. This means that we are born into relatedness, and that our coping capacities and our tangles develop, maintain, and transform relationally. Both agency and suffering are always situated, emotionally and temporally. Aging and dying means we are gradually losing our grip. Our work becomes to surrender to the loss of a sense of agency in the relational worlds that have enlivened, sustained, and troubled us. At every moment, we meet the patient within complexly nested lifeworlds more or less shared. We share common humanity – with all its potential for good and evil – and are the Other to each other, the You that meets the I in mutual dignity and reverence. I am human, said Terentius, and nothing human is alien to me.

But the psychoanalysts bear a special vocational burden – the requirement of asymmetry. Both Buber and Binswanger believed the teacher, the therapist, and the rabbi or pastor shared an obligation to treat the student, patient, or congregant as You without expecting, or even accepting, reciprocity. Levinas in turn defined the ethical relation – the infinite responsibility for the Other – as inherently asymmetrical. It is therefore no surprise that psychoanalytic phenomenologists seem drawn to dialogic theories and clinical attitudes that emphasize our responsibility to stretch empathically, to reach for contact, to understand, just as good enough parents do for many years, without expectation of any adequate recompense. The parent is primary support for the development of the child's personhood, and not vice-versa, except in the situation of the parentified (It) child for whom the needed support does not exist. Psychoanalysts and psychotherapists, I believe, work in a similar ethical relation of this asymmetrical type.

So the phenomenologist accompanies the troubled, usually traumatized, patient patiently. With good-enough attunement to emotional life – both same and other – we join with the patient in the search for understanding, without too much knowing. When we guess it may support dialogic reflection, we self-disclose a little. We attempt a "minimally theoretical" psychoanalysis, working with experience-near concepts, and holding our judgments and diagnostic impulses as lightly as we can. We stay close to our patients, finding our way together, we learn what we can from everyone, and we seek comfort and support – always needed, sometimes desperately – primarily from fellow phenomenologists. As we seek to move beyond postmodernism, we face our infinitely demanding work with radical hope.

Reference

Gadamer, H.-G. (2007) *The Gadamer Reader: A Bouquet of the Later Writings.* Evanston, IL: Northwestern University Press.

Index